On the Subj
of Values ...
and the Value
of Subjects

New thinking to guide
schools through
the curriculum

Edited by Bridget Knight,
with Mark Chater,
Neil Hawkes and
Mick Waters

With contributions from practitioners
and professionals across the nation ...

First published 2022

by John Catt Educational Ltd,
15 Riduna Park, Station Road,
Melton, Woodbridge IP12 1QT

Tel: +44 (0) 1394 389850
Fax: +44 (0) 1394 386893
Email: enquiries@johncatt.com
Website: www.johncatt.com

ISBN: 978 1 915261 29 8

Set and designed by John Catt Educational Limited

This book is thought-provoking and practical. It makes a strong case for a values-based approach to subject teaching and the whole curriculum, in order to help children develop into caring and responsible young people and the global citizens of tomorrow.

Patrice Baldwin, Chair, Council for Subject Associations, Former President of the International Drama, Theatre and Education Association (IDEA)

As this book shows so powerfully – education is about values and most people chose to work in education because they are led by this. However, in the business of the job and all its competing priorities and accountabilities it is easy to lapse into a lip service way of doing this. The authors show that it is possible to live and breathe values authentically and meaningfully. At a time when education feels more than ever like a political football this matters.

Prof. Samantha Twiselton, Director of Sheffield Institute of Education

This book is a timely and welcome read in a world where strong, ethically sound, transparent values are in short supply. Every page contains a gem of information that will help teachers and school leaders transform their school and the young people in their care.

Every child has a right to a values-based education system. This book will help you ensure … the young people you teach flourish in life.

Armando Di-Finizio, Educational Consultant

Values, depth and soul make education last a lifetime. Without them it is mere transitory instruction.

Sir Anthony Seldon, author and historian

Honestly, this is such a great book! The right mix of reflective thinking and clear examples that can be easily implemented. I'm looking forward to sharing it with subject leads.

A clear and detailed overview of how to deeply embed values into the school curriculum, enabling children to become reflective, critical thinkers.

Rebecca Williams, Head of School, Wigmore Primary School

Contents

Contributing Authors

This book is indebted to a diverse range of contributing practitioners, each of whom has offered their subject perspective on a values-based curriculum.

David Bartlett

David Bartlett founded Pear Tree Projects, providing care and education to children who have suffered adverse childhood experiences. He specialises in helping children recover from abuse by creating a highly therapeutic environment with an emphasis on the importance of role modelling good values. He was awarded an MBE in 2016.

Mark Chater

Mark Chater is an independent writer and consultant on education, religion, worldviews, ecology, theology, and dialogue. A former teacher, academic, policy adviser, and charitable trust director, Mark now lives in South Cumbria, UK, walking, writing fiction and supporting values-led educational initiatives. Currently he is an editor of the Reforming RE blog series; a theology and ethos adviser for Oasis Global; and a trustee/director of Good Shepherd Multi-Academy Trust; as well as a professor of Practice at the University of Cumbria.

He has written or edited eight books: three about RE, *Does Religious Education have a Future?*, *We Need to Talk about RE*, and *Reforming RE: Power and knowledge in a worldviews curriculum*; two on curriculum and pedagogy, *Teaching the Primary Curriculum*, and *Developing Teaching Skills in the Primary School*; and two on theology, *Jesus Christ, Learning Teacher: Where theology and pedagogy meet*, and *Mole Under the Fence: Conversations with Fr Roland Walls*.

Mark wants all schools to have a curriculum and ethos that is values-led, because it is the form of learning that will best equip young people to face the personal and planetary challenges of the present and future.

Geoffrey Coleman

Geoffrey Coleman is an Acting Coach and former head of Acting, Royal Central School of Speech and Drama, London University.

Richard Dunne

Richard Dunne is a thought-leader in education and sustainability, an expert in curriculum development and director of The Harmony Project. In his 30-year career in education (most recently as the headteacher of an Ofsted-graded 'outstanding' school), he has developed a school curriculum based on principles of harmony that enable systems in nature to be resilient, healthy, and in balance. These principles guide and inform the way a 'Harmony curriculum' is structured, providing a coherent and meaningful framework for national curriculum learning objectives to be delivered.

Huw Evans

Huw Evans has worked in education for over forty years and is currently an independent education consultant supporting schools. His career has included headships, school improvement work and being a maths consultant. He has never lost the joy of supporting pupils with their learning, either directly or through working with teachers and leaders.

David Gardner

David Gardner taught geography in a number of schools, before becoming a Curriculum Adviser and National Lead for geography at the Qualifications and Curriculum Authority. Since 2011 he has worked as a PGCE lecturer at a range of universities, including UCL IoE. He is the author of successful geography textbooks, including *Progress in Geography KS3*, for Hodder Education. David is now a freelance education consultant, leading training on curriculum design and assessment in geography.

David Gumbrell

David Gumbrell is senior lecturer at Kingston University and part-time education consultant. Founder of The Resilience Project, a company that seeks to start the conversation about the mental health needs of teachers. He is the author of several books and still passionate about the future of the teaching profession.

Neil Hawkes

Neil Hawkes is well known as an inspirational speaker, educator, broadcaster, author, and social commentator. He is a popular TEDx presenter. Neil's thinking is having a profound influence on education and more widely in society. He first gained international recognition as a headteacher in Oxfordshire, UK. Here he worked with a school community to devise and implement a pedagogical system that would give pupils a transformational vocabulary, based on values such as respect, tolerance, humility, and justice. The school community found that pupils were empowered to be self-leaders, with an active ethical compass that affected behaviour, their thinking, and the quality of their schoolwork. Today, Neil's philosophy of Values-based Living has spread. He is one of the V20 Task Group that is advising G20 leaders about the importance of values to humanity. He is also an Ambassador for the Foundation for Education Development (FED).

Neil founded The International Values-based Trust (www.ivetfoundation.com) and its educational arm Values-based Education (www.valuesbasededucation.com). His bestselling book, *From My Heart: Transforming lives through values,* celebrates the success of VbE worldwide. Neil's latest book, co-authored with Jane Hawkes, is called *The Inner Curriculum: How to nurture wellbeing, resilience and self-leadership.* More information can be found at www.neilhawkes.org.

Colin Howard

Dr Colin Howard has been involved in primary education for over 24 years, which includes 15 years as a successful headteacher in both village and large primary schools. He is an associate lecturer at the University of Worcester and has published books and articles relating to educational leadership, science teaching, mental health and wellbeing, and British values.

Colin Jackson

Colin Jackson has worked in arts & cultural education for 28 years, and is the founder of Creative Learning Partnerships, a consultancy, project management, and event management company specialising in working with young people and communities. He has played a fundamental role in the development of Arts Council England's Arts Award (www.artsaward.org.uk) and Artsmark (www.artsmark.org.uk) initiatives. His work has included the delivery of the annual Yorkshire Schools Dance Festival (www.artsaward.org.uk) and the development of a learning strategy for the UNESCO Guild of Media Arts (www.guildofmediaarts.com).

Sue Jones

Following a long teaching career in primary schools as teacher, deputy head, and headteacher, Sue now feels privileged to be the Senior Adviser for Values-based Education. She loves all aspects of this role, from visiting, advising, and supporting schools to communicating the importance and impact of a values-based philosophy for living.

Bridget Knight

Values have inspired Bridget throughout her career in education. Her background and experience includes a number of headships, national advisory and improvement work in a range of sectors, and curriculum development. She is currently the teaching head of a primary school and CEO of Values-based Education. Her practical experience illustrates the developed philosophy and impact of a values-based education. Among her current developmental work, she is working with The Harmony Project and developing values-based resources including values rhymes and reflections for the classroom.

Jane MacRae

Jane MacRae is the founder of Bloom (www.bloomeducation.co.uk), an educational enterprise which provides courses and workshops for secondary schools based on the principles of harmony in nature. Jane taught biology for over 20 years and held a number of senior posts. She has an MSc in the history and philosophy of science and PhD in cellular biology.

Lucy Marcovitch

Lucy Marcovitch is an education writer and PSHE consultant. She was a primary teacher in Leeds, spent ten years as national curriculum adviser at the Qualifications and Curriculum Authority (QCA), and then worked on the Subject Specialist team at the PSHE Association. She lectures on the BA in childhood, youth and education studies at Coventry University.

Emilie Martin

Emilie Martin is a journalist and former primary school teacher with a special interest in sustainability and education. She has first-hand experience of teaching a 'Harmony curriculum', having worked alongside Richard Dunne in the school at which the Harmony approach was first developed. Emilie has been a contributor to The Harmony Project since its creation, developing content and resources to help schools wishing to develop a Harmony approach to education in their own settings.

Claire McMahon

Claire has been a primary school teacher for fourteen years and has had the role of PSHE leader across various schools for most of her career. In her most recent position, her school has begun its journey to become a values-based school. She has therefore become interested in how to embed values through raising the profile of quality PSHE education.

Dr Helena Mitchell

Helena Mitchell is an educationalist with experience as an early years teacher and manager. She was head of the School of Education at Oxford Brookes University until 2013. Her research work has focused on a range of topics including early literacy, employability, the professional development of teachers, and the values underpinning education.

Liz Moorse

Liz Moorse is Chief Executive of the Association for Citizenship Teaching. The ACT is an education charity which supports teachers and all those involved in citizenship education in schools. This includes providing curriculum advice, resources, conferences, teacher training and professional development, and running funded programmes such as the Five Nations Network in the UK and Ireland. Liz has a MSc politics and public policy from Birkbeck London and a BA hons geography with archaeology from Manchester University. She has worked in education for over twenty five years and led the development of Citizenship as a new curriculum subject in previous roles for central government at the Qualifications and Curriculum Authority. Liz is on a number of advisory boards including the Industry Advisory Board to the University of Westminster. She is also the Department for Education's UK representative to the Council of Europe Education Policy Network on Democratic Citizenship and Human Rights and a member of the Advisory Board on Democratic Resilience with the Wergeland Centre and the Council of Europe.

Paula Owens

Paula Owens is an education consultant and author. Her career has spanned teaching and leadership in primary schools to curriculum development lead for the Geographical Association. Paula was the lead consultant to 'Go Jetters', the CBeebies' animated geography-based programme and continues to advise the BBC on their Geography Bitsize resources. Paula created resources for the Ordnance Survey Digimap for Schools (www. digimapforschools.edina.ac.uk) programme and is a judge for LESSCO2 (http://www.lessco2.org.uk). Paula is a co-designer of Meaningful Maps; a project researching children's ideas about their locality through maps, aiming to involve children from diverse backgrounds and geographical settings and find out what places matter to them.

Vikki Pendry

Vikki is the CEO of The Curriculum Foundation working with governments, business and groups of schools internationally to co-develop curriculum materials. Prior to this role, Vikki led music in three consecutive primary schools in England, became an Arts Award Adviser, and is currently the link governor for Music at a secondary school in York. Vikki sustains her own musicianship through choral adventures with The Chapter House Choir of York Minster.

Anne Phillips

Anne has been a passionately values-based teacher for 40 years, with 26 of those as a headteacher, in diverse parts of the country. Values have been a shaping influence over both her personal and professional life. Her school holds the Values-based Education Quality Mark, a recognition of the impact of the deep clarity, consistency and community of her uniquely values-based approach.

Hywel Roberts

Hywel is a teacher, writer, radio presenter, humourist, educationalist, and speaker working with many organisations across the UK and beyond. A true northerner, Hywel deals in 'botheredness', curriculum liberation, creative practice, learner investment, leadership, and teacher development across settings. Hywel's award winning book *Oops! Getting Children to Learn Accidentally* is a firm teacher favourite. His next, 'botheredness' is imminent.

Mark Sanderson

Mark has been supporting primary schools in Herefordshire in the educational use of technology for twenty years. The supporting role of computing for learning has always been upmost in his approach and Values-based Education has taken on an increasingly important status in this mix. Having seen the huge impact that a values-based approach has made to the ethos of so many schools, it's great to see a resource in development that will put it at the very heart of learning.

Sarah Somers

Sarah has worked in education for nearly forty years. Her roles have included headship, school improvement, and inspection. Sarah believes in the importance of the language of values through the whole curriculum. As an educator, parent, and grandparent, she believes in nurturing values-based learning in all aspects of life.

Dominic Seamer

Dominic has been teaching for twenty years and has worked at Wilds Lodge school for fourteen. Dominic's background is in primary education, and he is now head of education at Wilds. Wilds Lodge school has held onto the principle that everything we do is in service to our pupils at our heart. The school believes that the prior experiences of pupils should not limit their future opportunities and that our shared values underpin everything we do. Creativity, imagination and relationships are the holy trinity of education and VbE draws together these vital factors.

Rachel Usher

Rachel Ussher has been a teacher from Nursery to Y6 for over 20 years and is currently deputy headteacher of a two-form entry primary school in Herefordshire. She believes in developing schools through Values-based Education to offer warmth, laughter, and curiosity.

Mick Waters

Mick Waters has a rich experience in schooling. From teaching and headship to teacher education, the leadership of local education authorities, working at national level as Director Curriculum with the Qualification and Curriculum Authority in England, and higher education, Mick has always been close to the classroom. In recent times he has worked to support governments in different parts of the globe at policy and practical classroom levels. He also supports several charitable organisations as patron or director including the Curriculum Foundation, SAPERE, the Foundation for Compassionate Education (CoEd), the National Association for Environmental Education (NAEE) ... and, of course, Values-based Education (VbE). Mick is a regular conference speaker and has had many publications. His most recent books are *About Our Schools: Improving on Previous Best* (with Tim Brighouse) and *Our Curious Curriculum: Teaching Foundation Subjects Well* (with Claire Banks).

Klaus Wedell

Emeritus Professor Klaus Wedell was the first holder of the chair in Special Needs Education at the Institute of Education, University College London, in 1979. In his academic research and development work he has been involved in policy and practice to support the right to effective education for children and young people with special educational needs and disabilities.

Tessa Willy

Tessa Willy is deputy programme lead for the primary PGCE at University College London, Institute of Education, prior to which she was associate professor of teacher education at Kingston University, and a senior lecturer in primary geography at the University of Roehampton. She has been a primary school teacher in the UK and a secondary school geography teacher in the UK and Malawi. Her areas of particular interest are in the ethics of geography: climate change, sustainability, social justice, and global citizenship. She is on the Primary Geography Editorial Board and of the GA's Early Years and Primary Committee and Publications Board.

Acknowledgements

Dame Alison Peacock, Chief Executive of the College of Teaching for her foreword.

We would like to thank the following people for their quotes and comments:

Sue Brown

Kayleigh Evans

Maise Lou Gore

Oliver Gore

Chris Malone

Susan Mealand

Emma Mills

Sarah Peacock

Alison Philcox

Kate Phillips

Mike Salter

Katrina Small

The staff and pupils of Eardisley CE Primary School

The staff and pupils of the Marches Academy Trust

We give huge thanks to all who have supported and helped with this book along the way and are indebted to the education community who live out the values-based learning and ethics presented in this book.

The editors have agreed that all royalties from this book will be donated to the Values-based Education movement to support schools in the UK and across the world in promoting values-based learning and living.

The Subject of Values and the Value of Subjects

The vision of each school should be lived by all who learn there. It should resonate with everyone who comes into contact with the school – child or adult. The values we talk about need to be exemplified throughout everything that the school does. Typically, values are understood in isolation of the curriculum or may only be brought to the surface in particular subject areas or during assemblies. This book, however, powerfully illustrates the way that values can and should flow throughout both the taught and 'received' curriculum.

Our authors explore the curriculum and pedagogy of specific subjects, illustrating each with examples for KS1-3. In mathematics, for example, we pause to reflect on the beauty and universality of pattern, of geometry, of sharing. In science we consider how we can understand and improve our society and our world. Each subject chapter includes personal responses from teachers that illustrate how they seek to teach in a manner that responds to the heart and potential impact of their subject. Care is given to help the reader envisage various curriculum strands through the lens of the values which can be highlighted, reinforced, and understood in them. As the book progresses it becomes crystal clear that the choices that we make – not only in terms of what we teach but also in the ways in which we appreciate the process of learning – make all the difference.

I am reminded of Gordon Wells' insightful *The Meaning Makers* (2009), which shows how optimal initial language learning occurs when children are able to draw connections and make sense of the world around them. Similarly, *On the Subject of Values … and the Value of Subjects* shows us how to help children 'make meaning' in a wide range of subject disciplines. This approach shines a light on the way that values permeate every decision we make. We consider not only children's responses to a values-based education but also those of politicians and parents.

Essentially this book is about the core purposes of learning. If we want our children to flourish, we need to ensure that everything about their school experience is less focused on the transactional transmission of knowledge than cultivating an interdisciplinary appreciation of learning and a restless appetite for more. Factual knowledge is a by-product of a culture that promotes moral, ethical, cultural, social, and spiritual values. Let's ensure we get our priorities right. If we are teaching our children to live, love, and learn for an unknown future; then surely global sustainability, kindness, and consideration of others must lie at the heart of this movement.

Dame Alison Peacock

CEO Chartered College of Teaching

References

Wells, G. (2009) *The Meaning Makers: Learning to Talk and Talking to Learn*. Channel View Publishers.

'The Value of Values' in Subjects

A reflection of our understanding

Our collective experience consistently confirms that most teachers come into teaching – and remain in education – because they instinctively understand that the business of teaching and learning is about human values: how we all live and exist with ourselves, one another, and in our world. Teaching cannot therefore be simply the transactional imparting of knowledge and skills; it cannot even be values neutral. Teachers want the very best for their students – they want them to succeed in every way possible. They want to 'touch the future' and affect the lives and life courses of their students forever. We see, time and again, that the 'best' schools are compelled and propelled by strong values which inspire and guide their nurturing, encouraging, supporting and aspirational environment.

Teaching and learning are values-based experiences. We communicate lessons in values through who and how we are with our students; in turn, our students respond to the emotions and feelings evoked. Subjects carry their own values systems. In ourselves and in our subjects, values can be – and often are – submerged. By infusing our teaching with values, explicitly and implicitly, teaching and learning can serve a greater purpose, energising and nourishing us as human learners.

The values we describe throughout this book are not affiliated to any particular religion, faith, culture, or country. They are positive human values, relevant to our time and important for all times. These values – such as love, resilience, courage, joy and more – are the mainstays and meaning-makers of our very existence. Given that they are the very essence of our existence, all our interactions, and any achievements we make in the world, it is surprising we don't talk about them more.

This book makes the urgent case for values-based learning and offers both the theoretical underpinning and some practical examples of how to bring these principles to life in the classroom.

It is an invitation to all educators, everywhere, to channel their values and the essence of their essential selves and to bring them to the honourable profession of teaching, in the hope that in so doing we will awaken our children and young people to their own values system that they will use to make a better world.

CHAPTER 1

A Values-based Curriculum – What is it?

In this chapter Bridget Knight introduces us to a values-defined curriculum, illustrating its aspects and exploring its ramifications for a whole school approach.

Defining a values-based curriculum

A values-based curriculum is a philosophy: a way of thinking. It is about setting out to give children the very best that schooling can offer. The very best opportunities, experiences, skills, mindsets, and attributes. Better than we ourselves ever had, and so good that it enables them to be the people who create a world that is better than it is now.

The curriculum is an integral part of the journey of learning. It needs to do a lot of things – teach children about themselves, others, their world, and prepare them for a future that none of us has yet seen. So, it must work hard and achieve simultaneously many things.

Successful learning – the aim of every curriculum – means enabling every individual to flourish in any situation. It means having everything needed to engage in the day-to-day activity of being on every level: physical, emotional, spiritual, dispositional, social, linguistic, and cognitive.

Learning about positive universal human values enables children to learn more deeply than is normally expected and accepted. They permeate and guide the many dimensions that make up the whole picture of a successful learner. These learning dimensions enable learners to make sense of subjects, make meaningful connections between areas of learning, and better understand themselves and their world.

The values belief system infuses and guides the school's approach to the planning, content, and delivery of the curriculum. Schools that develop a values-based approach to learning provide a curriculum experience that is unique and fresh, engaging their learners and their teachers. They bring their curriculum to life, giving a greater meaning and focus that pervades each subject area and dimension of learning, and enables individuals to flourish regardless of their age, ability, or background. The values-based curriculum entitlement is broad, balanced, and rich, and succeeds in engaging, exciting, and empowering children for both their present and future needs.

This curriculum is realised as a dynamic entity, serving the pupils, rather than being served by them. It is conceived as the entire experience a child has in school, throughout and even beyond each school day. It is built upon the recognition of human needs, understanding that to be successful children need to be loved and valued, to be safe, to have positive relationships, and a growing mastery of the personal, social, and emotional, as well as academic, aspects of learning. Therefore, the curriculum in these schools first and foremost *nourishes* their children, enabling them to flourish ... and radiate their own special qualities, making a difference to the world through *who* and *how* they are.

Recent research (Lovat et al., 2009) has consistently found that a values-based approach to the curriculum leads to improvement in pupil well-being, self-esteem, behaviour, relationships, and emotional, moral, spiritual, and academic diligence. In other words, pupils are:

Self-aware

- Engaged learners.
- Reflective thinkers.
- Responsible participants.

Who become

- Values-led, able to make ethical choices.
- Academically successful.
- Emotionally literate.

They are more likely to exhibit strong self-identity, mastery of themselves and learning, agency and advocacy, along with a social conscience. If we believe that 'a childhood lasts forever' – that what happens in childhood and how we respond to it, is the model for our future lives, setting in train the mindsets, capabilities, and outlook that make us the adults we become – then what we place before children in a curriculum is of critical importance. The ambitious question becomes: 'what kind of people do we want to grow?' Meaning, of course, 'what kind of world do we want to make?'

This is where it starts. Every life has its kernel, its hub, the epicentre from which everything flows out. This essential self is both ephemeral and our core – and it is this that we nurture in education. It is nourished through learning – learning skills in reading, writing, maths, science and so on – all the skills that open up life's majesty for us. It is nurtured by the responses, messages and indications we receive from those around us. It is these responses that tell us whether we are cared for, valued, supported, liked, held in esteem – or not. Learning and emotional support are the combined elements that enable us to live our lives purposefully, well, or otherwise. Education is therefore about inviting children to take a step through life itself.

If we want children to flourish, to be able to create a better world, we need to set the right conditions for continuous growth … this is where values come in. Values pre-exist in nature and are seen in every culture throughout humanity. Think, for example, about respect, kindness, care (and, for that matter, greed, vengefulness, and selfishness): they exist in every culture and civilisation. We don't *make* them, but we can perpetuate them. And we can choose whether we align ourselves with positive or destructive values.

Positive values can come to fore and then recede in the hectic business of school, and the tumult of its inevitable inherent daily pressures and challenges. However, following the rhythm of a strong focus on values throughout the curriculum ensures that our intent and our outworking become anchored in these attributes, strengthening and accentuating their meaning and their effect.

A definition of values

Values are the principles we live by – and live up to. They intimately help us decide how to think, feel, and act. They are not fixed entities. We all bring our own contexts, perspectives, and emotions to bear in our understanding of them. However, when we affiliate to universal, positive human values – such as hope, love, peace, kindness and so on – and try to live through them, we try to live up to our own ideals, and in so doing build a more ideal world.

Through the lens of values, we become able to see ourselves, each other, and our world with ethical objectivity. In turn, this ethical objectivity feeds our intellectual and intuitive curiosity, enabling us to engage in deep consideration of issues – and develop an outlook of active care for ourselves, each other, and our world. Through this process our values become dynamic.

Values and the curriculum

When we look for them, positive human values are everywhere, inherent in all of life. So, of course, they run through the curriculum, conveyed through the teacher's words, actions, attitudes and relationships as well as through subject matter. A 'values-based curriculum' makes explicit the values that otherwise may only be implicit, or even lying dormant from disuse. By heightening awareness of values, we enable them to play a vital role in teaching and learning, strengthening understanding of moral, ethical, cultural, spiritual, and social aspects and bringing a closer attentiveness to what makes us human.

The national curriculum

The current national curriculum for England promotes this values-based approach, albeit using slightly different language:

> 2.1 Every state-funded school must offer a curriculum which is balanced and broadly based and which: promotes the spiritual, moral, cultural, mental and physical development of pupils at the school and of society, and prepares pupils at the school for the opportunities, responsibilities and experiences of later life ...

3.1 The national curriculum provides pupils with an introduction to the essential knowledge that they need to be educated citizens. It introduces pupils to the best that has been thought and said; and helps engender an appreciation of human creativity and achievement ...

3.2 The national curriculum is just one element in the education of every child. The national curriculum provides an outline of core knowledge around which teachers can develop exciting and stimulating lessons to promote the development of pupils' knowledge, understanding and skills as part of the wider school curriculum.

National Curriculum (2014)

Did you know the national curriculum is just one element?

Many teachers, when asked to consider the curriculum, will visualise the national curriculum. However, the national curriculum is only a minimum entitlement for children. The actual curriculum is everything children experience in our school; the entire planned learning experience includes lessons, events, routines, and what children do outside of school. Children learn in every context: whether we expect them to or not. It is the bringing together of these contexts under a coherent design that becomes the school curriculum.

The curriculum – the 'educational offer' – is the journey of learning. It needs to achieve a lot of things. It must equip children with the vital skills they need to function cognitively. It should also help children learn about themselves, others, and the world, preparing them for a future that none of us has yet seen. We need it to simultaneously achieve many things.

Aspects of a values-based curriculum

Ethical vocabulary

The basic premise of Values-based Education is treating one another with respect, civility and kindness and expecting same in return. Language shapes our beliefs and we become our language, so when we think, speak, and use values-based language, we start to define ourselves by these values. The language of values is exceptionally powerful: through values we come to define ourselves, our lives, and other people. We become our values. We think and act them. They propel us forward. They are where our personality resides.

The values words themselves – love, peace, honesty, for example – are more than just words, nomenclature, and names ... they are carriers of feeling, guides, comforters, prompts to conscience and aspiration, and bringers of understanding and meaning. They are also open to paradox, begging questions like can we ever care too much? What about loving the wrong thing? Can caring make us prisoners? In making values central it is important to move beyond the comfortable virtue element of values and set ourselves some real and meaningful philosophical challenges. For example, a simple and comfortable understanding of 'care', is a positive one – caring for ourselves, one another, and the planet. However, a deeper exploration of 'care' can and should lead us into consideration of – for example – which cultural or societal groups can get overlooked or attacked (e.g. through racism or homophobia); what meaningful care really looks like and what impact this has on our lives. Such questions can lead us to fundamentally examine our impulses and beliefs and help us to live with eyes that are wide open to the word.

A Values-based culture

It is important that a Values-based Education takes place in a culture of 'unconditional positive regard', meaning it is nurturing and guiding but non-judgemental. The relationships of respect and humility are at its core. Teachers can achieve this through tuning in to each child to realise their unique story. This approach helps teachers look beyond the initial self-presentation and see more holistically.

They can then teach children to do this for one another and to do it for themselves – through self-affirmation. But it is crucial that they also teach that the self isn't the 'be all and everything' – seeing the world through values means developing an objective lens through which we deepen our understanding of ourselves, others, and our world.

Values-based leadership

Leading through a values-base means the school's leadership is guided and inspired by positive, aspirational values. These inform every decision and action. Speech is consistent with action, lending a compassionate objectivity to decision making. Much of values-based leadership is discrete – the stuff that goes on behind the scenes. It's less the lone figure, boldly striding out in front, and more the person in the thick of things, responsible for keeping them in balance and moving forward at a rate, reading vibrations in school, listening, responding, noticing – guided by the notion of the collective good. Of course, these leaders also bring courage, decisiveness, and shrewd thinking, emboldening and nurturing others. In essence, it's wise and compassionate leadership: gentle, purposeful, serious, and emanating from integrity.

Role-modelling

So much of what children and adults learn is unintended – and that learning comes from experiencing the essence of who we are in that context. If you ever see young children playing the role of teacher at school, you will be very astonished to see the traits they have noticed! The culture and atmosphere of a school is an emanation of the vibes we all give off. An atmosphere that jangles, or even hints at unsafety is a direct reflection of bad tempers, frustration, worry and impatience. Values-based schools emit a tranquillity that is threaded through with a purposeful and joyful vivacity. The sense of forward-momentum is proceeds directly from their calm and cherishing ethos.

You will have heard of meme theory, coined by Richard Dawkins, and later developed by scientist Susan Blackmore. This theory is at the heart of Values-based Education. Memes – or behaviours – are passed from person to person: we copy or mimic the behaviours we see. Values, such as altruism, friendship, and sympathy, are shared and then deepened. Positive behaviours, such as altruism, 'work' because people like them! If people are altruistic, they become popular, and because they are popular, they are copied, and so these behaviours are spread. In a values-based school children and adults are inspired to be and behave at their best. This positive, self-perpetuating cycle, supports and strengthens everyone who is part of it.

Playfulness

When we ask children for their best memories of school (as we often do in preparation for their leavers' service, or some other occasion) they will invariably cite trips and visits, or perhaps some art project or sports event, or when something funny happened. They talk of their best memories involving their friends; times when they were just being themselves together. What does this tell us? It doesn't mean that children don't value or appreciate being able to master long division or knowing how to construct a formal letter to someone they have never met. What it does tell us is that moments of playfulness 'stand out' as times where there is a sense of liberation and fun – those chinks of light in the day – which help us all to learn and live better.

Remembering this, and purposely making time for 'playfulness', experimentation, humour, and even 'off-grid' learning, can help us all to appreciate being fully human, which in turn builds our capacity for the serious business of living and learning.

Contemplation and Reflection

> *The mind is everything. What you think you become.*
> commonly attributed to the Buddha

In values-based schools, reflections are a mainstay. Children are explicitly taught how it is possible to be physically still, then how we can turn that stillness to inner calm, relaxing our minds as well as our bodies. From that place, we are then able to think more deeply and maybe experience a sense of the numinous or 'other.' As adults, we can find ourselves in a perpetual state of internal harassment, fed often by self-admonishment. It so often becomes our natural state. As we learn to look with kindness when we look within, we can gently change our expectations of ourselves. If we can help children to develop this capacity from an early age, then they are in a much better position to care for and cope with their own wellbeing and emotional needs.

Making time and space for values-based reflection – using techniques of mindful breathing, guided visualisations, or simple focus on a particular value – not only contributes to our personal wellbeing, giving opportunity for resetting our inner senses, and to affirm our own self-worth, but also enables us to develop a reservoir that we can then share with others.

When we have enjoyed a deep surfeit of calm, joy, peace, and care – we can find that we have enough left over for it to share with those around us.

All these aspects of Values-based Education offer children a toolkit of self-supporting skills, techniques, mindsets, and attributes, which they can build upon and strengthen as they go through life.

The 'right kind of curriculum': Experiences and opportunities

A good curriculum is one that is aspirational for its pupils. This means getting the core learning right and aspiring to the highest possible standards, but not allowing learning to become polarised. So often, 'core learning' is seen in opposition to 'creativity', whereas in reality, they each feed and need the other to succeed. Secure knowledge and understanding gives the opportunity to use, apply, and further develop knowledge and understanding in real life contexts.

Emotional engagement is fundamental to successful, deep, and long-term learning. All of us – and children especially – are naturally inquisitive. A diet of didactic facts and knowledge, however worthy, can blunt our senses. We have to find ways to make learning personal to children, to arouse and awaken their full senses. Partly this is done through encouraging queries and curiosity: modelling, 'I wonder why … ?' thoughts and asking, 'what do you think about … ?'. Children who are used to being invited in to share the learning journey in this way, become able to respond readily; those who have been steeped in a didactic mode of learning will be unresponsive and even find it a distraction. The aptitude for asking critical questions, the ability to think deeply, to grapple with paradox and complexity are fundamental to great learning and to the ability to navigate through one's life.

To ensure learning is a rich and full experience, we also have to provide different ways of learning, e.g. go outside, have a speaker in, sketch your ideas instead of writing them. Neural pathways become ingrained, automatic, if they operate only by habit. They are highly attuned to alterations, to novelty. New sights, sounds, language, tastes, and smells stimulate different synapses to the brain, making different connection webs and increasing our neuroplasticity.

We can also offer to children a bigger stage than their immediate environment, a national stage and real-life contexts help them see that their ideas really apply and matter. Pupils2Parliament, for example, engages pupils in real issues, collating their personal views to influence real, living laws. The opportunity for children to use their knowledge, skills, ideas, and opinions to this end is intoxicating! Real experiences help children build a bridge between their cerebral understanding and the lived experience of own their lives.

Pedagogy: The values key to successful learning

Successful learning means enabling every individual to flourish in any situation. It means having everything needed to engage in the day-to-day activity of being human on every level – physical, emotional, spiritual, dispositional, social, linguistic, and cognitive.

Values enable children to learn more deeply. They infuse and guide the learning dimensions that make up the whole picture of a successful learner. These learning dimensions enable learners to make sense of subject disciplines, make meaningful connections between areas of learning, and to better understand themselves and their world.

A values-based pedagogy requires the capacity to combine structure with flexibility in both planning and teaching. Teachers need to be willing to take risks, not least in initiating open dialogue with learners. They have to be patient and act with humility so that the children's learning is centre stage, and not their teaching or their subject. Above all, they are required to teach the subject or the lesson *to the person of the learner* and not just teach the subject or the lesson as an entity in its own right.

What are we learning for?

At its core, learning is about our relationship with our world, our connections with the people in it, and our relationship with ourselves. When we study a text in English, for example, we find out about how people in different contexts and times think, feel, act, and react ... as we learn about these people, we learn about their world, and in considering them, we consider and wonder about ourselves. We all get used to thinking of learning as an abstract event.

How can we help children get the most from their learning?

Learning – just like living – is an emotional process. We all bring our own complex layers of emotions, memory and feeling to the business of learning. It makes sense that we present learning in a way that enables children and young people to connect at a personal level with the subject matter, allowing the learning to resonate more, mean more, and have a lasting impact in terms of both memory and use.

The key question is: how can our curriculum subjects teach their intrinsic elements (i.e. knowledge and skills) *and* help pupils to grow as people? How can they perform a bigger service, helping our students to understand themselves, to recognise, articulate and use their values more clearly – and then to use these skills to create a positive place for themselves in their world?

Staff often say they are unsure what they are 'allowed' to do in the scope of their subject. Learning as measured by tests and exams is of course important. Yet our society also prizes attributes like kindness, generosity, optimism, and peace – so shouldn't these values also come to the fore in our teaching? The rich diversity of the subjects on offer ensures a range of disciplines and skills. However, a deeper learning, beyond the surface, is invited as we look through a values lens.

> *Every learning, and teaching, experience is enhanced by the way we approach it. If we truly live values and they become an integral part of what we are, who we are, and how we grow, then those values become both the bedrock of learning and our inspiration.*
>
> Anne Phillips, headteacher

Engaging with learning

Values are in the air we breathe, all around us, implicit in all we do. We can think of them as a mirror, showing us our true selves; they are also a window, allowing us to look out to one another and to the world around us. Children often grasp this intuitively.

When we look at any subject through the lens of values it immediately invites the pupils voice into our teaching. The values radiate a warmth, transforming a lesson from a transactional exchange of knowledge into something that brings a human experience, and a meaningful connection.

A focus on values makes learning meaningful. We naturally have an *emotional connection* with values: they mean something profound to us as people. This makes a bridge, linking us directly with the associated learning.

This approach is about making the values that are already implicit within the subject matter explicit. Bring out the values in your activities. Help the learner to experience what they look like ... sound like ... feel like ... for them and others. And explore them in a range of contexts.

Further reading

Lovat, T.J., et al. (2009). *Values Education, Quality Teaching and Service Learning: A troika for effective teaching and teacher education.* Terrigal, N.S.W.: David Barlow Publishing.

CHAPTER 2

The Case for Values-based Education: Why We Should Have It?

In this chapter Neil Hawkes, Founder of Values-based Education (VbE), explores why we need Values-based Education in each and every school, and how this approach underpins high-quality curriculum provision.

The curriculum and pedagogy of Values-based Education

To begin to answer this question, I need to share with you a recent school experience. Jane, my wife, and I were with a group of Year 6 pupils at St. Peter Gowts CE Primary School, in Lincoln, talking with them about how they were putting their school's values into action in their lives. This multicultural values-based school is situated in a socially challenged area of the city. We had been asked by the school to conduct an audit to see if it merited being awarded the Values Enhanced Quality Mark.

Two boys, who staff told us had really benefited from learning about values, Diego and Cohen, told us that while walking to school they spotted a large scary knife under a car. They had wondered what they should do and decided to tell their teacher, as it seemed a very dangerous knife if in the 'wrong' hands. Their teacher, Emma Bradley, informed the police and the boys were praised by PCSO James Lingard for their wise choice and prompt action. Later the boys received a letter of thanks from the police and their photos, along with their story was celebrated in the local newspaper.

As the boys retold their story, I was overwhelmed by emotion and tears came to my eyes. I was deeply affected by how learning about values had shaped the choice these boys had made, and helped them solve their ethical dilemma. They were so values aware. My emotions were also triggered by the realisation of how effectively the school had understood the philosophy and practices of Values-based Education (VbE); powerfully affecting the current and future lives of their pupils, their families, and the community. At the end of the day, Jane and I were delighted to award the school the Enhanced Values Quality Mark – an outstanding achievement.

May I invite you to contrast that enriching experience with the substance of an email I received from a mum and psychotherapist who lives in Manchester. She is a qualified therapist in the internal family systems theory of psychotherapy (IFS) and is also a keen advocate of VbE schools. Her five-year-old had recently started school, but she was upset to discover that the school's pedagogy was toxic: with children regularly being shamed and humiliated by staff by, among other things, a traffic light system of discipline where the names of so called 'naughty' children were placed on the red light and named and shamed. Luckily, from my experience, such emotionally inappropriate behaviour checking systems are becoming less common.

The mother removed her child from this school, and he now attends one which the parent describes as being nurturing and supportive; not only of her child but all the pupils attending the school. This new school places a great deal of emphasis on mental wellbeing and helping children to understand why they have aspects of themselves that are unhappy. The mum told me that the headteacher is very interested and curious about how VbE can help the school support her pupils even further. I wonder how many other educators – you may be one – are curious about VbE and want to know why it is so powerfully successful and if they should embrace it.

If you were to meet me, you would soon discover that I am passionate about VbE and the life-enhancing impact it can have on individuals and school systems globally. My passion is rooted in many years of experience: seven years developing VbE in a school setting in Oxfordshire; then taking its methods to schools and other settings in many parts of the world; and seeing them transform and flourish.

So, what is VbE and why should it be in all schools and other settings? My stories above illustrate one of the main aspects of VbE; that it nurtures a cultural ethos and individual character; a spirit of awareness, based on an understanding of a community inspired set of positive transformational words called values. VbE is therefore an education that has its base or roots in universal, positive human values, such as respect, trust, co-operation, humility, peace, love, honesty, and compassion – the innate essence of all that is good in people.

St. Peter's, the school illustrated above, has a large label above one of its displays. It reads, 'Lived Not Laminated', referring to its values philosophy, which permeates all aspects of its life. I am aware that, for many reasons, highlighting values has recently taken on a degree of general popularity in schools and businesses. I am always keen to determine in these places, if the espoused values are lived in practice, or are merely aspirations that bear little relationship to reality in terms of how people behave towards each other. This was illustrated to me recently, when I was talking to a group of middle managers in a large national corporation. They left me in no doubt that the company's values were simply empty rhetoric to make the company look good on its website!

Not so at Aureus Secondary School in Didcot. On the 27 March 2018 I had the honour to open a suite of rooms in the school dedicated to mental wellbeing. Two of them – the sensory and thrive rooms – give students the opportunity to become aware of their internal world of thoughts and feelings that impact on their wellbeing. At the time of my visit, the school began each day with a mindfulness activity which helped the students to practise moment to moment non-judgemental awareness. This regular practice, the students told me, was having an enormous effect on creating a school that really lived its values.

I hope you are sensing that VbE gives young people an extended vocabulary, which helps them reflect on themselves, others, and the world, giving them the emotional and intellectual tools that will help them make wise life choices. This capability I describe as ethical intelligence, which is the ability to ethically self-regulate your own behaviour. I believe that for our planet to survive and thrive, this is the most important intelligence to nurture in people. It is the driving force that opens people's hearts so that they put their energy into life enhancing projects and achieve their personal meaning and purpose. Our planet's future requires local, national, and world leadership that thinks and acts from this awareness. I am looking forward to seeing schools making the nurturing of ethical intelligence an outcome of their curriculum.

This I could see, when I visited Eardisley CE Primary School, in Herefordshire. It had an amazing display, featuring a natural scene full of brightly coloured ladybirds, near to which were creatively written the school's 22 values. What especially caught my eye were the words written across the display: 'Our Values give us roots and wings'. This imaginative phrase I observed in practice when I was observing the school's assembly.

In the middle of the school's assembly hall was a candle burning steadily and brightly in the middle of a Mayan circle of figures. There was a globe and other artefacts that the head was going to use during her assembly. Bridget, the head, sat on one side of the hall and the children were grouped on the other three. What deeply moved me during this memorable assembly on the value of joy, was the quality of the atmosphere in the room which I can only describe as profoundly spiritual. By this, I mean that there was an atmosphere of love, peace, and harmony in the room, with everyone contributing to the feeling of reverence and joy for our world.

Bridget demonstrated her incredible skill as a teacher, by making meaningful connections with both individuals and the group of children as a whole. My words cannot do justice to the quality of the sincere connection that I witnessed during that assembly. One of the pupils read a prayer that she had written which said:

> *Dear God. Thank you for the value of joy and let's spread it across the world. Without joy we would not be happy and as grateful. Please help us to remember joy and keep it in our hearts. Amen.*

The child's prayer, quoted above, summed up the joy that was evident during the assembly. Bridget demonstrated what I consider to be the key skill of a teacher, which is to form meaningful connections with children that create the space for them to thrive and feel self-confident. These powerful humane connections are formed by the teacher first having an understanding, acceptance, and awareness of themself as a human being. Secondly, having the desire to form good interpersonal relationships, which give tacit permission for both adults and children to be authentically themselves. Such teachers put into practice the words of Goethe, which I have modified to suit the context of a school:

If you take children as they are you will make them worse.
If you take children as they could be you make them capable
of being what they could be.

VbE schools bring out the very best in children. They are curious about behaviour not critical, realising that each of us is on a journey of personal development and are grounded in love, which Carl Rogers, the renowned Psychologist, described as 'unconditional positive regard'. Good relationships are palpable in all VbE schools.

The author and journalist Frances Farrer captured the essence of a values-based assembly in her book *A Quiet Revolution* (2000). She wrote about the transformational values initiative at my West Kidlington School in Oxfordshire, which was the first explicitly values-based school. This state urban school inspired a quiet revolution in the school system by placing positive human values at the centre of its curriculum, as its beating heart. On assemblies, Farrer wrote:

A great deal of effort goes into the planning and presentation
of what looks like simple meetings to make sure that the precise
atmosphere of alert stillness is created in the hall, the correct
condition is for calm concentration, the exact balance of content.
As with all the West Kidlington school activities the continuity of
behaviour is exemplified by the teachers for the children.

As a Deputy Headteacher at West Kidlington, Bridget witnessed and was inspired by the power of these assemblies, with their focus on relationships, presence and silent reflection. She has taken these elements and this model into her own practice, and her own assemblies as head, as I witnessed at Eardisley Primary School.

Ledbury Primary School is an outstanding example of a school that actively nurtures good relationships throughout its community. Its head Julie Rees has made the building of meaningful relationships a cornerstone of her headship. Whenever I look back on my photos of Ledbury, they are full of smiles. Each member of the school is truly valued and accepted for who they are as a person. It is at Ledbury that I first witnessed children being taught class massage, which I observed created a feeling of calm as they practised routines such as 'the weather'. For this activity, the children sit in pairs and take it in turns to massage each other's shoulders, gently patting each other's backs to represent rain and moving in circular motions when the sun came out. The parents and children were asked to give permission for the lessons to take place, which are now very popular with both staff and children. Through these experiential sessions, which the children enjoy and take very seriously, they learn to respect each other – another central tenet of a values – based school.

Respect, not only for humans but nature in general, is the core value of another outstanding Herefordshire VbE school – Madley Primary School. It's head Lee Batstone has a profound understanding of the crucial importance of helping children to see that they are an integral part of nature and not merely an observer of it. His work reminds me of the great educator Sukhomlynsky, whose understanding of child development and how children should be educated is encapsulated in his must-read book, *My Heart I give to Children* (1966).

In my view, Lee has created the ultimate forest school. He is lucky that not far from his school is a forest which belongs to the Duchy of Cornwall; Lee has permission to use it. On several occasions, I have accompanied a group of children in the school's minibus to the forest and observed how the children have learned to be curious and respectful of nature. It is here, that children will lie on the ground when it is raining and feel raindrops on their faces and tongues – an experience I think many adults will have missed having! It is in the forest that children learn to use tools, which in many schools would be banned for spurious health and safety reasons. The result is that the children at Madley are grounded in nature, are confident learners and value each other and the environment – a guiding principle of Values-based Education.

Such experiences should, indeed I believe must, begin in early childhood: as Simon Poote demonstrates in his inspirational outdoor classroom at Long Crendon Primary School in Buckinghamshire. Simon, as early years coordinator, gives his pupils an outstanding start at school, providing a comprehensive range of engaging first-hand, values-based learning experiences that stimulate the children's intellectual curiosity, imagination, and senses, and which create a relevant context for other aspects of basic education to be taught.

I'm sure that you are aware, that in describing the nature of a values-based school, I have focused on several key aspects: underpinning your school's life with positive human values and importantly living them; creating an ethos, a climate for learning that takes account of the complex human needs of our internal world of thoughts and emotions; the centrality of good relationships and a deep respect for the natural environment, which is linked to how children best learn and how we as educators resource this learning.

Early in my own exploration of VbE, I realised that a school based on values can only be successful if the adults in the school actively and explicitly model the school's chosen values. This is challenging, as it requires each of us to have humility and compassion for others: none of us is a perfect role model. As a staff team, it was vital that we discuss the behaviours we are going to consistently model together and to agree that we would be accountable for them. For instance, if respect is one of the school's values, then what does this mean we do and not do? In my understanding, a school cannot be a values-based school if staff shout at children or use teaching techniques that shame children.

Great examples of appropriate staff modelling can be seen in several schools in Luton. One school I know particularly well is Chantry School. Its executive head, Cori Bateman, has been a values pioneer in Luton, encouraging many schools there to adopt VbE. She and a team of teachers organise an annual pupil values conference. All the points I have made so far can be witnessed in the behaviour of the adults that come to this empowering event. A teaching assistant readily comes to mind, who I saw teaching a boy how to weave. Her patience, encouragement, and explicit use of values – 'Well done, you are showing so much determination' – was a pleasure to watch. The boy quickly learned the new skill. Other excellent examples of relational teaching included experiential sessions led by Richard Jenkins, from The Meads School, who showed groups of pupils how to make their values rockets fly with the help of compressed air – great science teaching and leadership.

VbE schools rely on good leadership to be established. If the head and senior leadership do not understand the importance of VbE and actively set out to implement it in their culture, then despite the enthusiasm of individual teachers it doesn't happen. There are, of course schools that do not call themselves values-based schools – perhaps they haven't heard of the term – but nevertheless implicitly adopt many of these principles. My hope is that all schools will proclaim that they are values-based schools, as in that way we can create a movement for change in schooling systems that would give equal emphasis to the formal curriculum and ethical education, as shown in VbE schools, such as Hinckley Parks School in Leicestershire, part of the Owls Academy Trust. Its headteacher David Harding wrote on the school's website:

> *Values-based Education is a philosophy which underpins all of our thoughts and actions. It creates a strong learning environment that enhances academic achievement and develops students' social and relationship skills that last throughout their lives. The positive learning environment is achieved by the positive values modelled by staff throughout the school. It quickly liberates teachers and students from the stress of confrontational relationships, which frees up substantial teaching and learning time. It also provides social capacity to students, equipping them with social and relationship skills, intelligences, and attitudes to succeed at school and throughout their lives.*

Before David was appointed as headteacher, bringing VbE to the school (he had previously been the head of another VbE school in Bedworth), the school required significant improvement in terms of academic standards and behaviour. VbE has been embraced by the whole school community and what David has written on the website is evident in practice when visiting the school. The school attracts many visitors, which has recently included the Princess Royal, who was full of praise for what the school is achieving.

David's school is an outstanding example of one that has high standards and is based on a culture of ethics. This is also the case in two VbE Special Schools for young people up to 18 years of age. The first is Wilds Lodge Therapeutic School in Rutland. This is an independent school I know well because my home is in the same county. What I am writing about the school, I would like to be a testimony to the headteacher, Robin Lee, who sadly died last year. Robin was a big man with big ideas, who made wonderful things happen for young people – no glass ceilings here! It was always a deep privilege to visit Robin and be shown around his school – he was so very proud of all that happened there and was highly respected and loved by staff, pupils, and parents. He was a great defender of children's right to be given the highest quality of education and was very critical of institutions, privately owned, that were money making machines that didn't put resources into the young people's care and education. All rooms were beautifully furnished, nothing was too good for his young people. All external reports describe the school as outstanding in every aspect. A very proud moment for me was when I awarded the school the Enhanced Quality Mark as a Values-based School – Robin beamed with pride. Robin has left a great legacy which I trust will be maintained by the new owners of this remarkable Special School.

The second Special School is Pear Tree School near Darlington in County Durham. Its headteacher, David Bartlett is another headteacher who is values-driven with an inspirational meaning and purpose, which is about creating a culture that supports the needs of his young people who have all led very challenged lives. David provides so many opportunities for his students to develop the skills that are needed to navigate the complexities of life. The school is based on a farm; the students spend lots of time involved in caring for animals, particularly horses.

The school effectively uses horse therapy to help the students to form relationships and to gain in confidence and trust. David introduced me to the thinking of the American Monty Roberts and his unique humane approach with horses. I witnessed at first-hand how our inner world can be calmed and nourished by being immersed in the care of a horse. Needless to say, the students loved learning to be skilled riders too.

What both these Special Schools so skilfully demonstrate, is the importance of understanding the internal world of the child, something that I would like more mainstream schools to embrace. I call this the environment of the Inner Curriculum, which Jane and I have written about in a book of that name. The Inner Curriculum is an integral part of a values-based school, as are reflective practices, such as silent sitting, brain breaks, and guided visualisation. All aspects nurture what I referred to earlier as ethical intelligence.

In this chapter I have wanted to explain the nature of VbE through the examples of outstanding values-based schools that I know well. It is always invidious to select some and not include others. If your school is an outstanding VbE school that I haven't mentioned, then please forgive me. My only excuse is that there are now hundreds of VbE schools; it has become very difficult to choose exemplars. Through these examples, I wanted to highlight some of the guiding principles that should be adopted by schools that want to be values-based.

Over the years, I have realised that people learn about values, not by what I tell them but through their own experience. The movement of Values-based Education is a bottom-up phenomenon, growing as educators see the amazing potential of its simple yet profound transformative elements. VbE is having a global impact and its philosophy is helping to unite humanity. Currently, I am a part of a group of academics and practitioners called the V20, who are working on briefing papers that will help leaders of the G20 group of nations to understand that, for instance, the UN's Sustainable Goals will be achieved if the solutions are values-driven. VbE and its development of ethical intelligence is a significant part of the solution.

Here in England, I have been given the honour of being appointed as an Ambassador for the Federation for Education Development (FED, https://fed.education).The FED is dedicated to promoting a long-term vision and plan for education in England. I am pleased that through me, VbE has been seen as an essential element of England's future curriculum.

In conclusion, I hope I have inspired you, the reader, to understand what VbE is and why we should have it! I hope too, that you will want to adopt these principles and practices in your own school, or in your life in general if your work is not in schools. You can find out more about VbE and its impact by visiting www.valuesbasededucation.com. I invite you to become an advocate.

Further reading
Farrer, F. (2000) *A Quiet Revolution*. Rider, London.

CHAPTER 3

An Introduction to Values through Subjects

In this chapter Bridget Knight introduces us to how a values focus through subject disciplines works, along with suggested ways of using the exemplar material.

Working harder! (not you - the subjects!)

A values focus in subject teaching brings into sharp relief the matter in hand, underlining its human aspects and relevance for our own lives today. The subject then serves a double duty: teaching subject knowledge, skills, and techniques, while also offering unparalleled opportunities for life learning.

The advantage of this over a traditional thematic approach is that it avoids the dangers of incorporating 'random' elements, paying little heed to some aspects of the curriculum, or indeed inappropriately matching content to pupils' needs. It is about mining deeper for the values vein inherent in everything and so ensuring that learning can flow to where it needs to go.

> *Knowledge is like brackish water at the bottom of an old vase unless it flows somewhere.*
>
> Shams of Tabriz in *The Forty Rules of Love* by Elif Shafak

The following chapters suggest that our subjects in school should be working harder and doing more to educate our children and young people as human beings. Just scratch the surface, as these examples reveal, and values run through each subject like a stick of rock.

Bring your curriculum intent to life!

As values are intrinsic, they are ever-present in the teaching of any subject.

When we amplify values through the curriculum, we bring to life the broad purpose of education, to promote the spiritual, moral, cultural, intellectual, mental, and physical development of pupils at school and in wider society. In so doing, we are enabling them to make the best of their opportunities and to take responsibility for creating and shaping their life and their world.

Offering a rich, high-quality, values-based curriculum aims to set children and young people up for life as intelligent, cultured, thinking, and values-based people. It helps our students to think and see creatively and to be creative themselves. It's a curriculum that is fit for purpose – the purpose of living responsibly and responsively. It also supports teachers; who make a fantastic effort to bring learning to their pupils.

How to use the values in subject sections:

- Each section discusses values-application to each individual subject. This is followed in each case with sample lessons for KS1-3 showing: which values can be drawn attention to; how these values can be highlighted within the lesson; cross-curricular links; and then how the values message can be further deepened, taking these values into action.
- Here we are simply scratching the surface: the closer you care to look at any subject through a values-based lens, the more there is to uncover. This is about making values explicit at all times, while also recognising the power of messaging with implicit values.
- Values links can be passing ones – this is itself valuable as it demonstrates the omnipresence of these tenets – but it is important to guard against trite or tokenistic work. For example, if we talk about the value of self-belief, it is of less use to just say, 'Let's all have it' without going into what self-belief is, what it can look like and how it can be gradually developed over time.
- Practitioners can choose whether to champion their subject by making it the main driver for a values-based curriculum, or to just be more aware of the potential for drawing out social, cultural,

moral, ethical, and spiritual values as the opportunities present themselves. The following chapters show the potential for each subject area in this regard.

- It is worth just saying at this point that while certain values are suggested, there are no 'right' or 'wrong' values – any investigation and discussion of one value is worthwhile in itself and inevitably leads in any case to consideration of a range of other values.

- In every case, ask the children what values apply here, 'what values are at work?' Asking, 'what are the things that stand out as being contrary to our considered values?', is enough to elicit a values-connection in their learning.

- Most importantly, it is the person of the teacher who brings the values alive. Values reside in every subject and almost every aspect of every subject – but without a chorus of enthusiasm and approval from the teacher, they remain submerged and hidden. Values-based teaching needs the teacher to give it a voice, prominence, and importance – in your role, you could be that very person.

So let your curriculum subjects work harder for you and have more fun as you go!

CHAPTER 4

The Dilemma of Values in Subjects

In this chapter Mick Waters addresses the merits of subject disciplines both intrinsically and as transporters of values – showing how a values-based approach to subject teaching effectively serves a double purpose, enhancing and promoting individual subjects precisely through illuminating the values they convey.

The dilemma of values in subjects

Few books can cover everything within the scope of their title and this one is no exception. In seeking to encourage teachers to reflect on how consideration of values can be a natural part of the teaching of subject disciplines, it can only get so far.

Like any aspect of teaching, this question is complicated and not least because the issue of values is vast. Not only is each subject discipline intensely complex in its developmental history, but each is also taught by people who believe in it, are committed to it, and want to transmit these wonders to others. It is obvious that teachers value their subject disciplines.

This book emphasises the broadest human values and how they might fit into the disciplines of various subjects. It could be wrongly assumed that this search for fundamental values implies that the traditional aspects of subject disciplines are considered less important or insubstantial. The challenge is to try to shine a light on the values that can be explored within each subject discipline while enhancing the discipline itself, rather than casting a shadow across the landscape of learning that a subject can offer. Our subject disciplines have grown through values and are full of them.

The curriculum can be described metaphorically in terms of models or images. A common analogy is that of a plant which flourishes when we tend its growth, nurture its roots, and harvest its bloom. Let's consider the curriculum through the image of a tree.

For very young children, the start of their learning journey is like the base of the tree's trunk. Learning is simply part of life; nearly all of it. They are bombarded by new experiences and respond by assimilating them into their growing view of the world. In their early years in school and various other settings, they engage busily with the magic of the unfolding world around them as they meet scientific phenomena and experiment to test out theories. They explore noise that borders on primitive music making, make marks that appeal to them in the form of artistic impression and begin to learn all sorts of mathematical concepts. Good teachers and others put experience in their way and children begin to develop understandings of place and environment and concepts of future and past as little geographers and historians. Some get to trade their toys and we might claim the emergence of business studies.

As they reach the older end of primary and step into secondary school, children begin to appreciate that disciplines of learning and study are different, not just because we do the work in different books and have different lessons on our timetable. They begin to see the essence of history, or performing arts, or languages. We teach them that our tree of learning is beginning to branch out into the disciplines of science, or humanities, or arts. Those branches then sub-divide: science into physics, chemistry, and biology. Indeed, each of those disciplines might itself have off-shoots: botany, anatomy, mechanics, organic chemistry, or optics, for example, with each sub-field increasing and extending the reach and specialism of interest and expertise. In the arts, the branches lead off into graphic art or performance art, and into further sub-divisions including media, music, sculpture, photography, or fabric.

Further depth, specialism, and expertise sees yet finer twigs threading from one branch to overlap and interlock with those coming from elsewhere:

such as astrophysics or micro-biology. We see marine archaeology, for instance, bringing together history and science; computational linguistics bringing together technology, computer science, and languages; or photojournalism, which fuses art and English.

As we stand back from the tree, we see not the twigs and tendrils of new growth but the canopy where subject disciplines overlap and interlock to create an all-encompassing image of our world. The canopy is hundreds of times bigger than the base of the tree from which the journey through learning growth began.

Pushing the tree metaphor to its limit, as the leaves drop (yes, this is a deciduous tree) they in turn sustain its growth by fuelling the subject disciplines with a rising sap of those attitudes, attributes, and characteristics that enable the disciplines to extend: curiosity, perseverance, innovation, accuracy, improvisation, wonder, care, and commitment. These same sorts of personal qualities and values sustain musicians, geographers, linguists, mathematicians, historians, designers, and others, whether they are renowned in their field or a pupil in Year 4 or Year 9.

Some of those values are universal. They apply to the challenge of living a good life, of growing and maturing successfully as a person in our society and contributing fully to a community. Of course, that wider community includes specialists at the forefront of research disciplines, breaking new ground, but it also includes the amateurs enjoying their shared interest and fascination with like-minded enthusiasts. We are all geographers and musicians to a degree: some of us are more specialised than most but would any true expert want to deny someone else the interest and joy of their subject?

The essence of this book is to explore how subject disciplines can support the development of universal values. This development is not a replacement for the essential value of subjects, nor is it to imply that the value of subject disciplines themselves to society are not vital. What is sought is almost the reverse.

Values exist everywhere, including in the experiences children have in lessons as they explore subject disciplines ... and this is where we would hope such values would be learned: in context, where they matter. Indeed, trying to help children to learn values on a once-a-week timetabled basis can be counter-productive and create an artificial construct. A 'standard' lesson on say, 'tolerance' – complete with learning objectives, exposition or instruction, concrete examples and recording to gather evidence, possibly with a small assessment and plenary – is probably the approach most likely to *decrease* tolerance and stunt the very values we seek to support.

What we *do* know is that examples of human values sit naturally in subject disciplines. They can be found both within the content of the material covered and in the way the learning meets the pupils. By addressing each subject discipline in turn, this book tries to tease out some specific examples and encourages teachers to consider how their teaching of their own subject can contribute wholistically to the development of every pupil as an individual, in turn increasingly the likelihood of society at large benefiting fully from the schooling we offer.

Of course, a single book can only partially achieve such large aims. We could fill a book with the contributions each individual subject discipline could make to wider values in society. However, the purpose here is to spur thinking and stimulate conversation and action about how a department, faculty, or a year group of teachers in a primary school can use their subject interest to make the human qualities implicit in their disciplines explicit in their teaching.

Some might ask whether values from subject disciplines are collectively compatible when pooled together. Does the essentially collaborative nature of drama fit alongside the essentially competitive outlook of PE and sport? Any specialist knows that, below the headline image, a subject discipline relies upon and explores a plethora of outlooks. Sport might be competitive but winning with grace and losing with dignity are also watchwords. In every competitive encounter teammates collaborate and bring teamwork to bear. Mutual support enables team members to perform to their best individually and receptiveness to advice is essential for good coaching. Perseverance in training, pushing to the limit of performance, and refining skill through practice are values that sustain any competitor.

Similarly in music, members of an orchestra or band rely on each other, especially the leader, and offer advice or suggestion for improvement.

Artists experiment, scientists are meticulous, geographers precise, and historians imaginative: all bring their values into the satisfaction of enjoying a job well done.

Each of the following sections can do little more than offer a taste of the values within the subject discipline. Each offers a few examples for consideration, possibly ones already recognised and practised, though in these cases the reinforcement might spur further consideration. Each subject would require a book of its own to do it justice, but that's not the purpose here. The ambition is to provoke a school-wide conversation about how to make values matter in the place where children spend most of their time in school: in lessons.

Any reader whose specialisation sits within a specific subject discipline might read the relevant chapter and suggest several omissions. If they read other chapters with different subject disciplines in focus, they might be spurred to relate those to their own sphere. Maybe two or three different specialist groups could get together to compare notes and consider the range of values that could be addressed.

An extension, change of focus, modification, shift of emphasis or addition might be an enjoyable professional stimulus. The benefit to children would be felt in terms of a reinforcement of values secure in the context of real, authentic experience ... and a true spirit of enhanced value in the subject discipline for its own sake.

Subject Specific Chapters

The following subject-specific chapters are combined 'think pieces' from a diverse range of practitioners and specialists in their subject fields. These subject chapters are set out alphabetically and follow a similar structure:

- The values at the heart of the subject discipline.
- The importance of the subject discipline to society.
- The importance of the subject discipline in schools.
- The importance of the subject discipline to the individual.
- How the subject discipline can shine a light on spiritual, social, moral, ethical, and cultural values.
- Sample lessons for KS1-3 where the values are enhanced, along with examples of how a learner may be encouraged to extend their values-

based learning further. These lessons are deliberately often not obviously 'values' lessons in order to show how subject disciplines lend themselves at every turn to a values perspective.

- What the learners say ...
- What the teachers say ...
- Questions for staffroom or departmental discussion.
- Further reading.

CHAPTER 5

The Curriculum and Pedagogy of Values-based Education in Art, Craft and Design

Every child is an artist. The problem is how to remain an artist once he grows up.

Pablo Picasso

Values at the heart of art, craft and design

In the content and pedagogy of art, craft and design, the following values could be said to be core and of the essence of the subject: beauty, creativity, diversity, insight, persistence, resilience, and rigour. These are recurrent and characteristic. In the very act of studying this subject, learners will frequently come face to face with these values and practise them.

The importance of art, craft and design in schools

The arts, in all their forms, offer that most potent of gifts: the opportunity for the development of creativity and imagination. Using a range of media and processes, pupils explore in a tactile, sensory, and very personal way, colour, form, pattern and texture to express what they see, feel, and think. They explore ideas and meanings in the work of our 'great' artists, craftspeople, actors, musicians, and designers, thereby developing their personal aesthetic and practical responses as well as their own skills and abilities.

Let not, however, the arts conjure in the mind fey dabbling: underpinning all artforms is the rigorous acquisition of technique, and analysis of form and practice. Done well, the arts may be said to contribute the most of all the subject disciplines to the ability to learn.

The value of the arts to society

The arts are voice. The voice of people down the ages, of different societies, genders, classes, and cultures. They offers us perspectives: of wit and humour; spirit and emotion; and commentary, all the more seductive for being implicit, and open to interpretation.

When we share 'great' works of art with children, we are showing them the best possibilities of humankind through spoken and written mediums, which are the language of emotional as well as expressive thought.

The value of art, craft and design to the individual

Visual art can evoke emotional responses in a way that no other medium can. Surely the study of art and the engagement in the act of making, using the wonderful panoply of media so easily available to us now – paint, pencil, photography, clay, textiles, etc. – has a 'softening' as well as a civilising effect on us on a personal level. Knowing that you can communicate your feelings, views and inner most self in some way is surely cathartic. Having those responses valued is validating and can help you to develop self-respect, self-belief, and self-confidence. But you also realise that there isn't one single way to respond to the world: every piece of art is different, just as we are, and not necessarily better than the other.

Art can make us wonder, bring us close to what makes us human, and help us to see and really feel the interconnections we have with each other.

Illuminating the arts through a values-based framework

To honour art – and to critique it too – you need a framework to judge it by. Spiritual, moral, social, and cultural values interplay in art. By its very nature, art does not and cannot shy away from the 'big questions' that run through all our lives.

Moral and ethical values – while some artists would disown an intended morality in their work – art can and often does make sharp and explicit statements and can provoke sometimes uncomfortable questions that require us to examine ourselves, our own values and our society's values system. Conversely, sometimes it is the absence of explicit morality that makes for commentary. The prices art can command as a commodity is a very interesting topic in itself!

Cultural values – appreciation and understanding of other traditions and cultures. Art is an insightful and perhaps one of the most non-threatening ways open to us to the values of other religions, faiths, and cultures.

Social values – art reflects its context: who gets painted, who doesn't; what is shown in the background of paintings; what 'hidden messages' are purposely included by the painter; all these are fascinating indicators of the spirit and politics of the age. Being able to connect with the views, emotions, stories, and perspectives of others, across time and cultures is a binding act that also illuminates our own lives.

Spiritual values – opening ourselves to the inner and imaginative worlds of others can invoke what might be described as a spiritual response. Making a connection with something or someone outside of ourselves in turn can often tell us something about ourselves. Many – although not all – pieces of art, in both 2D and 3D, illuminate a strong sense of the spiritual, for example, much church architecture or stained glass windows. Other pieces may give rise to spiritual feeling in the 'eye of the beholder' – such as one might feel observing the natural artistry in an autumn leaf. What this does is say to learners that these responses are there, are valid, and perhaps they will want to pursue them further. Moreover, simply appreciating beauty and seeing the power and potential which art, craft and design has to enrich our personal and public lives can also in a sense be felt to be a spiritual experience.

What the teachers and practitioners say:

When I teach, I hope that my values flow out of me – and are an outworking of my true inner self. In practice though, I know I use a 'framework' of values as a subtle guide to prompt me to good action, courage, or perseverance. I think these values help me achieve a degree of objectivity in how I view others, the world, and myself – they help me to be curious because I see the world as one and I want to understand more about it. I have taught for over 30 years, and I believe that seeing the deeper intent of any subject enables us as teachers to honour it. This in turn enables me to feel a freshness in teaching and I hope the learners also feel it in their learning: it is akin to going on a learning exploration or journey together. I love teaching art with children because it is always the case that we go on a learning journey together. Through the children's eyes, I see new possibilities in artwork as we discover the awesome wisdom and talent the children possess. When they paint, and when they tell me about their painting – and the ideas the painting process itself has evoked – I often want to gasp out loud in awe and wonder. The process of creating is a both release of and a window onto their thoughts.

I think if we viewed more subjects through the lens of values it would help us to appreciate the overarching intent in pedagogy, help us to make those meaningful – and vital – connections, and bring to bear a more enduring quality to learning.

A values-based art, craft and design experience in the classroom			
Related Values	Curriculum Applications	Cross-Curricular Links	Taking Values into Action
KS1			
Hope Joy Beauty Service	Explore visual images of hope through nature, perhaps taking the artist Andy Galsworthy as inspiration - making your own images using fallen leaves, turn taking, negotiating, discussing as a group as you do it and then using photography to capture your naturally transient creations.	Science: the changing seasons and the role of weather.	Discussion: why is hope an important value for us all? Make a collection of images of hope from the world around you. What could you do to bring hope into somebody's life? It could be a 'small' thing, such as paying someone a compliment - or you could become involved with a charity that uses its collective power to do good.
Peace Hope Unity Care Consideration Respect Tolerance	Explore the symbol of the poppy for peace - explore the background to this. Look at Georgia O'Keefe's giant poppy paintings. How does its scale impact its message? Create your own image of peace.	English literature: stories of peace. History: the causes and effects of war.	Create your own image of peace using mixed media. Is there somewhere you could display it for maximum effect? Your room at home? Or maybe a local organisation would like to display it.

KS2			
Respect Diversity Self-belief	Explore the 3D images made by Alberto Giacometti. Look closely: all the people are walking about but each of them has a slightly different pose. What might it say about them and us? What values might they be showing?	English: base your sculptures on a story - or/ and write a story about them.	Make your own image using pipe cleaners and foil. Which particular values do you want your image to show?
Love Unity Co-operation Consideration	Explore the ways Barbara Hepworth and a host of other artists have used the symbol of the circle (the wedding ring, the heart) to show a purity and pleasing wholeness.	PSHE. RE.	How is love shown in your world and your life? Look for little acts of kindness as well as larger acts involving collective responses to disasters. Could you collate them into a class or school 'scrapbook'?
KS3			
Unity Co-operation Diversity Equality	Take a look at an artist like Tony Hudson to explore depictions of people living in cultures markedly different to our own, reflecting on their beauty and landscapes.		Research an artist from another time or culture. What do you have in common? What might they be able to teach you and what could you teach them from the benefit of your own experience?
Determination Persistence Resilience	Learn about how many of the artists we now consider among the 'greats' had to struggle to make themselves heard in their contemporary lives.		Discover more about these values through the process of making a pencil drawing of your own or someone else's face. Wow! Perseverance underpins achievement in any and every sphere! Now that you have had some success: how do you feel about trying again?

What the learners say

Art is a way to express your emotions and be creative in your own way. KS2 pupil.

To me, art is a treat: you can let your creativity show. KS2 pupil.

Art is my favourite subject: it helps you look at the world. KS2 pupil.

Art teaches us to have faith in our own abilities and to be patient and resilient. KS2 pupil.

Questions for consideration in the staffroom

How could values be better illuminated in your school's art, crafts, and design curriculum? Could, for example, you theme your art provision through a values-based framework?

How much opportunity do learners currently have to experience authenticity in art? In other words, how often do they visit (or create) an art gallery, see a play, or hear live music? Can you create more opportunities for this?

CHAPTER 6

The Curriculum and Pedagogy of Values-based Education in Citizenship

In citizenship, values education takes place not only through the nature of pupil-teacher interaction but directly through the subject matter.

Jeremy Hayward

Citizenship education has an essential role in helping to prepare young people for life in the real world and is especially important in the current age of uncertainty about the future. Citizenship develops both substantive knowledge and practical democratic skills. It is a subject that tackles the big issues and dilemmas of the day where there may be competing views or rights issues at stake. These might include the ongoing concerns about inequality, racism, and discrimination in society; the proliferation of misinformation and conspiracy theories, particularly online; or eco-anxiety and the challenges of climate change especially for young people and the most disadvantaged. The subject encourages critical and conceptual thinking and a positive, problem-solving approach to contemporary political and public issues, which are all crucial for nurturing hope in these challenging times. The role of citizenship in a values-based curriculum is clear in supporting more open, deliberative forms of democratic discussion, and positive participation in communities, which in turn nurtures young peoples' power and agency, thereby building resilience and enhancing democratic well-being.

The importance of citizenship in schools

At its heart, citizenship education develops the knowledge, skills and understanding that pupils need to play a full part in society as informed, active, and democratic citizens. Pupils explore complex concepts and sometimes controversial questions about politics, parliament and voting, human rights, equality, media literacy, justice and the law, and finance and the economy. They learn to consider and weigh up evidence, debate issues, and sustain reasoned arguments. They also learn the skills of active citizenship through practical opportunities to collaborate with others and address issues of concern to them. Teaching is brought to life using real and topical issues and case studies of people and events in local to global contexts.

In England, citizenship is a statutory national curriculum foundation subject in maintained secondary schools and has a national, non-statutory programme of study for primary schools. In the other parts of the UK there are different arrangements for citizenship education and its teaching.

In 1998 Bernard Crick and his advisory group set out the vision that effective citizenship education develops three mutually dependent and interrelated strands: social and moral responsibility; political literacy; and community involvement. The overriding goal of the subject is to cultivate an active and informed engagement in politics which links together the ideas of moral and civic virtue (or values), culminating in 'active participative inhabitants of a state exercising both rights and duties for the common good, whether in official or voluntary public arenas' (Crick, 2000).

This idea continues in the present 2014 national curriculum which sets out the overall purpose of citizenship as a subject.

'A high-quality citizenship education helps to provide pupils with knowledge, skills and understanding to prepare them to play a full and active part in society.' The purpose statement goes on: '… citizenship education should foster pupils' keen awareness and understanding of democracy, government and how laws are made and upheld. Teaching should equip pupils with the skills and knowledge to explore political and social issues critically, to weigh evidence, debate and make reasoned arguments. It should also prepare pupils to take their place in society as responsible citizens, manage their money well and make sound financial decisions.'

Good citizenship teaching involves exploring a wide range of political, social, environmental, economic, legal, and moral issues and topics as concepts are introduced and subject knowledge is developed. The choice of curriculum content – the issues and public problems that teachers choose to teach about – is a reflection of value judgments about what it is important for pupils to know and understand, and what citizenship education aims to achieve (Hayward, 2007). While the national curriculum teaching requirements are broadly value neutral, other national policies which have a bearing on citizenship set out a framework of values with expectations about the role of schools. For example, citizenship requires the study of 'parliamentary democracy in the UK' and 'other systems and forms of government including democratic and non-democratic' and this is likely to involve weighing up the merits and demerits of different systems. While there is no explicit suggestion that parliamentary government is better than other systems of governance, democratic rather than non-democratic government is promoted as best for society through the DfE fundamental British values, which includes democracy. Citizenship is at least in part to promote the importance of a liberal and free democracy with teaching about democratic government, local democracy, a free media, and religious freedom and tolerance.

As the national curriculum (2014) states: 'Schools should promote the fundamental British values of democracy, the rule of law, individual liberty, and mutual respect and tolerance of those with different faiths and beliefs,' and 'encourage respect for democracy and support for participation in the democratic processes, including respect for the basis on which the law is made and applied in England'.

The value of citizenship to society

Citizenship education instils a sense of citizenry and purpose, a respect for human rights, and a sense of belonging and wellbeing which is necessary for democracy to thrive. Heater and Oliver (1994) set out some ambitious goals for citizenship education:

To actively practise civic virtue and good citizenship.

To enjoy but not exploit civil and political rights.

Not to discriminate against others.

To teach citizenship to others.

If these goals are achieved, even to some extent, then democratic society benefits.

Democracy itself can enhance citizens' well-being, or flourishing – through their freedom of expression, through free association with kindred spirits, through a sense of belonging and purpose, and through the optimism that drives democratic renewal. These benefits contribute to what we can think of as a sense of democratic well-being (Moorse and Jerome, 2023). While schools are far from perfect institutions, for many pupils they offer a relatively stable and nurturing environment where equality and inclusion are consciously promoted and taught (through citizenship), and where good social relations are fostered. In both this school context and within the citizenship curriculum, pupils learn about and experience democratic values including freedom, rights, voting, equality, cooperation, and inclusion – and this contributes to the well-being of our democracy and supports the democratic well-being of our young people. In this sense citizenship provides a sense of optimism and hope for a better society and future where our actions and viewpoints are all valued.

The value of citizenship to the individual

Citizenship makes a unique contribution to preparing pupils for life and work whatever their background and beliefs and wherever their future takes them. The subject is ambitious in providing pupils with essential knowledge, skills, and an understanding of the political, social, and moral issues of the day, the legal and economic systems we live in, as well as practical experiences of the roles citizens play in a democratic and free society.

Through active learning in citizenship pupils develop the knowledge and skills required for weighing up evidence, sustaining arguments, holding those with power to account, influencing decision-making, and challenging injustice. It also fosters knowledge of how to play an active part in communities, and public and democratic life, as well as developing the understanding necessary to become empowered and have your voice heard in an increasingly noisy, information rich, and complex world. Opportunities to join with others, collaborate and take forward active citizenship can support pupils in building their sense of belonging, purpose, and agency. Giving them the tools to develop a more just sustainable and equitable world and to nurture informed participation in democracy.

At a glance: Illuminating citizenship through a values-based framework

Moral and ethical values – in citizenship pupils consider competing ideas of right and wrong, how to balance rights in conflict or tension, as well as different ethical debates in society both within the UK and beyond. These might include the rights, responsibilities, and moral dilemmas we face in relation to consumer choices and consumption; whether war is ever justified; how best to support the marginalised and most vulnerable in society; or the use of nuclear power as a means to counter climate change.

Cultural values – our sense of our own identities and connections with others are explored when considering ourselves in relation to the different communities and groups that we belong to, and which comprise the diversity of the UK and the wider world. This includes where personal and wider values are shared or differ, and how these relate to our own sense of national identity, citizenship, and belonging. Through citizenship we explore the different perspectives held by various groups about the big questions of the day such as: equality and gender; education; lifestyle choices; money; and types of authority and its influence.

Social values – our own role in society as citizens, our relationships with others in society, and how we see ourselves in relation to those who govern us are intertwined. Our actions and behaviours, and our own sense of citizenship and rights, develop as we build understanding of and contribute to democratic society – and as we show concern for others and the environment around us in our school, neighbourhood, the UK, Europe, and the wider world through active citizenship. Social values are explored through questions around: decision-making and how democracy works; rules and law-making; how we make sense of information and the media; and how we contribute to shaping a better society for all.

Spiritual values – citizenship also allows examination of our identities, what makes us unique as humans, and what binds us together with other similar people. This includes what drives religious and non-religious beliefs, and how identity is expressed through our sense of purpose and place; our actions and empathy towards others; and how these affect our view of the world around us and our role in society.

What the teachers and practitioners say

Values in citizenship is about promoting democracy, the rule of law and mutual respect but also about valuing student voice and our moral responsibility as teachers to provide high quality citizenship teaching and to enable students to use their voice in our classrooms. Teaching about the Equality Act, human rights, and diversity is really important. We do this in our curriculum, and we ensure that students can see themselves reflected in what we teach about the diversity of our school and community. This means we have to think about the stories we tell, the case studies we use, and the active citizens we champion.

For citizenship teachers, we need to think about controversial and sensitive issues, and we need to help our students use critical thinking as they explore these. The teacher-student interaction and relationship needs to be established with care and we need to understand which issues are sensitive for our students.

We have issues with far-right extremism in our city. Our teachers need to have the confidence to challenge viewpoints and the knowledge of how to present alternative viewpoints. This has become more necessary than ever since the Covid-19 pandemic. Helen Blachford, head of citizenship, Priory School, Southsea.

Schools as institutions need to become infused with democratic processes: this is equally true of classrooms. Alistair Ross, UCL, Institute of Education.

Exploring values in the citizenship classroom

Citizenship is at its best where schools teach the subject through a planned, progressive, and well sequenced citizenship curriculum in conjunction with opportunities for pupils to experience and practise democratic citizenship within the classroom, school, and wider community. However, sometimes there is a gap between the values promoted through citizenship and the practices used by teachers in the process of teaching. For example, if pupils are taught about democracy and the value of citizens having a say in decisions that affect them on the one hand, but teaching is directive, closed, and does not enable or allow pupils freedom to express their viewpoints on the other. Or teaching might address the democratic actions that citizens can take to address issues and problems in society, while pupils themselves are denied an opportunity to choose and take actions on issues of concern to them. Or teaching might focus on the roles of the media in democracy but be presented as a one-sided lesson on bias in the media (Hayward, 2007).

The citizenship teacher has a responsibility to create an open classroom climate for learning that is: safe and respectful; values diverse ideas and perspectives; encourages questioning and critical thinking; promotes discussion, deliberation, and reflection; and supports collaborative and positive action on issues of concern. Teachers need to be impartial when introducing issues and ideas and mindful of their role in providing a balance of perspectives especially on political issues and problems that are explored over time. Teachers also need to know their school's policy and how to respond when pupils express a view or disclose information that raises safeguarding concerns. However, we should also be realistic because teachers are not faultless. When pupils realise 'the teacher is human too', there is also an opportunity for powerful learning (Taylor, 1998).

Values at the heart of citizenship

Citizenship education has generally been discussed and considered alongside values and dispositions. There are many ways to consider and promote values in citizenship but one way to do this is to use the core values of democracy, justice, and responsibility, because these also act as key concepts in the subject.

Value	Disposition
Democracy and freedom.	Concern for the common good.
	Concern to resolve conflict.
	Practice of tolerance.
	Courage to defend a point of view.
	Willingness to be open to changing one's opinions and attitudes in the light of discussion and evidence.
Justice, human rights, the rule of law, equality and diversity.	Respect for the rule of law.
	Commitment to human rights and equality.
	Respect for diversity.
	Determination to act justly and speak out on injustice and discrimination.
	Concern for the environment.
Responsibility, democratic participation, and active citizenship.	Commitment to active citizenship and democratic participation.
	Disposition to work with and for others with sympathetic understanding.
	Showing initiative and effort.
	Proclivity to act responsibly: that is care for others and oneself; considering the effect actions are likely to have on others; and acceptance of responsibility for unforeseen or unfortunate consequences.

(adapted from Crick, 1998)

As discussed earlier, as well as the values that are promoted through teaching, we also need to consider the values promoted through the teaching process. For example, deliberation and toleration – which link to critical thinking, enquiry, discussion, and debate – support the development of pupils as informed citizens who can make decisions and take actions, thereby putting values into practice.

Related and supporting values

Related Values	Curriculum Application	Cross-Curricular Links	Helping learners put the value into action
KS1			
Democracy	Take part in a simple debate about topical issues. Agree and follow rules for the group and classroom. Understand how these rules help.	Developing purposeful talk through English/ literacy.	Use a simple 'hat' debate to help children express a viewpoint for or against an issue.
Justice	Discussion of what is fair, right, and wrong.	Developing concept of fairness through RE.	Use the Philosophy for Children methodology for exploring complex ideas in an inclusive way.
Responsibility	Listen to other people and play and work cooperatively.	Developing sense of self and relationships with others through RSHE.	Use a group decision making activity to choose which toys to play with and which to share with another group at playtime.
KS2			
Democracy	Introduce what democracy is, what politicians do for citizens, and where decisions for the local community and country are made.	Developing understanding of parliament through history and some significant politicians who shaped society.	Move from abstract to real by setting up an engagement with a local politician (in person or online) to introduce pupils to the role of MPs and parliament, or local councillor and council chamber.
Justice	Why and how rules and laws are made and enforced, why different rules are needed in different situations, and how to take part in making and changing rules.	Rules for managing risk in RSHE.	Consider situations in which rules are needed (safety, fairness, order) and link to the idea of why we have laws for the country, e.g. driving on the left side of the road. Consider what rules are needed in the school community.
Responsibility	There are different kinds of responsibilities, rights, and duties at home, at school, and in the community, e.g. the right to learn.		Use a class or school council as a place to consider children's rights and the different roles and decisions that children can make to help the class/school be a happy and safe place for everyone to learn.

KS3			
Democracy	Acquire a sound knowledge and understanding of the United Kingdom's government and political system, and how citizens participate actively in its democratic systems of government.	Developing understanding of the magna carta, and the historical development of parliamentary government in Britain.	Use deliberative debate to explore a controversial and topical issue that is currently in the news or being debated in Westminster – an approach that is exemplified in the ACT deliberative classroom resource.
Justice	Develop a sound knowledge and understanding of the role of law and the justice system in our society and how laws are shaped and enforced.	Develop understanding of different religious perspectives to crime and punishment in RE.	Critically explore how and why the justice system operates differently for young people who are victims or perpetrators and consider the role of the Youth Justice Board.
Responsibility	Develop an interest in – and commitment to participation in – volunteering as well as other forms of responsible activity through active citizenship to show concern for others and the environment.		Use the ACT active citizenship process (plan, act, and reflect) to explore issues that affect young people and how they can take different kinds of action collaboratively to address them, e.g. from eco anxiety to environmental action.
Democracy	Contrast the key features of a democratic political system with a non-democratic, for example a free media.		Develop media literacy to counter misinformation and to explore why and how different media cover a news topic. Build understanding of the role of a free media in democracy to hold government to account and inform citizens.
Justice	Explore how the law helps society deal with complex problems including human rights and international law.		Use case studies of human rights defenders to teach human rights issues from a personalised perspective and to explore the concept of universal and absolute rights and develop the skills to think critically and weigh up competing rights.
Responsibility	Investigate the actions citizens can take in democratic and electoral processes to influence decisions locally, nationally, and beyond.		Use the ACT parallel election process to teach about the nature of elections, the different voting systems that are used, and why voting matters.

What the learners say

We would never get these topics elsewhere in the curriculum ... citizenship helps you prepare for the world more than other subjects, it is real life stuff we learn. KS2 pupil.

[Citizenship] expands your knowledge of what is happening in society and helps us to understand how the government works. KS2 pupil.

Citizenship teaches you a lot about responsibility, and we value how we got to the point we have in our society, for example through equality laws. KS2 pupil.

Citizenship is important as it increases understanding of the world around us ... we need to become critical thinkers and find good sources of information. Citizenship helps us do this. Topics like democracy, voting and educating us on real news, not myths, around refugees etc. are really important. KS3 pupil.

Questions for consideration in the staffroom

1. Which values do you consider are the most important ones to promote when teaching citizenship?
2. Does your classroom practice reflect and include the values promoted when teaching citizenship?
3. What kinds of curriculum and pedagogical approaches lend themselves to promoting values when teaching citizenship?

Further reading

Citizenship Programmes of Study, KS1-2 (2001) London: Department for Education.

National Curriculum for Citizenship (2014) London: Department for Education.

Association for Citizenship Teaching (2017) *The Deliberative Classroom*. Available at: teachingcitizenship.org.uk.

Crick, B. (1998) *Education for Citizenship and Teaching Democracy in Schools. Final Report.* London: QCA.

Crick, B. (2020) *Essays on Citizenship.* London: Continuum.

Hayward, J. (2007) 'Values, beliefs and the citizenship teacher', in *A Practical Guide to Teaching Citizenship in the Secondary School*, ed. Gearon, L. Abingdon: Routledge, pp. 9-19.

Heater, D. and Oliver, D. (1994) *The Foundations of Citizenship*. Hemel Hempstead: Harvester Wheatsheaf.

Moorse, L. & Jerome, L. (forthcoming 2023) 'Citizenship Education: Building for the Future', in *Who's Afraid of Political Education? The challenge to teach civic competence & democratic participation,* ed. Tam, H. Bristol: Policy Press, chapter 11.

Ross, A. (2008) 'Organizing a Curriculum for Active Citizenship Education' in *The SAGE Handbook of Education for Citizenship and Democracy,* ed. Arthur, Davies, Hahn. London: Sage Publishing, pp. 492-505.

Taylor, M. (1998). *Values Education and Values in Education.* London: Association of Teachers and Lecturers.

CHAPTER 7

The Curriculum and Pedagogy of Values-based Education in Computing

Computing is not about computers anymore. It is about living.
Nicholas Negroponte

Values at the heart of computing

In the content and pedagogy of computing, the following values could be said to be core and of the essence of the subject: care, communication, consideration, opportunity, and safety. They are recurrent and characteristic. In the very act of studying this subject, learners will frequently come face to face with these values and practise them.

The importance of computing in schools

Computing is now an integral part of most people's lives. So, in teaching computing in schools, we are enabling pupils to develop their technical skills for their current needs as well as preparing them for the world of work. With this ubiquity, of course, comes opportunities for exploitation and thus digital literacy (often called online safety) is an essential component of learning.

The value of computing to society

Our recent Covid-19 experience has underlined how important computing is to all our lives: for communication; connection; knowledge; and support, etc. Many people have declared that they have improved their own digital skills by dint of need in this time – and there have been many heartening examples of generous assistance and sharing of knowledge. It is now almost impossible to imagine our lives without computing.

> *The 21 century has more potential than perhaps any other in our brief evolutionary history. We stand on the cusp of computing, genetic, and energy generation breakthroughs that were only recently in the realm of science-fiction. A golden age of humanity is tantalisingly within our grasp.*
>
> Clive Lewis

The value of computing to the individual

Computing, by its very nature, provides many very efficient tools for work and for learning. The ability of computing to elevate our knowledge, understanding, connections and achievements is manifold. Its impact for disabled, housebound, and aged individuals is well-recognised. Computing abounds with opportunities for children to achieve with technology where they don't in other areas of the curriculum, that is particularly true in coding where a heavily logical approach and strong element of there being very clear right and wrong answers appeals to some children.

Illuminating computing through a values-based framework

Moral and ethical values – these abound in computing: the ability to do good in the world always has questions and considerations attached. So, keeping safe online and free from exploitation is a necessary element of all this work. The big question of, 'just because we can, should we?' is a good one to grapple with.

Cultural values – computing is a reasonably egalitarian form of communication across cultures but of course cultures have developed around social messaging that have their own branding. Safeguarding messages are vital here so that children know how to keep themselves safe in a variety of contexts.

Social values – digital literacy strand. Helping children to use social media, messaging, blogging, etc. Children are usually grateful for the learning experiences they are given. Digital Leader/Online Safety Ambassador type initiatives are great for helping specific children by giving them school-wide responsibility for such things. By following safe practice rules, children can be taught how computing is a route to positive practical action in a whole range of spheres in the modern day.

Spiritual values – computing opens up worlds and vistas, communications and relationships that in their own right are a source of awe and wonder and can lead us to places we didn't know we could go.

What the teachers and practitioners say

I hope that I demonstrate a good set of values through all my work. A set of proper values, subscribed to by all involved is a vital component in every effective learning experience.

We need to really engage values in computing – this must not be a values-free space!

A values-based computing experience in the classroom			
Related Values	**Curriculum Application**	**Cross-Curricular Link**	**Taking Values into Action**
KS1			
Appreciation Understanding	Recognising common uses of information technology beyond school, looking at the things it can do to help people live well and live better.	PSHE	Ask family members about the information technology they use – how does it help them? What do they like or dislike about it? Can you make a drawn or written list of all of these?
Respect Self-Belief Care Consideration	Learning about keeping safe online. This is about self-respect and self-belief; using technology safely and respectfully; and keeping personal information private. Identify where to go for help and support when they have concerns about content or contact on the internet or other online technologies.	PSHE RSHE	Make a Staying Safe Online poster to take home to share with the family: what are the key points you need to get across?
KS2			
Hope Service Appreciation Gratitude Co-operation Generosity	How digital systems can be used to help people make efficient use of time and resources. Examine a variety of mechanisms in the home, e.g. fire alarms, fridges, etc.	PSHE Citizenship	Carry out some research into how technology is used in disabled aids to support those who need it most. What invention would you make to help someone who, for example, needed help with eating?
Respect Self-Belief Care Consideration Rule of Law	Use technology safely, respectfully, and responsibly; recognise acceptable/unacceptable behaviour; identify a range of ways to report concerns about content and contact.	RSHE PSHE	Look at ways in which technology has transformed care - each group looks at one service, e.g. hospitals or vet services, and reports back to the class.

KS3			
Respect **Care** **Consideration** **Empathy** **Rule of Law**	Communicating purposefully and respectfully; understanding our roles and responsibilities. What to do if something has gone wrong and understanding about the 'digital footprint'. Create a respect charter for online learning.	Citizenship RSHE	Take some examples of informal messages and use your respect charter to improve them!
Empathy **Understanding**	Animations.		Can you design a short animation using your computing skills to tell younger children about a particular value.

What the learners say

Computing teaches you how to be resilient through identifying bugs in programs. KS3 pupil.

Questions for consideration in the staffroom

How aware are staff of the values possibilities in computing and how explicitly are these links made in teaching?

Audience and purpose are some of the big benefits that technology can bring to children and their work. Can we enhance, for example, make routine use of peer assessment by using a class blog, rather than writing in an exercise book where the audience is the teacher alone? This can help to further develop values, resilience, and skills.

Further reading

UK Council for Internet Safety (2020) *Education for a Connected World 2020*. Available at: https://assets.publishing.service.gov.uk/government/uploads/system/uploads/attachment_data/file/896323/UKCIS_Education_for_a_Connected_World_.pdf.

If you want to look further Project Evolve (evolving!) is putting meat onto these bones for busy teachers in classrooms (https://projectevolve.co.uk).

CHAPTER 8

The Curriculum and Pedagogy of Values-based Education in Design and Technology

The inventor looks upon the world and is not contented with things as they are. He wants to improve things he sees; he wants to benefit the world.

Alexander Graham Bell

Values at the heart of design and technology

In the content and pedagogy of design and technology the following values could be said to be core and of the essence of this subject: care, cooperation, creativity, interdependence, resourcefulness, and service. They are recurrent and characteristic. In the very act of studying this subject, learners will frequently come face to face with these values and practise them.

The importance of design and technology in schools

Design and technology holds so much potential for enabling our children to develop creativity, ingenuity, resourcefulness, inventiveness, and wisdom. This subject requires students to play – to wonder, to experiment, take considered risks, evaluate, and adapt – and to generate inspiration. All the skills we need our young people to develop to be successful learners are here in design and technology.

The value of design and technology to society

As a society we need people who can dream, imagine, aspire, and invent so that we can live well. We need people who can create and develop from a values-based outlook to solve problems and improve the world. If we can innovate, be resourceful, and respectful of our planet, we might be able to continue to live on it into the future.

The value of design and technology to the individual

The gift of design and technology to us as individuals is immense and rich: discovering about and using a range of materials; learning about and from designs from other times and eras as well as our own; and designing and developing ideas and products on our own and with others. It is permission to play and experiment. It feeds our creativity and our imagination and offers us roads down which we can travel with our resourcefulness and ingenuity. It makes us think deeply about what it is to live well in our world.

Illuminating design and technology through a values-based framework

Design and technology goes right to the heart of human need, ingenuity, and our interdependence. When we look around our home, eat our food, do our daily jobs, we realise how much we have to thank unknown others for. The designer who designed my dishwasher, the people who made it, and those who came up with the detergent balls to put inside it all deserve my gratitude every day.

Moral and ethical values – the ability to create brings with it moral and ethical issues: what should we create? Who will benefit from it? Will it harm anyone? In creating one thing, are we depriving someone of something else? How can we build this idea without damaging the planet?

Cultural values – technology can swim across cultural divides, speaking a universal language and emphasising our connectivity. When we consider the origins of designs and products, we develop understanding of and respect for cultures through time and beyond our own.

Social values – the creation process demands that we consider our own needs, wants and values in combination with those of others. We have to work with others to understand their needs, benefit from their skills, knowledge, and ideas and acknowledge that we are playing a part in a collective whole.

Spiritual values – the creative and constructive process brings with it a tantalising glimpse of the ineffable: the sense that we have in a small way played a role in bringing about something that wasn't there before, that has made a contribution to the world and that may change it forever.

Natural values – the natural world around us inspires some of the great technological ideas, such as biodomes or velcrose. In borrowing from nature, we reinforce our respect for and wonder at our natural world. When we revere nature, we want to protect it, use it with a conscience, and feel a sense of our own place within a bigger system.

What the teachers and practitioners say

Design and technology, at its best, is a different form of creativity, using technology to solve real-life problems and issues. Values are inherent and run right through this subject because it's all about how we develop as people. There is scope in abundance for collaborative work, sharing ideas, working things out, using people's diverse skills, and for developing values such as resilience, industry, connection, and collaboration.

A Values-based design and technology experience in the classroom			
Related Values	Curriculum Application	Cross-Curricular Links	Taking Values into Action
KS1			
Co-operation Democracy Justice Rule of Law Unity Gratitude Appreciation Interdependence Harmony	Looking at where our food comes from - appreciation of nature and all the people who help get our food to us.	Science - parts of a plant; food cycles. PSHE - looking after ourselves and healthy eating. RSHE - looking after ourselves and healthy eating.	Can you draw a mind map of thankfulness for all the things (plant and animal) that are grown for our benefit? What sorts of things do we need to think about to ensure our plants and animals are well looked after? Invite a farmer to talk to the children about growing food.
Service Resilience Determination Courage Kindness Gratitude	Using mechanisms - create a moving thank you or congratulations card. Think about what the person would really like and how it can be made to move using a slider or leaver mechanism.	English - writing. Maths - carry out a survey to find out which of your designs people liked best.	How do we feel when someone says thank you or well done to us? Take a digital photo of their reaction to your moving card! What other ways can we show our support or gratitude - to people of our own age or younger, or the elderly?
KS2			
Equality Co-operation Unity Respect Fairness Justice Appreciation Understanding Service	Food technology, looking at where food comes from across different cultures and how it is used in celebrations in different cultures.	Research skills in geography and history. SMSC. RE and religious festivals.	Explore assumptions, e.g. although fish and chips are associated with UK culture they were first introduced here in 1860 by a Jewish boy. Can you design (and make!) a pizza that uses foods originating from different cultures?

Understanding Service Interdependence Compassion Kindness Altruism Empathy	Product design and how things that are made help us to live better. Look at a range of products to deduce how the manufacturer has tried to meet needs and appeal to the user.	Citizenship and RSE.	Analyse mechanical products at home ... how many of them have been designed to help someone with a need? Research disabled aids. What has the designer had to think of in meeting the needs of a disabled user.
KS3			
Compassion Empathy Respect Democracy Care Consideration	Understand the source, seasonality, and characteristics of a broad range of ingredients. Investigate food waste and how to minimise this in our own household. Making your own food composter!	Geography – countries of origin.	Get involved in movements to prevent/mitigate food waste, including the use of Food Banks. Research the range of options. Which appeal to you? How can you raise further awareness in your community?
Understanding Appreciation Respect Unity Co-operation Rule of law Kindness Altruism Generosity	Textiles and looking at different cultures to identify and understand need. Looking at the properties of materials (natural and synthetic).	Maths – reading, constructing, and interpreting data.	We think of natural fabrics as 'better' but what are the downsides to growing cotton, for example? Set up a debate on the pros and cons of growing cotton – what do you conclude?

What the learners say

I've still got the teddy bear I made in Year 2! I was so proud to have made it. Design and technology doesn't feel like work.

It's good [design and technology] because it's a helpful subject. It's mostly about helping things to get better.

I like it when we have to work in a group because it's fun and other people can help you.

Questions for consideration in the staffroom

How well do you think your learners currently understand the social, cultural, moral and spiritual values that underpin this subject? How would your staff respond if asked the same question?

How could you make more explicit the values-roots of any design project in your school?

Could your design and technology department agree on – say three – values they feel are most important to this subject and seek to promote them throughout their work?

CHAPTER 9

The Curriculum and Pedagogy of Values-based Education in Drama

Drama is a way of or seeing the world. Many learners have street wisdom. What drama does is offer them some world wisdom.

Hwyel Roberts

Values at the heart of drama

In the content and pedagogy of drama the following values could be said to be core and of the essence of the subject: appreciation, empathy, imagination, self-belief, and thoughtfulness. They are recurrent and characteristic. In the very act of studying this subject, learners will frequently come face to face with these values and practise them.

The importance of drama in schools

Drama brings other subjects to life! Who can conceive of Christmas or an end of year at school without a play of some kind? The Highway Man … the Vikings … the life of Jesus … who can imagine learning about these things without acting them out? And drama can do so much more! Drama is the enabling of scenarios and situations that invite children to think about the world but from a position of safety and care. For example, five-year-olds might be invited to negotiate the dilemma of discovering that the Big Bad Wolf is injured and needs our help. Dilemma-based learning is so important. It teaches us that binary thinking can be unhelpful, gently encouraging us instead to see and consider different perspectives.

The value of drama to society

From the days of the ancient Greeks, drama and performance have always been a way of representing ourselves, our thoughts, dreams and fears, and our attempt to make sense of our world. Drama education is not about making actors. Rather, it is about developing worth, spirit, and contribution. It also supports articulacy, oracy, and optimism. It is a currency of humanity. Dramatic presentations – whether in live theatre or through other media – enable us to see back through time and look on into the future; we see ourselves from angles we hadn't glimpsed before; we meet others we like and feel comfortable with (as well as those we don't). Drama always surprises. It prods our conscience; it feeds our soul; it suggests, infers, and enlivens our imaginations.

The value of drama to the individual

Drama allows us to play at and rehearse life. Like good literature, drama carries opportunities to look out at the world while also looking into ourselves, holding a mirror up to what it is to be human in all its complexity, and with all its paradox. You can be creative, confident, and yet, evil: drama enables us to recognise these traits. Becoming empathetic means being 'able to walk in someone else's shoes' – to enter imaginatively into their thoughts and feelings. Through drama we can do just this. It can help us be better people.

Illuminating drama through a values-based framework

Drama is all about what it is to be human. Threaded through are moral, ethical, social, cultural and spiritual elements. It offers a gateway to really meeting these values head on.

Moral and ethical values – drama invites and enables us to consider issues from a range of viewpoints. Stories and characters that twist and turn and invite us to weigh up information, knowledge, and facts, and cause us to see things through the eyes of others, thereby expanding our horizons, realisations, and knowledge base.

Cultural values – drama allows us to travel the world and travel through time: seeing, hearing, smelling, touching and feeling a connection beyond the immediate. New horizons safely open to us and open our eyes to different possibilities.

Social values – apart from the intrinsic value in working in partnership with others to decide, negotiate, discuss, and create, drama speaks to that most important question of how between us we create the best society. Storytelling and the negotiation of tension and dilemmas is key to this. We question ourselves and weigh up risk before moving forward. Dealing with difficulty is a great thing for children and young people to practise.

Spiritual values – the immersion of ourselves in the character of another – for however brief a time – and perhaps those precious moments when we 'lose' ourselves and momentarily become another, can offer a unique spiritual experience. The insight this brings is deeply meaningful, arresting, and long-lasting.

What the teachers and practitioners say

I feel that I'm lucky that my PGCE had prepared me really well for the moral quandary that faces teachers as they navigate the pressures of accountability and doing the right thing by the children in front of them. As an English teacher (and later a drama leader) I have tried to make curriculum decisions based on my values – for example, when I had issues with children using racist language in my classroom I dealt with this by choosing to teach them To Kill a Mockingbird. The curriculum served me, which is how it should be. There was, however, little guidance on this. Nobody told me it was the right thing to do. It just sat well with my values and what my training had brought out of me.

A values-based drama experience in the classroom

Related Values	Curriculum Application	Cross-Curricular Links	Taking Values into Action
KS1			
Honesty **Care** **Consideration** **Justice** **Thoughtfulness** **Forgiveness**	Retelling fairy stories and traditional tales using modelling, puppets, or toys, e.g. 'The Three Bears'. How did the bears feel when they saw what Goldilocks had done? Did Goldilocks reflect on what she had done to the bears? How did she feel? Where does consideration apply?	Maths – sequencing. English – speaking and listening, storytelling, reading, and writing. PSHE – relationships and emotions. RSHE – relationships.	In role, do a reflection as either Goldilocks or one of the bears. Think about what happened and how it made you feel. Write a letter to Goldilocks ... will you show forgiveness? Or write a letter from Goldilocks to the bears, saying how sorry you are. What can you do to make amends for your actions?
Peace **Happiness** **Friendship** **Love** **Understanding** **Thoughtfulness** **Service** **Kindness** **Altruism**	PSHE Scenarios: read, for example, *Peter's Chair* by Ezra Jack Keats. Explore Peter's feelings of jealousy about his baby sister through acting out the scenes of his 'run away' and tricking his mother, through to the reconciliation at the end. Freeze frame your scenarios to explore the depth of feeling. What brought him peace, love, and understanding? How did service help?	English – enjoying stories. Art – using collage and textiles like Ezra Jack Keats does.	Have a box of dressing up clothes and/or props for 'make-believe' and for children to use to become different characters – you will find uses for them at so many points in the term and children just love them!
KS2			
Hope **Service** **Appreciation** **Courage** **Unity** **Co-operation** **Justice** **Democracy**	Use stories that twist and turn and invite us to weigh up information, knowledge, and facts. For example, we considered an old, abandoned factory. We created floor plans and explored it via an unfolding teacher-led narrative. We were going to decide if there was anything in the old building worth saving before it was to be demolished. However, it was revealed that the factory was once a very famous chocolate producer owned by a man with the initials 'W.W.'. The children rebelled and wanted to protest against the demolition.		Look at social action groups that get together for a good cause – consider the range and scope of the things that unite people to try to help. What is your particular passion, and what might you be able to do to put your feelings in to action?

Hope Curiosity	Joan Aitken's *A Necklace of Raindrops* tells the story of a necklace that grants its owner wishes. Use silhouette cut outs to create your own wishes based on the Jan Pienkowski illustrations.	Science – light and dark. English – speaking and listening and performance.	Present these as play scenarios to the rest of the school or film them to share with families – great happenings come from values-based wishing!
KS3			
Self-Belief Courage Consideration	Public speaking. Experimenting with tone of voice to show emotions; pacing to confer self-belief and confidence and to give respect to the subject matter.	RSHE and PSHE – emotions and relationships. Computing – record these for playback evaluation.	Plan out a 5-minute speech to tell people about your chosen value.
Understanding Respect Consideration	Thought tracking. Study a range of still images for body language and facial impressions as conveyors of emotion, values, and beliefs. Experiment with still images to show different values or emotions.	RSHE and PSHE – emotions and relationships.	Choose a value to express visually as a still image through body language/expression. Have fun!

What the learners say

If I didn't know about values I wouldn't push myself to do as much as I can … reading about people who are determined and knowing about these values means I think about it and remember it. KS2 pupil.

Questions for consideration in the staffroom

How could we make more of drama in the classroom to heighten the subject experience across other subject disciplines?

Hywel Roberts describes drama as 'a vehicle for seeing the world'. Many learners have street wisdom. How can your arts curriculum offer some 'world wisdom'? How could it, for example, highlight issues of equality, justice, and tolerance?

Further reading

Digital Theatre Plus (DT+). Available at: https://www.digitaltheatreplus.com.

Drama Online. London: Bloomsbury. Available at: https://www.bloomsbury.com/uk/discover/bloomsbury-digital-resources/products/drama-online.

Farmer, D., *Primary Drama Ideas*. Available at: https://dramaresource.com/primary-drama-ideas/.

Kidd, D., & Roberts, H., (2018) *Uncharted Territories*. Carmarthen: Independent Thinking Press.

Kidd, D. (2020) *Curriculum of Hope*. Carmarthen: Independent Thinking Press.

Roberts, H. (2012) *Oops! Helping Children Learn Accidentally*. Carmarthen: Independent Thinking Press.

Taylor, T. (2016) *The Mantle of the Expert*. Norwich: Singular Publishing Limited.

CHAPTER 10

The Curriculum and Pedagogy of Values-based Education in English

Good literacy floats on a sea of talk.

James Britten

There are two reasons to read books: to illuminate your life, or to escape from it. Books set in another country may well do both.

Nicola Watson

Values at the heart of English

In the content and pedagogy of English the following values could be said to be core and of the essence of the subject: accuracy, appreciation, beauty, communication, diversity, meaning, and rigour are recurrent and characteristic. In the very act of studying this subject, learners will frequently come face to face with these values and practise them.

The importance of English as a subject discipline in schools

English is the bedrock for all learning and understanding in our school system: reading, writing, speaking, and listening, and learning the skills of critical thinking and reasoned debate. English carries positive human values such as love, care for others, the importance of community, and of equality and freedom for all. It is obviously true that English can be used to transmit negative values too. This emphasises the importance of critical reading. English can be a key vehicle for exploring values in terms of how characters behave in literature, but also in terms of developing the language of values and ethical vocabulary. English can teach the skills of debate and reasoning. It can be through English that pupils are given the means to express themselves and to listen to others respectfully.

As a world language, English is accessible to many people across the world. It has a wide vocabulary, enabling users to explore many ideas and beliefs. English is the vehicle for learning across all other subjects in the curriculum, and a confident use and understanding of the language is vital to effective learning. Terminology such as spiritual, moral, cultural, ethical, and social values all require definition, and those definitions may vary across users of the language, often because of different cultural perspectives. Simply presenting these values as implicit undermines the importance of very complex areas, which require much greater in-depth exploration.

The choice of texts for the study of literature raises issues about the values embodied in those texts. Texts such as *Whale Boy*, *Street Child*, or *Hiawatha* all demand discussion of the values which they illustrate. In analysing these texts, the teacher cannot ignore the messages about society that they clearly demonstrate. This is true too for picture books used with younger children ... *Dear Daddy* by Philippe Dupasquier raises issues of the pain of missing a parent, the joy of reunion with the parent, and the importance of love and loss. These may not always be acknowledged when reading with young children.

Teaching methods and approaches should aim to promote values for living in harmony in a democratic and multicultural society. They should enable pupils to develop the skills and knowledge to promote social cohesion, value diversity and appreciate differences. Pupils should be supported to be able to debate and discuss as well as settle agreements with a respect for other's opinions.

English can promote cooperation, teamwork, and critical thinking: through being able to work in groups, listening to others' opinions and asking questions, children test their own ideas and thoughts, and learn to modify or strengthen their views in the light of discussion.

The value of English to society

English, the language of international communication, the national media, and the internet, underpins all that we do and all that we achieve. It is essential for all aspects of life quality: educational, professional, and personal.

Any language incorporates the values of its users, and these values draw upon the cultures(s) in which it is used. Its many dialects and accents are imbued with values which relate to hierarchies. The use of received pronunciation is perceived as in the highest tier by some, while other dialects are less valued across the UK. One of the most notable disliked accents is that often used in Birmingham. In recent years there has been a greater acceptance of some less valued dialects, and a reduced emphasis on R.P. as the most valued dialect, at least in the media. Of course, prejudice against accents and dialects can also include dislike of the use of R.P., with a perception that it marks out those who consider themselves to be part of an elite group.

English can open the door to understanding others and to understanding other areas of the curriculum. It has huge power. Through literature, young people can learn to empathise and identify with the feelings of others. They can analyse motives and actions of characters without any risk taking.

The value of English to the individual

The ability to read perceptively, write cogently, speak articulately, and listen with perspicacity – are essential to be able to function effectively in and cope with the demands of today's society and workplace. Literature engages us, feeds our curiosity, nurtures a sense of wonder, and encourages an enquiring mind.

Literature also offers multifarious opportunities to exemplify values. Moral dilemmas explored in poetry and plays, for example, provide insights into choices made, and the reasons for these choices. They show how alternative behaviours could have resulted in different outcomes and enable children to engage in discussion about choices made and the values which underpin them. Take a young children's book such as the Ahlberg's *Burglar Bill* which, while entertaining and enjoyable, also raises questions about acceptable values and behaviour, which children love to ponder and pronounce upon!

Studying a range of texts gives an opportunity to reflect on our beliefs and opinions, learn about other cultures and socio-economic settings, and consider moral choices and decision-making. Through literature, we realise that other people too have internal worlds that are complex and rich, full of feelings, emotions, aspirations, regrets, opinions, and sometimes confusion. There is a reassurance that we are not alone in feeling or thinking as we do, and there is illumination in discovering new and different ways of being.

When we are writing, we discover more of our own thoughts and inner impulses; we learn to consider and balance views and arguments, and we engage in a reflective process that serves to deepen our critical faculties.

Literature takes us to new places, encouraging each of us to think of the world outside of our own experience. The ability to imagine, engage, question and empathise with a wide range of situations, contexts, and characters allows us to develop a sense of ourselves and our world on a far bigger stage.

Illuminating English through a values-based framework

The exploration of values can make the subject area of English more interesting, more relevant, and more exciting. If we are learning about the way the whole world communicates and how this helps us to build relationships, then learning through texts becomes very real and can profoundly influence our society. Through literature many experiences – and their inherent values – can be within our reach, e.g. we can read about Jewish experiences at the hand of the Nazis. Through characters, we can begin to appreciate the horror of this before we have even travelled to the museums and memorials.

Moral and ethical values – characters we meet in literature present us with a range of moral and ethical issues. Fairy tales, fables and traditional stories often pose moral dilemmas, but so too do contemporary fiction, poetry, and plays. Stories such as *The Selfish Giant* offer obvious openings for moral and ethical discussion, but opportunities arise more subtly in many, many other stories and non-fiction texts too. Discussion and debate widen and deepen our responses to dilemmas, helping us to see that very often morality and ethics do not have fixed points and easy answers, that our views require reasoned justification to have validity, and that the consequences of actions can be far-reaching and dramatic.

Cultural values – literature opens up the world to us, developing and deepening our understanding of its variety. Factual knowledge and understanding brings us awareness of needs and problems affecting our own and other countries. Researching world issues and learning the conventions of persuasive writing, for example, places us in a position to engage with issues of real significance in our world.

Social values – English is a deeply social and sociable subject. Literature is the sharing of what it is to be human, in all its countless forms. Discussion and sharing – and acting and retelling – of stories, plays, and poems demands that we listen and speak to others, disclosing our opinions and respecting and learning from those of others. Through this process comes greater self-knowledge and self-esteem.

Spiritual values – literature – perhaps especially diaries, journals, letters, biographies, and autobiographies – enables us to privately reflect on our own life in response to the lives of others. We can come to know and better understand our innermost thoughts and feelings.

What the teachers and practitioners say

It's impossible to effectively teach English without teaching about values … through literature, we teach children to develop their own reasoning and opinions, understanding that different social and cultural realities co-exist. They learn that the world is a complex place, but that values help us navigate through it – and that this is a thrilling experience.

Open a book: there are the values! They become like old friends to little children and they love pointing them out.

Values of all kinds are present throughout literature. It isn't about being preachy. Through literature, you come to see how values are just part of everyday life, and they can both help and hinder you. I find it endlessly fascinating.

A values-based English experience in the classroom

Related Values	Curriculum Application	Cross-Curricular Links	Taking Values into Action
KS1			
Hope **Joy** **Beauty** **Service**	Paddington - focus on his arrival in London as a homeless person. Write a diary entry as Paddington: what do you need right now; what are your feelings and emotions? Write Paddington a label for himself, describing his character for a potential new friend to be able to get to know him.	Geography - trace Paddington's journey from Peru to London.	Explore what we all need to survive - Maslow's hierarchy of need. Can you recreate it based on Paddington? For example, where does he find food and shelter? Look into charities that are set up to help homelessness.
Hope **Unity** **Care** **Consideration** **Respect**	Formal letter writing based on the book, *Dear Greenpeace*.	Science - species and their habitats and conditions needed to survive.	Research the work of Greenpeace and similar charitable groups that work together to protect the planet.
KS2			
Peace **Love** **Courage**	The use and effect of metaphor, simile and personification in poetry, drama, and fiction writing - Longfellow's *Hiawatha*, Emily Dickinson, and others provide good starting points. Use these literary techniques to describe one another, what do we notice about the values they display?	Art - draw or use mixed media to depict your values person. Make a values line - drawing of someone's face or profile, using values words to form the lines.	Create your own personification of a given value - such as a personification of peace - what does your person look like, sound like, say to you? What aura does your person emanate? Do they have a special message for you or the world? Will you base this writing on someone you know or a well-known role model?
Courage **Hope** **Friendship** **Compassion** **Empathy**	Writing in role as a displaced person. Use current examples in the news about refugees and their plight. Can we use our value of empathy to put ourselves in their shoes? Write a letter to a humanitarian friend or to God.	Geography and history of diaspora.	Start to look out for news stories of refugees and displaced people. Little acts of kindness as well as larger acts involving collective responses to disasters.

KS3			
Unity Co-operation Diversity Equality Justice	Formal letter writing. Pick a current local or national issue to write to your local MP about. Research the issues carefully and make at least 5 reasoned points to argue your case, then make your polite request for action.	The geography and history of the issue.	Research local and national charities and groups that are also supporting this issue. Is there anything that you can personally contribute at this stage?
Love Courage Altruism Justice	Shakespeare. What are the moral/ethical dilemmas posed in the play and how does the principal character approach them? What would you have done in their shoes and what factors would you have to consider?		What are the modern-day parallels to the issues raised in this play? What are the main messages you would extrapolate for a modern-day audience? Develop a set of advice for a person of your age?

What the learners say

When you ask what values mean to me in English or any subject, it's a question that makes you go into a new nook and cranny of your brain. It's finding something new in yourself, like being in a house and finding a new room you didn't know was there before, or like Narnia – going into a cupboard and finding a new world! KS2 pupil.

English teaches us love because you learn new words and languages to use in our writing. We create our own stories which enhances our imagination and language skills.

Questions for consideration in the staffroom

How do you choose your curriculum texts? Would an audit show they provide a good range of opportunities to consider moral, social, cultural, ethical, and spiritual issues?

How much importance is placed on discussion and debate, including philosophical debate, in your English curriculum? Could there be room for more?

What do your pupils say they would like to learn about?

Further reading

Campbell, E. (2003) *The Ethical Teacher*. Maidenhead: Open University Press.

Cribb, A. (2009) 'Professional ethics: Whose responsibility?' in, Gewirtz, S., Mahony, P., Hextall, I., and Cribb, A. (eds) *Changing Teacher Professionalism: International Trends, Challenges and Ways Forward*. London: Routledge, pp. 31–42.

Janmaat, J. G. (2018) 'Educational Influences on young people's support for fundamental British values', *British Educational Research Journal*, 44 (2), (April 2018), pp. 251-273.

Johnston, B. (2003) *Values in English Language Teaching*. London: Routledge.

Rayner, S. (2014) 'Playing by the rules? The professional values of head teachers tested by the changing policy context', *Management in Education*, (2014), 28 (2), pp. 38-43.

Rees, T. (2018) *Wholesome Leadership: The heart, head, hands and health of school leaders*. Woodbridge: John Catt Education.

Sant, E. and Hanley, C. (2018) 'Political assumptions underlying pedagogies of national education: The case of student teachers teaching 'British values' in England', *British Educational Research Journal*, 44 (2), pp. 319-337.

Teaching English and Teaching Values: The Debate. (2021) IATEFL. Available at:

https://oupeltglobalblog.com/2021/06/03/English-teaching-values-debate-iatefl-2021/.

CHAPTER 11

The Curriculum and Pedagogy of Values-based Education in Geography

The study of geography is about more than just memorising places on a map. It's about understanding the complexity of our world, appreciating the diversity of cultures that exists across continents. And in the end, it's about using all that knowledge to help bridge divides and bring people together.

Barack Obama

Values at the heart of geography

In the content and pedagogy of geography the values of appreciation, curiosity, global responsibility, respect, and wonder are recurrent and characteristic. In the very act of studying this subject, learners will frequently come face to face with these values and practise them.

The importance of geography in schools

Geography *is* our world: both the physical and the human. 'Thinking geographically', means thinking of ourselves as global citizens. Being global citizens means being environmentally aware and informed and being thoughtful, enquiring inhabitants of our earth.

Geography is the study of the earth's key physical and human processes: places, people, resources, and natural as well as human environments. It tunes us in to the world around us. With a deepening understanding of this world comes a sense of connection; a geographic awareness that becomes imbued in us as a way of thinking, a way of life.

Geographical knowledge, understanding, and skills give us the tools to appreciate how the Earth's features at different scales are shaped, interconnected, and change over time. As we develop knowledge and understanding of how our world works, it stands to reason that we are more likely to respect this world and to want to work in harmony with it.

Practitioners agree that this subject is centrally placed to offer rich gifts to our learners in the way it teaches concepts and skills. These in turn, stimulate learners' curiosity to know more and to understand more about the world they inhabit – and in doing so, learn to love it and learn to want to live in a way that is compatible with those around us. When learners understand and use the myriad skills required to take part in enquiry-based learning in this subject, the doors to their world are opened wide.

The value of geography to society

Geography raises our level of understanding and appreciation of the complex wonder that is the world we live in. It is precisely about our relationship with our world, and therefore how we have relationships with one another, through time and space – and across physical, societal, cultural, religious, racial, and economic boundaries. Ultimately, it concerns us as individuals: how we live, how we spend our time on this planet and what we leave as our legacy. Geography is everywhere and everything ... it is through being aware of geography's fundamental, simple and ubiquitous concepts that we are able to understand our world, our connections with and within it, and predict and plan for the future.

The value of geography to the individual

Geography opens our eyes to the world around us. It is about understanding and appreciating the world – and as such, it is about developing our relationship with it. Geography helps us to understand how interconnected and interdependent the world is, and therefore how connected we are to it, and to all our fellow human beings, animals, insects, plants, and trees that share it with us. The more we understand and appreciate, the more we can value it and the more enduring the sense of wonder that will perpetuate a respectful personal outlook. While geography lessons do not tell us how to live, thinking geographically and developing our innate geographical imaginations can provide the intellectual means for envisioning ourselves on planet earth.

Illuminating geography through a values-based framework

Geography offers us our world; implicit in this offering is hope. Some practitioners argue it is in fact the only subject in the national curriculum to really focus on and tackle the futures dimension, in a real and empowering way by helping learners consider what futures are possible, probable, and preferable.

Moral and ethical values – wow! Tricky, contentious, and challenging issues are central to geography, the matter of our world's very sustainability being just one. There are numerous other moral and ethical dilemmas that geography explores: for instance the dilemma around livelihoods and food export systems; the use and abuse of maps and cartography; euro-centric maps focusing on the west; and the nomenclature used to describe countries as 'more' and less (e.g. 'Economically Developed', what do we mean by 'Developed'?). How do we measure a country? Measuring by economic value alone and not considering well-being and happiness leaves much in question. Understanding our colonial past through mapping, location and place, and recognising colonialism's enduring legacy and damaging impact is another example of how geography can and does cause us to confront moral and ethical values. There is so much to question around moral and ethical values through geography that in our teaching and learning it is impossible to avoid these issues. If we ensure our approach is one of enquiry, always asking questions and avoiding definitive statements we can uncover these big themes, open them up, and encourage our pupils to appreciate the complexity of our world and their actions within it.

Cultural values – these are 'the bread and butter of geography' for many people, recognising the fundamental truth that there is far more that humanity has in common than is different about us. The more we know, understand, and are amazed by other countries: their landscapes, wildlife, and their people, the more we respect and are enhanced by them. There is therefore the opportunity to celebrate the rich diversity of myriad lives across the globe and to appreciate natural world values. Understanding that people live with the physical geography of their landscapes and that lives can be both enhanced and inhibited by them causes us to question and think about the elements that form us as humans.

Social values – to understand that we share the world and it's precious resources means appreciating: how we all live together; how we interact and communicate; how we work with and against each other; how we have developed using and exploiting what is around us; and how we have changed and how we will continue to do so. All of these are rooted in the study of geography. They lead us inevitably to a greater awareness of the need to take care of the earth, to know that we must consider issues of fairness and equality, and the tensions between need and desires. The impact Covid-19 and its huge implications for our social geography will be a big consideration henceforth. We can use the subject to help us to understand much about social values, and crucially examine what will happen next, and what we need and want to happen next.

Spiritual values – seeing, perceiving, and understanding (even in small part) how the natural world works can bring moments of spiritual awareness: the sight of a waterfall; understanding the water cycle; erosion creating sand out of rock ... the list can go on and on. There are so many awe-inspiring aspects of the earth at our feet and the sky above us that the subject of geography can lay out before us. There is an obvious connection here with Forest Schooling, enabling children to simply be in the outdoors, experiencing its sounds, sights, and smells for themselves creates relationships with the natural world. Children are so readily at home in and inspired by nature that it is an effortless way of enhancing our emotional health.

What the teachers and practitioners say

It is how geography can inspire learners to behave in their lives that is of great importance: it is about understanding other people and places and empathising with and appreciating different viewpoints. All of this is of great significance to becoming successful young people who are enquiring citizens, globally and environmentally informed, and equipped to see the world with ethical objectivity.

I think if we viewed subjects through the lens of values it would help us to appreciate the overarching intent in pedagogy, help us to make those meaningful and vital connections, and bring a more enduring quality to learning.

In geography, along with factual knowledge, I've seen how children learn to apply their own values and to recognise values in other people, irrespective of geographical distance in order to gain fuller and richer understanding.

A values-based geography experience in the classroom			
Related Values	Curriculum Application	Cross-Curricular Links	Taking Values into Action
KS1			
Love Peace Co-operation Joy Fairness Justice Rule of Law Unity Tolerance	Settlements: what do people need to be able to live in a place? What would your design for a perfect settlement look like? What values do you think people would need to be able to live together well?	English: speaking and listening; debate; writing.	Encourage and follow children's own questions. Hold a class debate – each child or pair presents their charter of values as a way of living well. Discuss and debate the most important values.
Happiness **Beauty** Peace Joy	Features of our local area. Use a values lens to look at our local area ... which areas inspire us with joy/beauty/ peace/happiness, etc.? Why is this? Identify features of the local landscape that help human wellbeing. Photograph them for a display.	Art: photography. English: letter writing. Maths: carry out your own survey to find out what your family or schoolmates would like to see in their local area.	Community project: how can manifest our values in our local geography for everyone to appreciate? For example, with permission, take a piece of 'unloved' ground and replant it with spring bulbs. Write a letter of congratulation or suggestion to the local council to improve the local area.
KS2			
Equality **Co-operation** **Unity** **Respect** **Fairness** **Justice** **The Rule of Law**	Look at the world's natural resources – what are they? Where do they come from? What can they be used for? What is some of the impact on the environment of their use?	Research skills: use various media to hone research skills to extend knowledge and understanding, and then summarise and condense information.	At home, challenge your family to reduce, reuse, and recycle or carry out a food mile audit. Where does your most frequently used food come from, and can you reduce the food miles you use as a family? Get out the calculator to keep track!

Respect **Justice** **Equality** **Compassion** **Understanding**	Look at sustainable development in relation to e.g. farming: pollution and pesticides; soil erosion; deforestation, etc., and the range of possible mitigating factors or solutions. Case study: what would happen if...	Research skills.	Do an analysis of your own family's consumption of non-renewables. How respectful are you being of our planet, and what more could you do? Write a letter to your MP to get something actioned. Consider Alexander McCall-Smith's saying: 'We think the world is ours forever, but we are mere squatters.' How could this change our approach to using the world's resources?
KS3			
Compassion **Empathy** **Respect** **Rule of law**	The study of climate and climate change and its environmental, economic, and human impacts.		Conduct a climate change management exercise.
Determination **Resilience** **Unity** **Co-operation** **Rule of law** **Kindness** **Altruism** **Generosity**	Employment structures in this country and around the world. What personal values do you think you need to bring to any workplace?	Maths: reading, constructing, and interpreting data.	What values would you hope to see governing a workplace or industry you choose to work in? Carry out your own research into the declared values of some major companies. How apparent are they on their websites? How would you expect to see these values enacted?

What the learners say

Geography makes me want to travel the world! KS2 pupil

We learn to love our planet and respect other cultures even though they are different to ours in geography.

Geography doesn't only teach us where places are in the world or what a country is like. It also helps us understand how other people live and how lucky we are in comparison. We have easy access to food, water, medicines etc. ...and we can easily take that for granted.

Values I use could be appreciation, gratefulness, and to be humble. Secondary pupil.

Questions for consideration in the staffroom

Could your geography department agree on – say three – values they feel are most appropriate and ensure these are given prominence through the subject teaching?

Could the approach to learning in geography be grounded in values through the use of enquiry, by always asking questions and avoiding definitive statements?

How much opportunity learners currently have to make a practical application of their learning in geography?

Further reading

Baggini, J. (2018) *How the World Thinks*. Granta: London.

Catling, S. & Willy, T. (2018) 2 ed. *Understanding and Teaching Primary Geography*. Sage: London.

Dolan, A. M. (2020) *Powerful Primary Geography*. Taylor and Francis: London.

Hicks, D. *Future perspectives for Sustainability in Education*. Available at: https://teaching4abetterworld.co.uk/future.html.

Gardner, D. (2018) *Progress in Geography*. Hodder Education: London.

Gardner, D. (2020) *Progress in Geography Skills*. Hodder Education: London. Available at: https://www.hoddereducation.co.uk/geography/progress-in-geography.

Pickering, S. (2017) *Teaching Outdoors Creatively*. Routledge: Abingdon.

Pike, S. (2015) *Learning Primary Geography: Ideas and inspiration for the classroom*. Routledge: Abingdon.

Roberts, M. (2013) *Geography through Enquiry*. Geographical Association: Sheffield.

Scoffham, S. (Ed) (2017) 2 ed. *Teaching Geography Creatively*. Routledge: Abingdon.

Scoffham, S., & Owens, P. (2017) *Teaching Primary Geography: Everything you need to teach primary geography*. Bloomsbury: London.

Scoffham, S., & Rawlinson, S. (2022) *Sustainability Education – A classroom guide*. Bloomsbury: London.

Scoffham, S., & Owens, P. (2017) *Teaching Primary Geography*. Bloomsbury: London.

Willy, T. (Ed) (2019) *Leading Primary Geography: The essential handbook for all teachers*. Geographical Association: Sheffield.

The Geocapabilities Project. Available at: http://www.geocapabilities.org.

Owens, P. (2020) *Primary Geography CPD Pack 2: Enquiry and critical thinking*. Geographical Association. Available at: https://www.geography.org.uk/eBooks-detail/695c513e-e36c-4cc3-8354-d0a5bc4d0245.

For resources on maps and mapping in the early years and teaching map skills in the primary national curriculum see the ordanance survey (ordnancesurvey.co.uk).

CHAPTER 12

The Curriculum and Pedagogy of Values-based Education in History

We are not makers of history. We are made by history.

Martin Luther King, Jr.

Values at the heart of history

In the content and pedagogy of history the values of diversity, the rule of law, understanding, and identity are recurrent and characteristic. In the very act of studying this subject, learners will frequently come face to face with these values and practise them.

The importance of history in schools

History invites learners to journey into their own past. In undertaking this journey, we see the diversity of human experience, and understand more about ourselves as individuals and members of society. We learn about how the past influences the present, what past societies were like, how these societies organised their politics, and what beliefs and cultures influenced people's actions. As we do this, we develop a chronological framework for our knowledge of significant events and people. History helps pupils to understand the complexity of people's lives, the process of change, the diversity of societies and relationships between different groups, as well as their own identity and the challenges of their time.

The value of history to a values-based society

History's value is intrinsic; it is contained, as it were, in its very subject matter. Our attitudes, perceptions, outlooks, and actions create history and, in its turn, history creates us. We respond and react to our immediate as well as our distant past, learning – or recoiling – from past events. History can be seen as looking back in order to look forwards. Every era views its history from its own time. Recently the debate around statues of figures connected to slavery has highlighted this very issue. How do we balance understanding the past in its own terms and applying today's values to yesterday's events?

The value of history to the individual – for their life

History connects us with ourselves, one another, and the wider world; with our past, present, and future. Our curiosity cannot help but be kindled as we examine how our forebears lived, worked, fought, and adventured. We cannot help but make comparisons between their actions and our own views and imaginings. What we learn can influence our own decision-making, attitudes, and values. Therefore, our lives and our images of ourselves, one another, and our world, become anchored in our knowledge and understanding of our antiquity.

The skills that history demands – reading, researching, sifting through and evaluating evidence, creating hypotheses and conclusions, and developing coherent arguments are all skills to be cherished life-long.

Illuminating history through a values-based framework

History is filled with examples that connect us to moral, ethical, cultural, social, and spiritual choices, conundrums, and events. These are precisely the values that create the dynamic we continuously live in and respond to throughout our lives.

Moral and ethical values – looking at how moral and ethical values shift and move across the ages is fascinating. The use of corporal punishment is a gory and ghastly case in point. Henry Vlll's treatment of the monasteries, and their inhabitants, not to mention his own wives continues to horrify and engross today. What these lessons of history can have to teach us about our own belief and values systems can be immense.

Cultural values – almost all topics in history tell a tale about the cultural attitudes and norms of their time. For example, the study of people such as Florence Nightingale and Mary Seacole – and changes in attitudes, provision, and responses to sickness and illness at large – resonates loudly with our current times.

Social values – shifts in living conditions and social expectations never fail to interest and intrigue us, as they are so close to our own concerns. Local studies of amenities in our own neighbourhoods: the once-present Poor House with all its terrors and garden wells all have a story to tell about how people had to live and work, and how society was formed to enable this life to happen.

Spiritual values – historical buildings abound with messages about devotion and religious faith. What, for example, does the sheer scale of our city's cathedral, soaring so high and in such marked contrast to the surrounding housing, tell us about people's relationship to God at this time? Studying how far some people – like Thomas Cromwell perhaps – were prepared to go to defend their own religious views and beliefs provide stark examples against which we can set our own convictions.

These values intertwine throughout the subject matter – they are an implicit and integral part of the material. However, being explicit about these aspects of the curriculum subject during lessons and activities helps define them for learners. It is entirely possible, and justifiable, to look at the subject matter through one value alone, e.g. how do the events leading up to and during World War II, such as appeasement, reflect the value of peace. Was it a worthy aim then and is it still now? Or there can be an exploration through another value – such as unity – as a way of preventing war? Either way, the values focus brings into sharp relief the matter in hand, underlining its human aspects and relevance for our own lives today. The subject is then serving a double duty, teaching subject knowledge, skills and techniques while also offering unparalleled opportunities for life learning.

What the teachers and practitioners say

To be an effective teacher in any subject discipline, you need to be able to connect with people. There is a need to resonate with your audience and the best way to achieve that is to have an overlapping set of values. History is the perfect medium for this: in questioning the past, we can question the present. Who are we? What are we trying to achieve? What values are central to us? In this way, we can and should inspire learners to enact their values.

I always notice when I'm teaching history how much of it speaks to the choices people have made – values-based or not. There's always an ethical underside to historical facts. When we explore history, we're learning more and more about ourselves. I think the children really get that.

When children respond with empathy and compassion to focused studies in geography, history, or RE, sensitive exploration of values can transform rote knowledge into a dynamic curriculum of memorable moments. In this way, children learn to conceptualise, explore, and debate.

A values-based history experience in school			
Related Values	Curriculum Application	Cross-Curricular Links	Taking Values into Action
KS1			
Empathy Care Gratitude Justice Co-operation The Rule of Law Democracy	The Great Fire of London - effects of the fire on human lives and livelihoods. 100, 000 people were left homeless and King Charles promised there would be changes as a result. Write a piece about finding your home has been destroyed by the fire: What have you lost? How do you feel? Did anyone show empathy to you?	English: writing a diary entry. Maths: ordering and comparing statistics. PSHE: emotions and feelings. Study Skills: Research skills.	Think about your home, your bedroom and all the things in it. What are you most grateful for? If you didn't have them, what would you miss most? Look at homelessness in a democracy like Britain today through the care of homeless charities. What can people do to help homeless people? How can we best co-operate to help one another? Is there anything in the rule of law that is there to help people?
Peace Justice Tolerance Love Unity Forgiveness	Remembrance Day and the Armistice - look at the events that led to peace. Did it bring about justice? How do you think soldiers, leaders, and ordinary people would have felt about the armistice? Did it establish a sense of unity? Where do you think forgiveness could come in? Can you create your own memorial picture to the people who died?	Art: creating a still image or moving piece about peace, perhaps taking inspiration from nature. English: inspiration from stores.	Read, for example, *Tusk Tusk* by David McKee - why do you think the story ends as it does? What does it tell us about human nature? What is the best way of preventing intolerance and war? What place can forgiveness play? Could you create a tribute to peace in your school - something that will remind others about the importance of a peaceful world?

KS2			
Understanding Respect Unity Co-operation Interdependence Empathy	The Stone Age - life and living. Draw out the ingenuity of early humans, the way society worked through co-operation and interdependence. Also, the vital link with the natural world - using materials like wood, plants and animals for their needs and showing respect for them.	Art: creating images of reverence and respect.	Consider cave paintings and the respect we think these drawings confer about the animals that were hunted and killed. What pictures would we paint today... how can we really show our respect for the natural world and what more can we do to really carry these values into action, inspired by our ancient ancestors?
Respect Understanding Co-operation Gratitude Generosity	Romans in Britain – Roman settlement and their many amazing skills and ingenuity in building, making, and organising their society. Much of which we still benefit from today in roads and sewage systems for example. What have we got to be grateful to our Roman ancestors for?	English - writing a letter.	Write a thank you letter to the Romans. Looking with 21 century eyes, are there any of their values systems that you would critique and why? What legacy would you like to leave for the future - what can you do for the world?
Diversity Love Individual liberty Tolerance Justice Understanding Rule of Law Determination Empathy Courage Gentleness Love Peace The Rule of Law Equality	20 century conflict, World War II, and the Holocaust. How Hitler whipped up antisemitic feeling. How can we be aware of negative 'group mentality', e.g. at a football match or similar. What characteristics and values make us truly human? The importance of independent thought and critical analysis of information we are given.	PSHE: emotions and feelings. Study Skills: Research skills.	Research countries and groups of people where there is persecution today. Write a manifesto to secure the human rights of all living people - to ensure nothing like this can ever happen again. Debate: what is the place of gentleness and peace in a scenario like this one? Debate: is war ever good? What about standing up to injustice in this instance? Write a poem or create a piece of artwork dedicated to the people who died in concentration camps that will touch people's hearts - so that they will feel the human sorrow and vow to love and protect all of humankind.

KS3			
Co-operation **Unity** **Peace** **Justice** **Equality** **Beauty** **Democracy**	Who were the Anglo Saxons and how did they live? What do the artefacts we have found tell us about their culture and the things they found important? The Anglo Saxons were a warrior people, yet capable of making beautiful pieces of art … what kind of values might they have had? The Lawcodes – what do they tell us about the values of the Anglo Saxon society? Beowulf and the attributes of a leader – what made Shieds Sheafson 'one good king'? What values would he have shown?		What are the values systems on which our current society is built (reference 'British values': rule of law; individual liberty; respect; mutual tolerance; and democracy)? Choose your top 5 values for society and justify your choice. What would your society look like and how would it function as a result? Design an emblem for a society based on your value choices. Create a values-based character description for a great leader for society today. Compare and contrast to Anglo Saxon society.
Tolerance **Understanding** **Unity** **Respect**	The Islamic Golden Age – what was the value of learning in this age? In what way does learning matter to you? How did the Islamic scholars show they valued learning? How do you show you value learning?		What, if anything has surprised you about this topic? Has it altered your understanding about the Islamic world? What important elements have made you respect the Islamic legacy from this age? Take time to research some of the stunning examples of Islamic art from this time.

What the learners say

I love history because you can imagine what it was like to live all that time ago. KS1 pupil.

History teaches us about the past and so we learn respect for where we have come from.

You realise that people had to work very hard at living and that makes you really appreciate your life. KS2 pupil.

Questions for consideration in the staffroom

How can the focus on values through history help you to bring your school's Curriculum Intent to life?

What Cultural Capital can be found through the study of this subject, and how could it be brought into even greater focus?

Further reading:

Gumbrell, D. (2019) *LIFT.* St Albans: Critical Publishing.

Gumbrell, D., (2020) *RISK.* St Albans: Critical Publishing.

Gumbrell, D. (2021) *SPIN.* St Albans: Critical Publishing.

Gumbrell, D. (2021) *The A-Z of Resilience.* London: Jessica Kingsley Publishers.

CHAPTER 13

The Curriculum and Pedagogy of Values-based Education in Mathematics

If people are encouraged to immerse themselves in nature's grammar and geometry – discovering how it works, how it controls life on Earth, and how humanity has expressed it in so many great works of art and architecture – they are often led to acquire some remarkably deep philosophical insights into the meaning and purpose of nature and into what it means to be aware and alive in this extraordinary universe.

Charles Mountbatten-Windsor, Prince of Wales

Values at the heart of mathematics

In the content and pedagogy of mathematics the values of determination, fairness, honesty, interdependence, and understanding are recurring and characteristic. In the very act of studying this subject, learners will frequently come face to face with these values and practise them.

The importance of mathematics as a subject discipline in schools

Mathematics is a universal language, connecting us all and offering the same to all of us. Increasingly, especially through the Mastery Maths programme, schools focus much more on being able to express oneself and reason or prove a given problem. Problem solving and reasoning in maths demonstrates that, like values, things are rarely black and white in their nature.

Making links to the real world is a great way to bring maths to life. Statistics and information about real world poverty, for example, give both understanding to maths and to ethical and moral problems. The incredible intricacy of nature's patterns can really be appreciated when a good understanding of maths is added. This sparks curiosity and wonder at how amazing the natural world is.

The value of mathematics to society

Mathematics is apparent in almost everything we do: buying our food, cooking, eating, building and heating our homes, putting fuel in our car, etc. Have you ever considered how mathematics can also make difficult things easier to understand? For example, how often do we give a numerical value to an emotion or feeling ('on a scale of 1 to 10, how painful is that?') or see statistics emphasising a news story?

Of course, mathematics in its truest form supports being able to function in a monetary world where an economical understanding at all levels is vital for our emotional, social, and physical well-being, all of which are at the heart of Values-based Education.

The value of mathematics to the individual

Which of us can forget the surge of joy at achieving a complete page of correct sums? For a moment there, we are masters of our universe. In an uncertain world, where so much does not conform to our will, we have – albeit briefly – ruled supreme. And when it doesn't work out like this for us, well, mathematics gives us the opportunity to find resilience. We begin to relish the challenge rather than the outcome, taking pleasure in the struggle and developing strategies along the way. Success following a struggle can be empowering and those feelings can stick, making a good reference point for future learning. Mathematics unlocks the ability to make connections, find a way, think systematically while giving the opportunity to adapt and adjust to the situation and one's individual way of thinking.

Illuminating mathematics through a values-based framework

The study and use of mathematics, as with all subject disciplines, requires us to embody a host of values: determination, patience and perseverance, humility, and appreciation. The elements that are perhaps less often associated with mathematics as a discipline are those of social, cultural, moral, ethical, and spiritual values.

Moral and ethical values – the use of money, the cost of goods and services, and the division of resources are mathematical but also moral and ethical matters and these of course are deeply rooted in our daily lives.

Cultural values – mathematics is a glue, binding cultures together. Personal financial management is directly related to how our own culture promotes and supports saving and investment and is an important part of personal education. Looking at how some cultures and faiths approach the matter of charity and support for those in need is a fascinating slice through the subject.

Social values – mathematics takes us to the heart of values: we connect with one another through maths on a daily and pragmatic level. How the world shares its resources, and the value we place on lives and livelihoods, are values-based issues.

Spiritual values – there is a sublimity in the workings and patterns of mathematical calculations and geometry that connects us with aspects we feel are greater than our individual selves. The purity of a mathematical calculation can be an outworking of spirituality for some; for others, understanding patterns, formulas, equations and so much more helps us to know that we can find these in other aspects of our lives. To suddenly see why those numbers fit together, why those connections are so powerful, says things about ourselves as much as mathematics.

What the teachers and practitioners say

Values have become one of the most important aspects of life. More and more I find myself considering how values fit or what values are needed for a certain situation. Within my personal life I am aware of the values that are most dear to me. Having two teenage sons has made me consider not only the values that I want them to have but also the values that are part of their worlds and how they are evolving.

Within teaching, values are the letters running through the stick of rock, the ground on which we walk, and the air all around us. After many years of being in a truly values-based school, decisions about what and how we teach always consider values, but often subconsciously.

I live values every day in all I do and know that they have helped to shape and guide me. When I reflect on my day and the whole range of experiences and emotions that every day brings, I know that I can always find a value to attach to each aspect. It helps me to focus and to understand and to plan a way forward. I could say that one day appreciation comes to the fore but then alongside that sits; peace, understanding, hope, love, happiness, and the list could go on. Values are intertwined and prevalent. They are powerful and beautiful because of what they are and can be for everyone.

Values are important to me. As a Catholic my core values are Christian. They are my 'guidebook' to how I live my life, how I make decisions and how I interact with the world and with people. Religion does not have the monopoly on values though and a secular set of values is not a diluted one.

A values-based mathematics experience in the classroom			
Related Values	Curriculum Application	Cross-Curricular Links	Taking Values into Action
KS1			
Equality Justice Fairness Care Co-operation	Division of numbers and shapes.	Citizenship and PSHE.	Bring in a cake or pizza to share. When is it important to share? Why is equal sharing important? Can you think of examples in your own lives of when you have shared things - or when someone has shared with you? How did it make you feel?
Peace Tolerance Unity	Learning number bonds, counting in rounds, times tables - any number-based learning as a class.	RE and PSHE - being a good friend, being part of a group and the behaviours that go with them.	Notice how we all help each other and how we need each other to play a part. Notice what we all do instinctively when someone is stuck or unsure - those are our values in action!
KS2			
Understanding Respect Unity Co-operation Interdependence Empathy	Problem solving and reasoning. Planning a family holiday on a budget, working out the activities that offer the best value and experience.	Geography: using mapping skills.	Build on this budgeting to plan a small saving to go to a charity of your choice?

Diversity Determination Empathy Courage Gentleness Love	Area and perimeter calculations, e.g. a wildlife shelter for hedgehogs in the school field, designed for different numbers of wildlife.	Science - animal habitats and sustainability issues.	Turn this into a project for creating the shelter itself - include costing, positioning, and materials, having researched what is necessary for this animal's survival.
KS3			
Co-operation Justice Equality Democracy	Using percentages to calculate differences. Calculate percentages from monthly /annual wages to be given to charities.		

Consider this scenario

This scenario focuses on a group made up of mixed ability and gender: Sebastian (S), greater depth ability; Fiona (F), middle to high ability; Charlotte (C), low to middle ability; and Adam (A), lower ability.

The teacher (Mrs Day) has split the class in groups of four. She has introduced the activity and given out 16 lots of percentage, fraction, and decimal dominoes. She explains to that class that every member of the team must end up with a set of four dominoes which join to form a 'doughnut' where touching ends have equal value.

She stresses the fact that the task is only successfully completed when everyone on the team has completed their domino doughnuts. They go to their table. Immediately all except Fiona look at the dominoes. Fiona is chatting to a girl on the table behind her. The teacher approaches to re-focus Fiona but realises that she is helping the girl by re-explaining the instructions and decides not to intervene, though she makes a note to praise her later.

The conversation in the group starts:

A (pushing the dominoes away from him into the centre of the table): I'm hopeless with fractions.

C: I don't like it either – I always get mixed up with which is the top number and which is the bottom number.

S (who has already started on one 'doughnut' and grabs another domino from across the table): it won't take us long to sort this.

F: but we have to do it together.

A: I don't mind Seb doing it for me.

C: he can do mine too.

S: come on Fi – you can help – you're good at equivalence.

A: yes, we can be the first table to finish C (smiling at Adam): that will be great – I am never the first one to finish.

Both C and A push the pile of dominoes in S's direction.

F (pushing them back into the middle): no, we've got to do it together

A: but Miss will never know.

C (looking concerned): oh, I think we will have to talk about how we did it, won't we?

A: yes, but Seb or Fi can do that, and we can hold the dominoes and nod.

F: but what if Mrs Day asks you to explain Charlotte or you Adam?

Both A and C look fed up.

S (stops moving the dominoes and stares at F): why does she do this all the time? I just want to get on with it and finish so I can do something hard.

A (almost to himself): this is hard ...

F: she wants us to work together and help each other.

C: I don't think I will be able to help Seb – he's the best in maths in the class.

S: thanks Charlotte but you are good at loads of things.

C (laughs): I am not in any of the top groups.

F: you are better than me in Netball.

S: ... and you're better than me when we have to read to the reception class. They all love you. I think they're scared of me.

They all laugh. Mrs Day asks the class to focus on the activity and reminds them that they have only ten minutes left.

(looking at C and A): is there any of these you know?

C: I know that a half is 50%.

S: look for that pair. What do you know Adam?

A: don't the decimals go up in 0.1 and percentages go up in 10%?

F: yes they do – well remembered – you find those pairs.

All four work together to find the pairs. They are not the first group to finish but they are all pleased with how they have worked together.

Now let's look at that from the values point of view: they go to their table. Immediately all but Fiona looks at the dominoes. Fiona is chatting to a girl on a table behind her. The teacher approaches to re-focus Fiona but realises that she is helping the girl by re-explaining the instructions (friendship a thoughtfulness are at play here) and decides not to intervene, though she makes a note to praise her later (showing respect and love). As the students start to work together, they display varying values of honesty, optimism, self-belief, determination, assertiveness, friendship, appreciation, cooperation, respect, courage, and reflection. Values are subliminally part of the maths group work and the teacher could have chosen to make these aspects of learning very much more explicit, encouraging also of course curiosity, and therefore helping students on the journey to joyful success.

What the learners say

It's so satisfying when you get a question right. I love it. KS2 pupil.

Maths gets me educated. KS1 pupil.

It helps you learn everything. It's good when you learn about money because you have to know how to take care of it. KS1 pupil.

I really enjoy maths but I find it really challenging sometimes. I use the values of determination and perseverance to keep trying until I can get it right. In the end I feel really proud of myself. It makes me feel happy knowing I didn't give up. Secondary pupil.

Questions for consideration in the staffroom

What are the values that you think come to the fore in mathematics?

How could your maths curriculum ensure that values can be put to explicit and practical use?

Further reading

Barton, C. (2018) *How I Wish I'd Taught Maths*. Woodbridge: John Catt.

Doherty, S. (2021) *100 Ideas for Primary Teachers: Maths*. London: Bloosbury.

Jones, K. (2019) *Retrieval Practice*. Woodbridge: John Catt.

Mackle, K. (2020) *Thinking deeply about Primary Mathematics*. Woodbridge: John Catt.

Sherrington, T. & Caviglioli, O. (2020) *Teaching Walkthrus: Five-step guides to instructional coaching*. Woodbridge: John Catt.

CHAPTER 14

The Curriculum and Pedagogy of Values-based Education in Modern Foreign Languages

To have another language is to possess a second soul.

Charlemagne

Values at the heart of modern foreign languages

In the content and pedagogy of modern foreign languages the values of cooperation, friendship, persistence, respect, and understanding are recurring and characteristic. In the very act of studying this subject, learners will frequently come face to face with these values and practise them.

The importance of modern foreign languages in schools

Young children are refreshingly inquisitive about language. They will squeal with delight at the shape and texture of a new word on their tongue. Introduced to a new phrase, they often look around the room at one another, sharing the ecstasies of these exquisite new sounds that they are allowed to produce. When they realise these words have meaning, there is a quiet sense of awe: *People say that? And it means that?*

Learning a foreign language does far more than teach linguistic competence: it opens the door to social and cultural experiences that give an insight into our own culture and those of others. It creates a cognitive connection between us and another country and its culture, enabling us to feel and experience a little of what it is like to be from and in that different place.

Confidence and fluency in a modern foreign language – be it French, German, Spanish, or Portuguese – is essential in today's world. In the UK language learning lags behind our foreign counterparts. So how do we fire our children and young people with a love of languages? We have been 'missing a trick' with our MFL teaching. Can taking a values-based approach can make all the difference?

The value of modern foreign languages to society

Languages play an important role in global diplomacy, security, and international relations. They contribute to UK prosperity and provide value-added skills across a wide range of occupations. Languages connect us to the rest of the world and open educational, cultural, and business opportunities. Ian Collen, lecturer in modern languages education, Queens University, Belfast says: 'It is vital for the future of the UK that all school pupils have access to high-quality language teaching.'

There is also increasing understanding of the personal and societal benefits of bilingualism, recognising the 'soft power' of language skills, and the 'cultural agility' from knowing other languages and cultures that comes into its own in conflict areas. This is all because language learning supports us in understanding one another, and feeling a sense of connection with others, which enables us to focus on what might be achieved together. As Elif Shafak, acclaimed Turkish-British author, reminds us, languages help us look closer at our own culture and country as we examine another's: 'languages shape us while we are busy thinking we control them'.

The value of modern foreign languages to the individual

Being in command of another language emboldens an individual. It extends our own borders. It allows us to enter, intimately, the head of a fellow human being; to feel soothed and reassured that they like the things we do, that they think the things we do (albeit more poetically of course). They might even consider – and have words for – things we do not. At one level, language is a plaything, a hoot, a charming encounter; at another it is a profoundly affecting extension (as Charlemagne described it) to our own soul, and an enduring reminder that we are far less limited than we might have imagined. Through the medium of language, we share and discover similarities and differences, dissolving barriers and inculcating respectful fascination. Another language takes us beyond our own borders. To be a successful linguist is to be successful at life itself!

Here are just some of the personal and social skills to be found in a well-conceived MFL curriculum: communication, social skills, relationships, understanding of the self, intercultural understanding, and the ability to take positive action. These need to be pivotal if we are to develop and embed language learning that has lifelong meaning and significance.

Understanding more about the culture of other countries prompts us to wonder, 'What do I think about that? How do I fit into that?' This is a really important value-added part of the curriculum. Learning a foreign language gives a unique opportunity to grow our own understanding of who we are: who you are changes in response to the world opening up for you.

Illuminating modern foreign languages through a values-based framework

To speak, read and understand another country's language is to become part of its culture, to absorb some of its values, outlook, and insights. It is to have a sense of that country's history – the things it holds dear and the episodes that have shaped its people. And to have all of that is to have a deep connection that extends beyond your own self.

Moral and ethical values – through learning another language we can compare and contrast the values of its country as espoused in that language.

Cultural values – language is cultural transmission. When we learn another language, we are naturally introduced to its culture: its food, its art, and its buildings. Language reflects the values and beliefs of a culture. The differences between two cultures are reflected in their languages. Mastering the nuances of a language means really being able to understand – and therefore appreciate and respect – people's values, beliefs and where they may have stemmed from.

Social values – take France, for example, where the social norm of eating out (stemming from the concept of self-nourishing and looking after oneself) is very important. This is reflected in the myriad words for 'restaurant', including, restaurant, bistro, café, cafeteria, brasserie (to name but some) – many of which have become absorbed into our own language. How people live, work and play is embedded in the language they speak. How we appreciate and respect – or even just tolerate – the difference social norms of other countries is influenced by how far we are able to share in them through language.

Spiritual values – speaking in the language of another, seeing the world through their eyes, seeing the things they hold dear offers an empathetic experience which can be described as spiritual. Moreover, when you are able to speak another language, you are able to leave behind your usual self and temporarily enter the shoes of another – this can at times be a cleansing experience and can give an unparalleled insight into the human condition and our fellow man.

What the teachers and practitioners say

When I am teaching MFL I am very aware that the attitudes I bring to my subject are instilling values in the learners. I hope I convey a respectful fascination. Even when teaching, for example, the colours in another language, all my implicit values messaging is about respect, tolerance, and unity.

I love teaching French because of the sense of possibilities it conveys – there's a real freedom that comes in being able to express yourself in another language and I want the children I teach to experience that for themselves.

A values based MFL experience in the classroom

Related Values	Curriculum Application	Cross-Curricular Links	Taking Values into Action
KS1			
Self-Belief **Resilience** **Understanding** **Friendship** **Co-operation** **Unity**	Learning to converse in a different language itself builds our self-confidence and self-esteem. Learning the rudiments of self-description, including parts of the body, members of our household, likes and dislikes, and so on, helps reinforce our sense of ourselves.	Both communication and language skills support the 'Who am I? Where do I fit within the world?' elements of learning. English: speaking and listening and writing. Geography: knowledge of the world's geography. PSHE: understanding of the self; parts of the body.	You can explore every aspect of learning through a different scenario. Even a virtual visit to another country can start children on journey to asking 'Who am I?' 'What do I believe?' 'Who can be my friend?' Understanding of ourselves grows in direct relation to our understanding of others. Using puppets can be a great way in to exploring ourselves through others.
KS2			
Understanding **Appreciation** **Unity** **Tolerance**	There are myriad opportunities with MFL for building inter-cultural understanding, e.g. national foods!	Design and Technology: making a French or Spanish breakfast, for example.	… and it's not just another country and culture that we get to know! There's nothing like having a visitor from another country to help you get to know your own land! So, rather than just going on an exchange, work on a joint project, e.g. investigating different religions, and invite some friends from abroad to join. Develop an exchange programme. Work in two languages. Video conference on a weekly basis. Compare, contrast, share and celebrate your new knowledge and understanding. Fire young people with enthusiasm for languages!
Unity **Co-operation** **Respect** **Friendship**	Cultural differences in greetings; the formal and informal; the actions that go alongside the words.		Localise what languages you offer; look at talent and opportunity within local community. This in turn provides a valuable opportunity to validate linguistic skills and talents within the local area, as well as to use these to build a strong platform for achievement. Before you know it, you have a virtuous cycle: success at community level breeds success at school level and both are mutually reinforcing.

KS3			
Self-belief **Love** **Joy** **Courage** **Determination** **Respect**	Using adjectives to describe a person's emotions. Learning this key vocabulary gives insight into the human condition, the fact that all humans experience similar emotions at different times and can even help us process our own emotions through the lens of another language.	PSHE	Compiling an emotions chart for the classroom in another language with visual symbols alongside is a useful and purposeful visual aid for giving acknowledgement and permission for human emotions in the context of schooling! Use this for a simple language-based game of 'How are you feeling today'?
Friendship **Respect** **Tolerance**	Describing ourselves and one another: likes/ dislikes; pastimes; etc. This encourages us to respect and celebrate the 'uniqueness of me', recognising similarities and differences between ourselves and others.	Geography History Research skills	Research some famous French, Italian, Spanish, and German people. What is it that they are famous for? In what ways are they making a significant contribution to the world? What do you admire them for? What attributes or traits would you like others to recognise you for?

What the learners say

It's like trying out new clothes! KS2 pupil.

French teaches us to respect other languages – and to be resilient because sometimes it can be really hard to learn.

I think values help me be responsible and a more caring, kind person. They make me a better friend and a good role model. Sometimes I don't even realise I have used my values. They are just something that is part of me. Secondary pupil.

Questions for consideration in the staffroom

Languages taught well in a coherent way brilliantly lend themselves to a values-based approach to learning and teaching. Just as with the values approach itself, a whole school (or whole department) approach to the development of MFL is essential.

Wouldn't it be fun to have the school's values translated into the languages taught in school?

How much opportunity do learners currently have to experience at first hand the cultural and social values of the country whose language they are learning?

Further reading

For more information and resources see the British Council (www.britishcouncil.org).

CHAPTER 15

The Curriculum and Pedagogy of Values-based Education in Music

Music doesn't get in. Music is already in. Music simply uncovers what is there, makes you feel emotions that you didn't necessarily know you had inside you, and runs around waking them all up. A rebirth of sorts.

Matt Haig, *How to Stop Time*

Values at the heart of music

In the content and pedagogy of music the values of appreciation, beauty, cooperation, diversity, harmony, patience, persistence, and self-belief are recurring and characteristic. In the very act of studying this subject, learners will frequently come face to face with these values and practise them.

The importance of music in schools

Music is part of every life; as a backdrop, taking centre stage or as something that is visited periodically – or a combination of all of these. Making music, either on our own or with others is a powerful and usually pleasurable experience. So, teaching children to compose, play, learn about, appreciate, and discriminate between the vast range of music that is open to them connects them to their lived experience. It opens opportunities to discover personal skills and talents, and, taught well, puts us on course to live a musical life.

Opportunities to learn a how to play a musical instrument have historically not been open to every child. Now, with Wider Opportunities in primary schools, many schools can address the inequalities that can otherwise exist in music education provision.

Music in all its forms offers a rich layer of beauty and creativity across a variety of contexts and cultures. Consequently, studying music opens doors to understanding both our own and other cultures. But it also brings with it a complexity of form, innovation, and sensation that is worthy of study in its own right.

When we learn about music as a phenomenon, we learn how composition and structure can evoke a great range of personal reactions and experiences. We also learn the value of our *own* subjective experiences. In music we have the liberty to have and feel our own responses, and these can change and evolve depending on our exposure, our age, where we are, how we are feeling, and so on. Our responses (and therefore our very selves) are valued in music as much as the music itself. How utterly liberating, self-affirming, and self-empowering this is!

Music is a unique form of communication enabling us to project – and even change – our feelings and emotions. It brings together intellect and feeling and enables personal expression, reflection, and emotional development. As an integral part of teaching and learning about culture, past and present, it deepens our roots and invites us on journeys. In listening to a wide variety of music it helps pupils understand themselves and relate to others, forging important links between the home, school, and the wider world. In making music, children and young people develop a host of skills, not least co-operation, resilience, ambition, creativity, aesthetic appreciation, and self-belief.

The value of music to society

Music is part of every society. We know that early man created music; we know that every culture has evolved musical forms. Music expresses togetherness, identity, and intent. It can impel feelings of pride and joy, or lamentation; speak of a country's fortunes and misfortunes, or triumphs and disasters; it's history, or it's hope for its future. Music can – and does – cross boundaries and barriers of communication, time, and place, often articulating for us feelings and responses which surpass words.

A great question to consider with children is, what would life be like without music? Imagine it for a moment. Count the myriad ways music plays a part in our everyday existence. What would they miss the most? What would we have lost? No listening to music on the radio on a long drive. No music to dance to. There would not be any soundtracks in movies, and concerts and musicals would be non-existent.

The value of music to the individual

Music evokes emotion, rippling through us like a river, taking us to places and giving us experiences we could never have imagined. It can be both an enhancer and bringer of joy; equally, it can prick our conscience, cause us to think new thoughts and inspire us to individual and collective action.

To be able to delight in something is surely adequate reason itself! Beyond this, however, music has the power to build our confidence, our ability to listen, to communicate, to express ourselves, and to develop our sense of likes and dislikes. For children and young people, developing their sense of self and their place in the world, music is connection and communication – they discover through music that they can share, collaborate, and make links in a way that goes right to the heart! Alongside this comes an appreciation of the achievements of people down the ages and across the globe, speaking to us of our own cultural heritage and opening new eyes to the culture of others. As such, it is the builder of bridges – both to our own self and others.

Illuminating music through a values-based framework

Music offers us an authentic and immediate experience, with real purpose, because it is almost always created with another listener in mind. Through music we engage in both an intellectual and an emotional experience – exploring and analysing the composition and impact of music – all by immersing ourselves in sound, listening to the sound of our own emotional response as it were.

Moral and ethical values – music can lead us to peace or accompany us into battle: it is by no means without morals and ethics. Music, therefore, is power. Take protest songs, for example. They have enabled messages to be communicated across social, cultural, geographical, political, and economic boundaries time after time. Look at the enduring impact of

John Lennon's 'Imagine', for example, Bob Marley's 'Stand Up for Your Rights', or Billie Holiday's 'Strange Fruit' – to name just a very few. Knowing the potential of music to stir the emotions is to also know that it is to be handled with care.

Cultural values – music is critical in defining who we are and how we determine our identity. It often serves to communicate emotions, beliefs, and abstractions that may not have been comprehensible otherwise. Throughout history, music has broken down cultural barriers – look at Jazz, Reggae, and Blues for obvious examples. Live music is a vital element of our cultural life

Social values – like perhaps no other subject, music has the power to connect and bind us, most powerfully realised of course in a joint choral or instrumental performance. Its key message is equality – the soloist needs the choral parts; the violin is offset by the double bass – each instrument or voice working individually to create a harmonious whole. Using music to collaborate and make links is one of the oldest forms of communication.

Spiritual values – who hasn't experienced the euphoria that comes from immersing ourselves – and losing ourselves – in sound? Whether it is a piece of church music or a current pop song, music's transcendent qualities enable us to glimpse something that goes beyond our own selves. Put simply, music can move the soul.

What the teachers and practitioners say

Values help me to make decisions. I am particularly aware of my values when I need to make difficult decisions as they guide me and encourage me to look through various lenses. Values are critical in the teaching of music, particularly in developing creativity as we uncover the skills, knowledge, and beliefs needed to both compose and perform. For me, music also brings opportunities for honesty and autonomy – as through music we are able to express emotions and describe experiences in a way that is unique to ourselves.

A values-based music experience in the classroom

Related Values	Curriculum Application	Cross-Curricular Links	Taking Values into Action
KS1			
Unity Cooperation Appreciation Friendship	Musical imitation – listening to instruments, copying one another, and following tuned and untuned instruments playing melodies to copy. All humans learn through copying one another and experiencing this unique form of unity through cooperation is a privilege – but we need to be mindful about who and what we are copying and why!	English: musical imitation to tell a story. PSHE: awareness of our own perception and behaviours, likes, and dislikes.	What types of behaviours do you notice in others? What sort of behaviours do you appreciate and want to copy? Who are your heroes? Think carefully about the values they show and what you want to copy.
Unity Cooperation Appreciation Patience Tolerance Self-belief Service	Instruments of the orchestra – each instrument has its own contribution to make and is necessary to the whole harmonious sound. It only works with patience, co-operation, and appreciation. Which instrument do you like best/associate with? Can you say why?	PSHE/RSE: special me.	Think carefully: what is your unique contribution or service to your family or class? Are you sweet-tempered, energetic, funny, or kind perhaps? How does that make others feel? Look around you – what contributions are other people making to your family or class? How will others appreciate you?
KS2			
Resilience Determination Humility Generosity Self-belief	Music composition – compose a piece of music independently or in a group, with one or more instruments. This will require all your values of resilience, determination, humility, generosity, and self-belief!	Maths: number patterns and sequencing.	Share your musical composition with others. How does it feel to be sharing your work? What emotions does it evoke in others? How might you comment with generosity on their contributions and respond with humility and self-belief to their reactions?

Cooperation **Unity** **Diversity** **Tolerance** **Gratitude** **Self-Belief** **Harmony**	Singing in canon and harmony - this is co-operation, unity, diversity, and joy in action!	Maths: number patterns and sequencing. Geography: look up the countries of origin of these pieces of music. History: look up the history of your musical genre.	Remember that feeling of singing in unison with others! At what other times in your life do you feel you are working in harmony with others? What values are involved? How can you ensure you are able to work in unity with others?
KS3			
Unity **Respect** **Appreciation** **Cooperation** **Unity** **Harmony**	West African drumming and how this is used in communication. What do you appreciate and respect about this music? What do you find surprising, beautiful, or wonderful about what you have learned?	Geography. Mathematics: recording beats in the bar.	Taking the idea of polyrhythms, what do you feel these simultaneous contrasting rhythms can say to us about the way we need to work together in unity or harmony in our society? What place does discord play?
Peace **Love** **Beauty** **Joy** **Generosity** **Service**	Protest songs - examine how they are composed and the effect on the listener. What do they have to tell us about generosity, peace, love, and beauty?	English: poetry. Citizenship. History: apartheid, oppression, and political songs.	Research songs that have been used as a call to action or service; explore the place of music with its own beauty in protest. Can you compose your own poem or song to bring people's attention to a cause you feel passionate about?

What the learners say

When we sang together back then, on that stage, that was the best moment of my entire life! KS2 pupil.

I've learned to think of values like pens and pencils in my pencil case. Which one shall I choose now?

Questions for consideration in the staffroom

How could music illuminate your schools' values or be used to promote and support values-based behaviours?

Do you have access to good quality musical instruments? How are they displayed? Are children encouraged to touch, use, and find out about them?

What about musical appreciation? Does your school have a way of introducing children and young people to a wide range of musical styles? Is there ever time for listening for pleasure or while children work?

How much opportunity do learners currently have to experience authenticity in music? In other words, how often do they hear live music? Can you create more opportunities for this?

How can you use learning in your school to enhance the wellbeing of learners and/or those in your wider community?

Further reading:

For further resources see for example the Huntington School Music Department, York (https://huntschoolmusic.com/index.html) and *Primary School Music*, a website dedicated to free music resources (https://www.music-education.co.uk).

CHAPTER 16

The Curriculum and Pedagogy of Values-based Education in PE and Sport

I believe in the impossible because no one else does.

Florence Griffith Joyner

Values at the heart of PE and sport

In the content and pedagogy of PE and sport the values of cooperation, perseverance, resilience, and responsibility are recurring and characteristic. In the very act of studying this subject, learners will frequently come face to face with these values and practise them.

The importance of PE and sport as a subject in schools

We take it for granted that physical education will be on the curriculum in every school – an unalienable right. It fits so very well with all we expect of childhood. The actual process of physical development into competence and skilfulness is not only enjoyable but an intrinsic part of our human development. It is increasingly recognised by sports bodies that, used in the right way, PE and sport are a perfect carrier for a values-based curriculum, promoting positive values in action. The Youth Sport Trust has this year produced a set of personal development posters for schools (My Personal Best) to promote the 'personal development characteristics' of responsibility, respect, tolerance, equality and diversity, inclusion, self-motivation, integrity, co-operation, confidence, resilience, aspiration, and how to resolve conflicts. Each poster sets out how physical activity can help personal behaviours in PE, in school and in life.

The value of PE and sport to a values-based society

Analogies to the sport field in our English language are legion: 'Fair play', 'playing by the rules', 'it's not cricket' are all references to 'good sportsmanship, which is still upheld and honoured. Allegiance to, for instance, a football team can be visceral. For this reason, sport is well positioned to promote equality and diversity – fairness in the way we treat and talk to others.

The value of PE and sport to the individual – for their life

Physical confidence and competence often go hand in hand with personal competence. The relationship between physical exercise – both individual and team sport – and mental health are now widely recognised. On the football field and in the gym learners learn how to think in different ways, to be adaptable and flexible to suit the demands of the situation. Independently, and as part of a team, they learn how to plan, perform, and evaluate actions, ideas, and performances to improve their quality and effectiveness. Through practice we learn how to improve on our personal best but alongside this, we inevitably learn values of humility, resilience, unity, equality, gratitude, and graciousness.

Illuminating PE and sports through a values-based framework

PE and sport, like any subject discipline, has the strong potential to bring out the best or worst the in humankind. Competition, in the right amount, resilience, but not a 'win at all costs' mentality. In order for a PE and sports curriculum to have the positive effects highlighted above, it needs to set about illuminating its inherent positive values.

Moral and ethical values – these run through sports and physical activities: adherence to the rules of a game, not cheating, and playing fairly are paramount if the game is to work. The para-Olympics of 2012 showed us all that we don't have to be a 'standard human' to be good at physical activity.

Cultural values – appreciation and understanding of the way sports and sporting heroes have contributed to our culture and economy form the bedrock of our appreciation of sport in both our country as well as other countries around the world. For this reason, it is often described as a 'great leveller', showing us how we can be united in both playing and watching a game.

Social values – engagement in sporting activities help us to realise and see the part we play in creating the whole. Responsibility, unity, co-operation, tolerance, and respect are all enacted here.

Spiritual values – the utter joy of 'losing yourself' in physical activity. This is perhaps all the more enhanced when the activity is outside and among the natural world – it can be said to be a spiritual response, as can the elation of 'winning' a team game or beating a personal best.

Being explicit about these aspects of the curriculum subject during lessons and activities helps define them for learners. The subject is then serving a double duty, teaching subject knowledge, skills, and techniques, while also offering unparalleled opportunities for life learning.

A values-based PE and sports experience in school			
Related Values	Curriculum Application	Cross-Curricular Links	Taking values into Action
Co-operation and Unity	This is applicable to any team game. It is about finding the joy in using individual skill and talents to work towards a shared goal. Emphasise how turn taking in playground games, sharing the ball in a match, helping one another during a game - and so on - brings its own reward in the unification that comes with putting the group's interest above our own.	PSHE	Review a team game together and note where co-operation was used during the game to good effect. How did it make you feel? What parallels are there in 'real' life?
Respect Tolerance	These values underpin co-operation and are about being patient, understanding, and accepting other people's differences. In turn we hope that others will treat us accordingly. In a team game we need to accept that people have different abilities and aptitudes and need our support and encouragement.	RE PSHE	

Perseverance Resilience	Discover more about these values through being willing to have a go and persevere through; learn about how many of the sportspeople we now consider among our 'greats' had to learn self-discipline, patience, and perseverance, to acquire self-belief.		Set yourself personal goals in physical fitness or any other sphere.
Responsibility	To enact this value in sport, you see your role in the team and so you can offer advice and encouragement to teammates; positively contribute to the enjoyment of the game, both on and off the pitch; and start to be creative in how you approach things.	Citizenship PSHE	What areas in your life do you have responsibility for? Do you feel equipped to deal with them well? If not, is there someone who could help you? What responsibility for yourself or for others might you develop more of so that you can feel on top of your game?

What the teachers say

Whether at a school sports day or at elite competition level, I think the most valuable lessons to be taken from sport come not from physical prowess or victories, but from the values displayed by participants. Examples of sportsmanship and values abound: take Flintoff and Brett Lee's iconic handshake in the 2005 Ashes; the recent conduct and victory of England's women's football team at the 2022 European Cup; or the Brownlee brothers where one stopped to help other during a triathlon, to name just a few.

Values thread through PE and sport and are made explicit through all team games. In Herefordshire, sporting values are rewarded at competition level and the children are really proud to receive this acknowledgement. What's more, they really understand how the values of self-belief, determination, and unity, for example, play out.

From PE And sport, I've learned commitment and dependability: having to attend weekly training. Moreover, in team sports your commitment not only impacts you, but your fellow teammates as they expect you to show the same level of commitment.

I've also learned about honesty; something I learned recently is the importance of being honest with yourself. In terms of how you are feeling mentally and physically. The first stage of the behaviour change model (contemplation) requires this initial honesty. For example, rethinking behaviours, the risks of these behaviours, and a thorough analysis of yourself and your actions. If we are not honest in this respect, we will not change our behaviour. This example shows how something learned through physical activity is transferable to other aspects of life.

Perseverance: if you are losing, learning a new skill, or if you are teaching a difficult group of children; perseverance is crucial to win back the game, conquer that skill and get the best out of those children. Nothing good in life comes easy! Undergraduate Student.

What the learners say

We do lots of sport. I like that we try to do as much sport as possible. KS2 pupil.

PE teaches us honesty and teamwork through fun activities that value fair play and rules.

Sport and PE have been consistent fixtures in my life ... they often kept me motivated to go to school, were integral to my mental wellbeing, and a channel through which I have been able to support myself and others to be the best version of ourselves (both physically and mentally).

I've had problems with my feet since I was little which means doing some sports is really hard or causes me pain. However, I really enjoy playing cricket with the school team and use the value of resilience and determination to make sure I do my best so I don't let the team down. KS3 pupil.

Questions for consideration in the staffroom

How could the values outlined be promoted to reinforce how learners develop their behaviour both on and off the sports field?

Would it be helpful to include a self-perception review at the end of sport activities to ask students which specific values they have shown or how they could draw on a set of values to help them in a specific situation?

Could PE and sports lead the way in the values-based curriculum for your school to help learners develop personal characteristics, good health and wellbeing, and to pursue and develop their own interests and talents and become active citizens?

CHAPTER 17

The Curriculum and Pedagogy of Values-based Education in Personal, Social, Health and Economic education (Including Relationships and Sex Education)

The main thing in life is to know your own mind.
Snuffkin in *Moominsummer Madness* by Tove Janson

Values at the heart of personal, social and health education – including relationships and sex education (PSHE and RSE)

In the content and pedagogy of PSHE and RSE values of care, diversity, health, kindness, and respect are recurring and characteristic. In the very act of studying this subject, learners will frequently come face to face with these values and practise them.

The importance of PSHE in schools

Personal, social, health, and economic (PSHE) education is a school subject through which pupils develop the knowledge, skills, and attributes they need to manage their lives, now and in the future. It helps children and young people to stay healthy and safe, while preparing them to make the most of life and work.

The PSHE Association

PSHE specifically enables children to learn about and discuss things that are key to their lives now and in the future. They'll talk about relationships, feelings and emotions, differences, how to be healthy, how they are growing and changing, and discuss key social issues in our society – such as racism, homophobia, or equality. Statutory guidance is broad and for both the non-statutory PSHE programme of study and the now statutory health and relationships guidance. Both of these present opportunities to exemplify values and help learners recognise their importance. The non-statutory programme of study puts values at its core. This subject is all about *us* and as such is about thoughtful and reflective learning. As one practitioner writes, you never hear students saying, 'When am I ever going to use this?' The skills learned through PSHE are applicable to life in and outside of the classroom.

PSHE can lead the way in pedagogy. By its very nature, the learning in PSHE is open and honest and enables pupils to grow and develop. It establishes a learning atmosphere that is safe, non-judgemental, and promotes ideas, thoughts, and questions, developing a sense of mutual respect which in turn can permeate the entire curriculum if it is embedded within a whole-school approach.

The value of PSHE to society

The big contribution of PSHE is to our future. It offers markers and signposts to help children navigate life. This is perhaps most notably seen through the guidance it gives on the building blocks and characteristics of positive stable relationships. As these are the basis of the family and therefore of society, this is of paramount importance to the present and future happiness and health of the nation.

PSHE sets out to teach children about the character traits and positive personal attributes (sometimes referred to as 'virtues') that will underpin their lives – respect, tolerance, understanding, appreciation, honesty, integrity, courage, humility, respect, kindness, generosity, trustworthiness, and a sense of justice – and enable them to be of service to and in the wider community. Perhaps more uncomfortably, PSHE also addresses the aspects of our world that are of sources of harm – for example threats on social media or adults with malign intentions.

The value of PSHE to the individual

Good PSHE equips children with the tools to look after themselves, to be kind and thoughtful to each other, and to recognize, respect, and celebrate differences. It enables children to recognize that they need to maintain a healthy mind and body and to value a kind, respectful, and positive atmosphere in order to become effective learners in school and in the wider world. If children feel valued and celebrated in school, in their friendship group and within themselves, they will equally feel empowered to take risks within their learning and to develop effective learning habits.

Through PSHE, children are supported to examine, evaluate, and even challenge their own values. This is essential grounding for enabling children to become aware thinkers, able to make reasoned choices for themselves in the future. Teaching about values is central to PSHE. Without a values-framework the subject is an empty husk.

At a glance: Illuminating PSHE through a values-based framework

Moral and ethical values – learning about what is legal and right and wrong, as well as the reasons behind why we should avoid certain behaviours or treating people certain ways, is an integral to PSHE. The specific values of consideration, gratitude, forgiveness, humility, self-control, and service thread through our decision making and our actions. In turn, this approach leads us to valuing human life through celebrating our self and others. Other 'big questions' that can be explored in PSHE, include the environment and sustainability.

Cultural values – our sense of connection with those in and beyond our immediate environments are critical to PSHE. Our cultural beliefs and values should be shared, considered, and understood in an atmosphere of respect, tolerance, compassion, and appreciation. Diversity and difference should both be both respected and celebrated.

Social values – relationships are at the very heart of PSHE studies. Our own behaviours, communication, and interactions with others, intimate or otherwise, inform our inner world, colour our individual day to day experiences – and form the fabric of our society

Spiritual values – PSHE allows us to examine the aspects that make us unique as a person, inviting us to identify and question our responses to ourselves and one another. Where do our personal value systems come from, and what influences our core beliefs? It can lead us into consideration of our sense of otherness, beyond ourselves, leading to a sense of hope, unity, and harmony.

What the teachers and practitioners say

All the practitioners and teachers interviewed for this subject said values are an essential part of their life and how they teach. They see values as a dynamic entity contributing to a personal code for living as well as to their teaching. They describe a connection with learners that fuses teaching and learning experience:

Oneness or a sense of unity is another essential value for living and teaching: not seeing the pupil as 'other', but empathising, aiming to really meet their needs and respond to them in a way that both teaches them the subject and helps them overcome obstacles.

To achieve this, they purposefully create a climate for learning in their classes that is 'calm and kind'. They are mindful of the need to model these values in their teaching, discussing the behaviour and values that they want the children to show, for example, being kind, listening to each other, and valuing each other.

Teachers of this subject are very conscious that their own values are informed by the vast arenas of politics, education, upbringing, cultural background, social groups, role models, literature, media, and politics.

Through PSHE they hold a steady course, helping in turn their children to navigate the waters of *life.*

Values underpin everything I do: they are a key part of my teaching – and my life.

A values-based PSHE experience in the classroom

PSHE lessons should inspire children to think specifically about universal human values and provide a framework in which they can be discussed. By its nature, PSHE will encourage children to use the language and meaning of values in their exploration of relationships and their place in the wider world.

PSHE should also include elements of mindfulness and opportunities for children to ground themselves, and to reflect upon how they are thinking and feeling. It should provide tools to recognize the things that are really important and how they can look after their own mental and physical well-being.

PSHE lessons should also allow opportunities for children to discuss how their choices and attitudes can have an impact on the wider world. It should allow children to discuss what it means to be a member of a school community, a local community, and a global citizen. Framing the discussion with an awareness of positive universal human values should empower children to check that their interaction with the world has these values at its core.

A values-based PSHE experience in the classroom			
Related Values	Curriculum Application	Cross-Curricular Links	Taking values into Action
KS1			
Respect Tolerance Understanding	How behaviour affects others; being polite and respectful - use puppet play to explore feelings and consequences, good manners, and respectful language.	English: speaking and listening; turn taking; developing vocabulary. RSHE: relationships.	Create a class Smiley Suns display to exemplify each time a child uses good manners and respectful words - see how many Smiley Suns you can collect over one day!
Kindness Honesty Self-Belief Compassion Trust Empathy Unity Respect Loyalty Trust Co-operation Patience Tolerance	Relationships -through the use of Special Person Circle Time. In a circle, children say why they think a certain person is 'special'.	English: speaking and listening; turn taking; developing vocabulary. RSHE: relationships.	Affirmative comments build our own self-belief and help us reach out to others. Consider your own special qualities: what are they and how can you use them well today?
KS2			
Kindness Honesty Self-Belief Compassion Trust Empathy Unity Respect Loyalty Trust Co-operation Patience Tolerance	Relationships - Special Person - as above but use a post-it so that everyone writes down their affirmative messages. Introduce modelled phrases, such as 'I think ... is special because they are self-reflective and will always apologise if there has been a misunderstanding' etc.	English: writing and vocabulary development.	Encourage children to use these phrases as self-affirmation as well as in the course of their conversations with others.

Friendship Kindness Care Compassion Respect Peace	Respectful Relationships. Anti-bullying. Learning about respectful behaviour in friendships – including but not exclusive to physical, psychological, racial, emotional, or/and cyber bullying. Examine the difference between bullying and teasing. Knowing how to get help.	Computing: safe use of the internet.	Make an anti-bullying poster for the school or classroom. Put together an anti-bullying charter for your school playground, or for internet use. Make a Help Box for your classroom for children to post requests for help.
KS3			
Generosity Care Happiness Self-belief	Health and wellbeing and the factors that affect this. Understanding it is not about being happy all the time but how we react to different circumstances. Using reflection.		Connecting with others: look out for others and their mental health and wellbeing.
Friendship Kindness Empathy Altruism Service Unity Co-operation	Physical and mental wellbeing. The contribution of hobbies and interests. The importance of making connections with others. Record – write or draw – all the different things you enjoy as a hobby or interest. Consider 'good' or 'unwise' connections to things.		Think about how concept of joining up 'good causes' – for example, a sustainability movement or a local charity can move us beyond our immediate circle. This takes us beyond the 'self' into the more abstract concept of friendship as a channel through which to lead one's life.

What the learners say

I love it when I'm the Special Person because it makes me see what makes me me! KS1 pupil.

You should show respect for others. KS1 pupil.

I think learning about values and using them day to day has made me more responsible, self-aware, and sensible. I didn't realise until I thought about it how many values I use day to day, in my lessons.

Determination … [is] to keep trying if I don't get things right first time.

Integrity … [is] to learn more and do what's right.

Efficient … [is] always going to class with the right equipment and ready to learn. Secondary pupil.

Questions for consideration in the staffroom

Which values do you consider the most important ones in teaching and learning about relationships?

Do you think that a considered set of values could provide a stable underpinning to your PSHE/RSHE offer?

How can PSHE/RSE become more of a driving force in helping children develop and maintain healthy self-image and healthy relationships?

Further reading

Carroll, J., Howard, C., & Knight, B. (2018) *British Values in the Primary Classroom.* London: Sage.

Knight, B. (2019) *Can I Tell You About Friendship?* London: Jessica Kingsley Publishers.

The PSHE Association (www.pshe-association.org.uk).

CHAPTER 18

The Curriculum and Pedagogy of Values-based Education in Religious Education

Two things are infinite, the universe and human stupidity,
and I am not yet completely sure about the universe.
Attributed to Albert Einstein

I did then what I knew how to do. Now that I know better, I do better.
Maya Angelou

Values at the heart of religious education (RE)

In the content and pedagogy of RE the values of respect, reason, open-mindedness, and care are recurring and characteristic. In the very act of studying this subject, learners will frequently come face to face with these values and practise them.

The importance of RE in schools

We are all born into a world of beliefs. As individuals and societies, we develop our worldview, live with it, change it (or not), and die with it. Our worldview might be religious or secular or a mixture of the two. Encountering differences and divergences in worldview – I believe this, you believe that – is a fascinating daily reality in schools. The journey towards learning how to understand oneself, and how to live in a diverse school, society, and world, starts with a curriculum offering clear knowledge of what worldviews are and how they influence us all.

Schools can flourish when they encourage knowledge and understanding of different worldviews. They can operate as seedbeds of democracy and civilisation when they give children and young people the vocabulary to say: 'we are different, here's why we are different, and this is what we can still do together.'

In primary schools, finding out about the variety of worldviews that exist – from the belief systems of pre-colonial civilisations; to dharmic traditions in Asia; to the deities and values of the classical world; to Abrahamic religions such as Judaism, Christianity, and Islam; to secular post-religious philosophies; ecologically-based spiritualities; and many more – helps children to understand the stories, rituals, life-moments, and ethical commitments of the world.

In secondary schools, knowing about the disciplinary frameworks that can be used for studying and reflecting on worldviews – for example, philosophy, theology, religious studies, sociology, anthropology, and psychology – helps young people to pursue the study of worldviews rigorously, and provides them with a wide repertoire for interpretation, in ways that interface with many other disciplines, skills and professions.

And at all stages of education, knowing about worldviews, and understanding how they can be approached and interpreted, contributes to children and young people's personal sense of meaning, identity, belonging, purpose, and role in life. It empowers them to define themselves as human beings in a changing and fragile existence.

The value of RE to society

Human society in all its diverse forms is a beautiful adventure, but it is now threatened by two global forces: violent fundamentalist extremism, and an accelerating climate and species emergency. A violent fundamentalist worldview is one that believes 'I am right, you are wrong, and it is my duty to destroy you and your culture.' The climate and species emergency is caused by a worldview that we can continue consuming and abusing the planet with impunity – with consequences that will be faced by someone else, somewhere else.

The subject called RE (or, in some schools, worldviews) cannot directly solve these threats, but it does equip young people to understand the mindsets that got us here, to critique hateful or wasteful thinking, and to come face to face with a wide range of positive values, such as beauty, courage, cooperation, hopefulness, reason, and truthfulness. The pathway through the threats and towards a better, safer existence for society, runs through the systematic study of beliefs and worldviews, and reflection on them.

The value of RE to the individual

A worldview is simply an individual's way of making some sense of the fact of existence – to understand life, experience it to the full, and respond to others. Some people call their beliefs a philosophy of life, others call them a religion or a set of ideas and values to which they are committed.

Many children are born into a systemic worldview, such as an ancient religious tradition, and they become part of its beliefs, rituals, culture, and ways of life. Later in life, they might question it or move on from it, but it still influences them. In secular societies, many children are raised with a set of values that may be more or less articulated through stories, ethical examples, and commitments. There are also many children and adults who inhabit a worldview without being fully aware of its influence over them.

Studying a wide range of worldviews, noting how they have changed historically over time, observing how they influence people's values and behaviour, realising that each worldview is internally diverse and nuanced, is a journey of fascination, bringing ever deeper awareness of the self and others.

Illuminating RE through a values-based framework

RE takes children and young people up close to the beliefs, experiences and values that motivate and influence people, the taproot of culture, work, community, society, and spirituality.

Moral and ethical values – RE frequently explores the difference between right and wrong and the consequences of behaviour and actions. For example, in learning stories from the Jewish, Christian, Humanist and other traditions, where someone stands up against oppression and injustice, learners encounter values such as courage, compassion, empathy, equality, freedom, hope, justice, and persistence. Debates about ethical issues, such as animal rights, just war/non-violence, or relationships, can contribute to moral and ethical development by giving learners direct experience of seeing a different point of view.

Cultural values – RE provides opportunities for learners to appreciate the beauty of sacred buildings, art, music, decorated texts, or dance, and to consider the place of imagery in devotion or reflection. This process enables learners to experience and enjoy more of their own heritage, and to encounter a diverse range of cultures. Learners will also acquire mastery of some key words in a range of languages that have influenced theology and philosophy, including Sanskrit, Latin, Greek, Hebrew, Arabic, and Punjabi. Immersion into a range of key terms deepens learners' understanding as well as strengthening their interest in, and respect for, cultures different from their own.

Social values – in RE, learners often share their views on an issue, their interpretations of stories, and their experiences of belonging to a worldview. They learn to express themselves with confidence and in interesting and appropriate ways, and to receive the views of other people, both children and adults. They can enter into dialogue and discussion by active listening, taking turns to speak, and disagreeing well with mutual respect and humility. They can experience how it is possible to change one's mind without losing face or self-respect. They learn to see the world as a diverse place, in which diversity of views and experiences can be a positive, not a problem.

Spiritual values – RE deals directly with faiths and worldviews, and the individual faith or spirituality of key figures such as Guru Nanak, Gandhi, Doreen Lawrence, or Greta Thunberg. In RE learners realise how these outstanding spiritual examples have underlying values that guide and strengthen them: forgiveness, goodness, love, peace, service, transcendence, and truthfulness, to name a few. By studying the lives of these examples, learners can reflect on the beliefs and values which they held dear, and then think, speak, and write about their own values, hopes and dreams. Images and stories which stimulate the creative spiritual imagination, such as the earth from outer space, the campaigners who faced bullying and intimidation to protect the rights of others, and rescue operations to save refugees on land and sea, can also be used to promote spiritual reflection on what values matter most to them.

What the teachers and practitioners say

The role of RE in preventing radicalisation and prejudice is important. Secondary RE teacher.

I am saddened when I hear of schools … teaching RE as just a 'let's do Divali' approach where there is not context or meaning attached to the children's lives. Primary RE teacher.

A very, very large number of beliefs are relevant to the workplace, e.g. if you work in education or health. Employer.

Religious education done well helps children understand where values overlap and where they diverge … it allows children to understand how their own faith relates to the wider world, both in terms of attitudes and the prevailing law. Amanda Spielman, HMCI.

A values-based RE experience in the classroom

While RE (or worldviews) explores many values in its study of belief systems, there are three that can be permanently embedded in the curriculum and pedagogy, to such an extent that making successful progress as a learner means understanding and practising them repeatedly until they become habits: respect, reason, and reflection.

Related Values	Curriculum Application	Cross-Curricular Links	Taking Values into Action
KS1			
Respect	Setting up rules for dialogue and discussion, reinforcing them regularly, and applying them to a range of questions, e.g. on bullying, sharing, and interpretations of stories.	PSHE: sharing opinions or feelings, listening to and valuing contributions from others.	Make use of the Philosophy for Children methodology for exploring complex ideas in an inclusive way.
Reason	Using sophisticated sorting techniques to react to the plot of a story, e.g. 'Gautama should have …' or 'the Good Samaritan should not have …'.	Computer studies: using ICT to develop skills in co-writing and editing a piece of reasoning on ethical issues.	Make use of the Godly Play methodology to explore motivation and reason in famous stories.
Reflection	Taking time in silent reflection, looking at or copying an image or a piece of decorated text.	Art, craft and design: understanding and appreciating an icon or portrait of an inspiring ethical figure.	Playing meditative music while decorating or copying a famous text such as a psalm, poem, prayer, or story.

KS2			
Respect	Discovering the range of worldviews and the hundreds of different names for God in a range of languages.	Geography: locating the places where specific worldviews began, and how they came to this country.	Planning and implementing a local study that interviews believers to elicit their views in a constructive way.
Reason	Debates about the existence of God.	English: writing to argue or persuade on a philosophical or ethical issue.	Holding a debate on the question 'does God exist?'
Reflection	Considering a story such as Moses, Gandhi, or Rosa Parks: what values would be needed to follow their example?	History: comparing histories of civil rights movements.	Creating a 'shopping list' of the personal qualities needed by leaders, such as courage, determination, and self-sacrifice.
KS3			
Respect	Studying the holocaust and theological responses to it.	History: understanding the roots and causes of antisemitism. Citizenship: understanding how societies can fall prey to 'othering' which excludes and generates hate towards a specific group.	Planning and implementing activities for Holocaust Memorial Day.
Reason	Understanding that 'proof' means different things in theology, philosophy, history, science, and maths.	Designing a comparative diagram of 'proof' examples from maths, science, history, and philosophy.	Generating lists of 'proofs' in philosophy and theology and 'scoring' them for their credibility.
Reflection	Studying the causes and consequences of the Reformation in Europe, and the birth of secularism and the Enlightenment. Thinking about the consequences of religious wars and the necessity of tolerance.	History: the significance of Erasmus, Luther, Calvin, the Thirty Years War, the Peace of Westphalia, and the conflict between Henry VIII and Rome.	Designing a timeline of events and organising a debate: 'are the differences between Christian denominations still significant?'

What the learners say

Respect: *I get why you go on about RE Miss. It matters to people. I need to know why people are like they are. I don't have to agree but I do have to know about it.* KS2 pupil.

We learn to accept differences in each other as understanding breeds tolerance in our diverse communities. This allows us to create a Safe environment that benefits everyone. KS3 pupil

Reason: *After taking RS A level it becomes hard to ever blindly accept a proposition again ... before we studied RE, we'd have been more egocentric. Our discussions have stopped being celebrity gossip and more talking genuinely about genuine things.* KS5 pupil.

Reflection: *We are lucky to have a specialist teacher who helps us to go deeper with our learning. Your teacher needs to have a good understanding of religious and non-religious worldviews.* KS2 pupil.

Questions for consideration in the staffroom

1. Do the teachers have a strong understanding of the purpose and aims of RE in your school?
2. Does the RE curriculum balance a generous and open range of religious and secular worldviews? Does it balance breadth of coverage with depth of research and reflection?
3. Is your school networked into supporting groups and networks that operate nationally and locally, providing CPD opportunities?
4. What is the impact of the RE curriculum on learners? How does it continually deepen their understanding of complexity in religions and worldviews?

Further reading

Bennett, W. (1993) *The Book of Virtues: A treasury of great moral stories.* New York: Simon & Schuster.

Blaylock, L. (2013) *Values: What matters most: exploring right and wrong with Christians and Humanists.* Birmingham: RE Today.

Blaylock, L., Christopher, K., and Moss, F. (2015) *Religious Education and British Values.* Birmingham: RE Today.

Chater, M. (2020) ed. *Reforming RE: Power and knowledge in a worldviews curriculum.* Woodbridge: John Catt Ltd.

Reforming RE (2021) *Blogs on Curriculum Design in Worldviews.* Available at: https://reformingre.wordpress.com/.

Religious Education Council (2018) *Commission on RE: Final report: religion and worldviews: the way forward: a national plan for RE.* London: RE Council. Available at: https://www.commissiononre.org.uk/final-report-religion-and-worldviews-the-way-forward-a-national-plan-for-re/.

CHAPTER 19

The Curriculum and Pedagogy of Values-based Education in Science

Science is more than a body of knowledge. It's a way of thinking.

Carl Sagan

Values at the heart of science

In the content and pedagogy of science the values of accuracy, beauty, gratitude, interdependence, responsibility, unity, and usefulness are recurring and characteristic. In the very act of studying this subject, learners will frequently come face to face with these values and practise them.

The importance of science in schools

The subject of science pivots on and thrives through questioning. The ability to formulate as well as respond to questions is fundamental to successful learning in any subject discipline. Fuelled by curiosity, learners are guided to seek out answers, carrying out their own research as well as their own experiments.

As pupils learn more, they may begin to appreciate the incompleteness of scientific knowledge. This stimulates their curiosity to find out more. The most striking example is that we say 'science is the study of life', but do we actually know what life is?

When actively involved in the scientific process, students can begin to learn to work with others, a process underpinned by values. They also use and consider values when reflecting on what they are doing in science, how this might impact upon the world around them, and other living things. A values-based approach allows them to think through the host of moral and ethical issues that come with working in the field of science.

Science can open people's eyes, minds and hearts to the beauty and wonder of nature. It can make people aware of humankind's total and utter dependence on the gifts of nature, from the air we breathe, the water we drink, to the food we eat and much more besides. Thus, it can engender a love and respect for the living world and encourage them not to mistreat and exploit it. Science, by its very nature, has the potential to promote the universal values of love and compassion for our world.

The study of the natural world through science has the potential to allow pupils to connect with nature more deeply; through this connection they can feel at one with nature and experience a sense of peace and well-being. This inner quiet is a strong and stable basis from which to learn effectively.

The value of science to society

Science allows individuals to understand the world in which we live in terms of both its fragility and the enduring nature of life on our planet. It allows people to understand the complexity of their existence – in biological, physical, and chemical terms – through information and concepts that underpin life and the physical world in which we live. It can show us that laws can be derived to explain our complex existence and that some things are as of yet beyond our understanding. Science can show us how we can manipulate life as well as helping us understand how such knowledge can be used as a tool for good and evil. Science can help us to understand how we fit into the universe. It allows us to consider the ethics and morality of what we do to ourselves and the world in which we live.

The vast amount of research carried out in the biological sciences in particular benefits society in myriad ways, for example in medical and pharmaceutical developments, materials science 'copying' materials found in living organisms, genetics, agriculture, and ecology. The astonishing detail of the living world that is revealed through research adds further dimensions of wonder. However, it has to be said that like any other science, the biological sciences are in need of an ethical and moral framework – not all developments are beneficial or are used for good.

The value of science to the individual

The idea of caring for ourselves, one another and our planet should underpin all science. Through science therefore, we are encouraged to value ourselves and the life in the world around us. Through the study of science, we find ourselves considering how we interact and can contribute to our society and the world as a whole. We are encouraged to consider the world's unique ecosystem and how if we do not care and have compassion for humans and non-humans, we can cause harm and grief to them. Science helps us to both see our personal responsibility towards the world, and gives us the tools to help us enact that charge.

Illuminating science through a values-based framework

Moral and ethical values – a moral and ethical code with its associated values is necessary if we are to act responsibly with the knowledge that science gives us. The moral and ethical values implicit in sciences could be said to be restraint, patience, generosity, courage, kindness and service, compassion, trust, integrity, and honour.

Cultural values – science can better help us to understand how we can improve our society and our world. Conversely, our ability to create can have a negative impact. For example, the development of medicines and energies have had an impact on us as humans. The cultural values implicit in the sciences could be said to comprise: respect, gratitude, unselfishness, and service.

Social values – science embodies the social values of respect, responsibility, honour, compassion, and kindness by helping us to co-exist with others and life on earth. For example, understanding how our body works can inspire us to care for our physical, mental, and emotional health with respect, gratitude, and care; we can think about what good health enables us to do for others, and how it is needed to fulfil one's potential and function in life. In other words, this knowledge can serve a wider purpose. Science can help us in our relationships too. Research clearly shows that no-one can exist in isolation: relationships are vital for flourishing. We can learn from this that values that lead to harmonious relationships – such as forgiveness, patience, love, and tolerance – are worth working at. Understanding about interdependence in biology from studying ecosystems could inspire learners to enact values such as respecting, caring for, and valuing individuals, as each has special qualities to give to the whole class/family/friendship, etc.

Being well informed and understanding about ecosystems, climate change, greenhouse gases, deforestation, etc. – while learning about the generosity and abundance of nature and our total dependence on it – could lead learners to have an attitude that enacts values of respect, gratitude, care, love, and restraint in how they treat the resources they use. Because we are nearly always taking, we could ask how we could give back.

Spiritual values – both science and spirituality can be said to coalesce around the values of love, hope, beauty, peace, and understanding. Science seeks answers through means of enquiry such as observation and measurement. For example, the science behind why the sun is yellow and bright in our sky. A spiritual desire to understand this same phenomenon might move us to awe and wonder, or to consider why we feel a sense of warmth and contentment when it shines on us. Anyone who has observed the joy of a pupil who has discovered a scientific phenomenon through their own endeavours has witnessed a spiritual moment.

What the teachers and practitioners say

Values are an essential part of my life and how I teach. Unselfishness – putting the other person's/pupils needs before one's own – is a special one for me which I learned from my parents. I would love my pupils to understand that if they do this it is difficult to be unhappy. Oneness or a sense of unity is another essential value for living and teaching: not seeing the pupil as 'other', empathising, aiming to really meet their needs and respond to them in the right way that both teaches them the subject and helps them overcome obstacles.

Values are embedded in Science. Finding answers to 'why' pushes children to question, research, and form their own opinions. It builds co-operation, confidence, and communication skills to help make sense of the world around us ... and to respect the natural world.

Values guide my thoughts, feelings, and actions so that I engage positively with others. They also allow me to develop a route map to make a positive contribution to the society that I live in. As an educator it is not just about the learning of facts and conceptual ideas that can help underpin our understanding of the world. Through values we can teach those we educate to show, for example, hope for the world by considering our daily routines and actions as we go through life.

I think science should encourage the universal values of love and compassion for our world. It should also nurture an unfaltering belief in all students' abilities and potential.

Personal responsibility is something that science should teach, as without it science can be used for many negative things.

A values-based science experience in the classroom			
Related Values	Curriculum Application	Cross-Curricular Links	Taking Values into Action
KS1			
Unity Co-operation Diversity Respect Tolerance Peace Love Generosity interdependence	Living things – looking at what we all need to survive – shelter, food, and love.	English: research skills using non-fiction material.	What values do we all need to work together? Can you describe to someone how a given animal uses co-operation to survive? A social action project in our own community, e.g. preserving the habitat for hedgehogs.
Love Understanding Compassion Service Kindness	Staying healthy – hygiene, food, medicines, and care.	History: famous people – such as Edward Jenner, Florence Nightingale and Mary Seacole – who have worked to keep people healthy. RSHE: keeping healthy and safe.	Research people in our society who help us – who work in service to show compassion and kindness to help us stay healthy. Can you devise a set of questions you would like to put to them. Design a thank you poster for the people who help us. Think about the things you can do to help other people stay safe, e.g. washing hands.

KS2			
Gratitude **Restraint** **Service** **Empathy** **Tolerance** **Unity** **Interdependence**	Life cycles of humans, birds, animals, and insects, trees, and plants. Cycles are a fundamental aspect of how nature works to maintain overall harmony and balance at all levels, from the molecular to whole ecosystems. Cycles keep going, i.e. are self-generating, do not create waste or pollution, and cause no harm.		Responsibility to take care of the species on this planet. Become an expert on a given species – find out all you can about its life cycle and what it needs to thrive. Values that can be made explicit here include not doing anything that causes harm for example, to nature and the environment, or even words spoken face to face or on social media. All this requires awareness that actions can have wider effects than we may realise at first.
Responsibility **Care** **Consideration** **Rule of Law** **Friendship** **Kindness** **Compassion**	Changes as humans develop to old age. This topic illustrates the principle of interdependence throughout nature and the human world.	Citizenship: how we all need to work together for a safe society. Consideration of different job opportunities for the future.	Values in the context human evolution and change are concerned with emotions and relationships: friendships, family, relationships, authority figures, or our relationship with nature. This may be taken forward as a social action project looking after the elderly in our local community, e.g. choral singing visits to care homes, or partnering and pen pal for an elderly person.
KS3			
Respect **Democracy** **Consideration** **Care** **Gentleness** **Equality**	Biodiversity in the study of ecology. All organisms play a vital and specific part in the whole, so each is of value. Biodiversity in an ecosystem gives it resilience, strength, and richness.		Respect for all people, equality i.e. that each person or organism is of value and has something specific to give; being humane.

Care Consideration Empathy Generosity Beauty Peace Gratitude	Reproduction. This is one of the few opportunities secondary level biology gives pupils to look at a whole structure. Seeing the symmetry in flowers when studying plant reproduction is an opportunity to open pupils' eyes to symmetry throughout nature and start to spot it in other areas of biology. There is beauty in the structures plants make to hold their seeds.		Values that can be made explicit here (and in other parts of biology) arise from focussing on beauty. Beauty can be extended to include beauty of action, of thoughts, of ideas. This leads to values such as empathy, generosity (putting other's needs before one's own), harmony, quietness, and peace. There is also the value of generosity, i.e. of nature in producing such vast numbers of seeds from one plant.

What the learners say

Science helps us have faith that we can cure illnesses and disease in the world. It teaches us to be a team when we are working scientifically.

Science teaches us about the world around us and the values of interdependence and diversity so much! KS2 pupil.

Questions for consideration in the staffroom

What further potential is there to promote social, cultural, moral, ethical, and spiritual values in your school's science curriculum?

How much opportunity do learners currently have to use and develop their scientific knowledge for real through projects, such as Reduce, Reuse, Recycle?

How could your science curriculum be used to open people's senses, minds and hearts to the beauty and wonder of nature?

Further reading

Berry, W. (2018) *The World-Ending Fire*. London: Penguin Books

Blackmore, K., Howard, C., & Kington, A. (2018) 'Trainee Teachers' Experience of Primary Science Teaching, and the Perceived Impact on Their Developing Professional Identity,' *European Journal of Teacher Education*, pp. 1-20.

Cooke, V. & Howard, C. (2014) *Talk: Using dialogic talk in science*. Available at: http://eprints.worc.ac.uk/3518/.

Cooke, V. & Howard, C. (2015) *Practical Ideas for Teaching Primary Science*. St Albans: Critical Publishing.

Howard, C. & Blackmore, K. (2015) 'A hard nut to crack – improving primary trainee teacher confidence in teaching physical processes topics,' *Science Teacher Education, 73* Available at: http://www.ase.org.uk/journals/science-teacher-education/.

Howard, C. & Cooke, V. (2016) 'Key Concepts in Primary Science: audit and subject knowledge,' in *Surviving and Thriving as a Primary NQT*, Robinson et al (eds). St Albans: Critical Publishing.

Howard, C. & Blackmore, K. (Howard, C., Carroll, J., & Knight, B. (2018) *Understanding British Values in Primary Schools: Policy and Practice*. London: Sage.

Howard, C., Burton, M. and Levermore, D. (2020) *Children's Mental Health and Emotional Well-being in Primary Schools: A Whole School Approach* (2nd Edition). London: Sage.

Juniper, T., Skelly, I., Windsor, C. (2010), *Harmony: A new way of looking at our world*. London: Blue Door.

Sacks, J., (2020) *Morality, Restoring the Common Good in Divided Times*. London:

CHAPTER 20

Where do Subject Discipline Values Fit? A Theme ... a Topic ... or Integrated Studies?

In this chapter Mick Waters contemplates the issues around curriculum design and looks at how a values-based approach can underpin a whole school way of life.

Many schools follow an integrated approach to their curriculum, especially now that Ofsted has recently thrown a focus upon the link between *intent*, *implementation*, and *impact*. So how do we integrate an approach to values?

We don't 'do' values in school in the way we 'do' history, or maths, or art. Values are not on the timetable of most schools: children don't journey to a room where they get out the exercise book and have lessons or 'cover' 'values' which they are then tested on.

As we say in the introduction, values run through the lifeblood of our schools. Values are within the curriculum because the curriculum itself is at the heart of why we have schools. The curriculum is that which we have decided we want our children to learn, and schools are the places we have devised to help this to happen. We use every moment in school to enable that learning: in lessons, events, routines, and even all that we arrange beyond walls of the school itself. For we know that children will learn all the time that they are with us, whether we intend them to or not. They learn from the people they spend their time with, which includes their teachers and other adults in school, as well as the other pupils.

We are all teachers of values. In the best schools all staff adopt the same learning intentions about values in the same way that they share subject discipline content, and they are clear about how they can help children to acquire these values. They are also clear about the ways in which we behave toward our world, our community, and other people, all of which of course includes the people we teach (and ourselves).

When we are enjoying a special event at school – such as a sports competition, a performance, charity function, or a residential visit – the values we exhibit and encourage will be transmitted to children. As we go about our everyday routine in school, whether using a library, taking part in assembly, dining, or playtime, the respect we have for people and property will be absorbed by children. As we lead lessons and take children through passages of learning in our various subject disciplines, we have an opportunity to make values explicit and encourage children to relate those values to their own context, depending upon their maturity.

Values exist across every aspect of this broader description of curriculum. Thus far we have delved into various subject disciplines to explore ways in which values can be addressed within the context of structured pathways through concepts, knowledge, and the acquisition of skills. Our consideration has drawn out the ways in which each subject discipline in turn lends itself to the potential exploration of values in the place where children spend the majority of time in school: their lessons.

In schools where all teachers recognise and work together to enable the development of values there is a clear understanding that they are the lifeblood of the school. Values are not simply something we do for twenty minutes in Friday assembly as our 'value of the week'. Values are not simply special 'kindness' days (though it would be good if *they* occurred seven days a week). Values are not just the things we mention when something wonderful, terrible, poignant, or moving happens. Values are more than all of these things. They are present even when they are not articulated; in whether we feel valued, respected, appreciated, or not. Values are part of our contribution, worth, and spirit.

Yet it is in lessons that we can also bring an intellectual or cognitive consideration of values to support our on-going effort. In our reflection on subject disciplines we have highlighted some of the ways in which we can address values through, for example, the exploits and circumstances of people in different times or parts of the globe, or the ways in which artists have portrayed their thoughts and experiences. We have seen how the subject disciplines can help pupils to appreciate the natural world and the phenomena that exist all around us. We have noted the incredible discoveries made by humans as they have sought to influence their world, as well as some of the errors and consequences that have led to wars or scientific calamity. We have looked at the way the sports, performance, and technology have influenced life – helping us to exist together, shrinking our planet and bringing us closer and helping us to appreciate differences of culture, orientations, and sensitivities – while sometimes also creating challenges in terms of the way people relate to each other. When our subject disciplines explore such issues with children, they are addressing what is so often written in the vision for learning within the school. Making explicit the values that pervade our school bind this learning tighter so that the achievement of children, even as measured simply in tests and exam outcomes will be more secure. The richer prize will be sustained personal development which will continue long after the grade, level, or score has lost its meaning.

We know that the format of lessons makes a particular difference to learning and we know that some schools organise their teaching of subject disciplines in an integrated way. They teach through themes, topics, or projects. In doing so, they are recognising that our world is not arranged in separate, distinct, and discreet sections called subject disciplines but is an interwoven mass of interactions. Primary schools typically use a thematic approach more than secondary schools do though many of the latter are now organising learning in KS3 around a thematic concept to be explored in distinct subject discipline lessons for a half term or so at a time.

The reason our schools teach in subject discipline-based lessons is historic. Schools began with the few rich families who wanted to send their children to the few universities, paying for a tutor to help with study to pass the entrance exam for the university in the subject discipline that they wished to study. As universities grew, schools developed where tutors gathered, each to teach their own discipline. The logic went that, the earlier children began to study a subject discipline, the better their chances later. Only in the post war years did teachers begin to question this and bring learning, particularly for younger children closer to their starting point rather than working from the 'top down'.

Arguments have raged for more than fifty years about how the school curriculum should be structured at the point where it meets the child, and how far it should start from their understanding of the world. Most primary schools seem now to have settled for a linear pathway in mathematics and English, usually followed in the morning while children are at their freshest, with other subject disciplines in the afternoon, when children are less fresh, presumably because these aspects of learning are deemed either less taxing or less important.

Most primary schools seem to have those subject disciplines beyond mathematics and English addressed through some sort of integration arrangement of theme or topic, or a hybrid of separate and collective subject disciplines.

So, are the insights we have offered in values for subject disciplines applicable for schools that approach learning through themes? They are ... and they can be further explored though the careful and thoughtful management of learning within a theme.

A useful starting point is to consider how we want our children to behave as learners. The importance of 'audience, purpose and process' is well appreciated in the teaching of English. Applying the same principles to the wider curriculum, we would see our children behaving as organisers, activists, scholars, performers, inventors, collaborators, and guides. In order to do this, they need to become young historians, scientists, artists, mathematicians, technologists, cooks, and engineers ... the list is extensive. If they are going to become these sorts of people, pursuing the disciplines in depth, they are going to need to know how to use equipment, work with texts, understand and use research techniques, and develop high quality 'products' – models, artwork, experiments, writing, music, maps, calculation – all of which emanate from good teaching which sets appropriate contexts, uses visits out and visitors in, and uses quality literature, real archives, and proper experiments well.

The previous paragraph touches on the sheer number of facets involved in the work of any good teacher in what is a complex world of organisational decisions. It is difficult to imagine and hard to get going but, once established, is rewarding in every respect: children's attitude, tangible learning ... and even test results.

How is this achieved? Is the required content of subject disciplines simply shipped into a theme and re-ordered? Well, to an extent; the outlined content in each subject discipline is just some of the potential content to be explored in the realm of values.

Within any curriculum, however it is presented, content fits three 'ways' of learning.

- Things we learn *about.*
- Things we learn *how to.*
- Things we learn *though.*

Learning *about* is often called subject knowledge: it is about the dates, the people, the reasons, the location, the causes, and the effects.

Learning *how to* is often called the skills: to use a brush, construct paragraphs, use scientific equipment, build, make, and create.

Learning *through* a subject discipline is more complex. It is when we gain insights about, say, history *through* a dramatic re-enactment, or learn mathematics or science *though* cookery.

Perhaps you would like to try it! Read through a chosen subject discipline section of any curriculum, at national or school level, anywhere in the world with three coloured pens and highlight: first, in yellow, all the things that children are expected to *learn about;* then go through and highlight in green all the things they are expected to *learn how to;* and finally go through and highlight in blue all the things that children might *learn though* the subject discipline. You will have the text covered with yellow, green, and blue and there will be nothing left unhighlighted: all of the content will be covered.

Most learning about values in subject disciplines comes *through* the study of a discipline.

It is important to recognise that, while values are important in the way we act, and there are skills that can be practised to make us more accomplished in our valuing, we can also learn about values. Sadly though, few governments have ever judged it important to develop a curriculum for values, with programmes of learning appropriate for each key stage. However, while this omission might mean less prestige, it also mercifully spares us from centrally specified expectations about common and uniform values ... or even the possibility of a values test!

Many of the suggestions in our examples explain where values can be explored and learned *through* the subject disciplines. They are sort of 'while you are here' moments, 'don't miss the chance to' make explicit, think about, draw children's attention to or emphasise the values aspect of these facts, this knowledge, these skills.

An important issue to recognise is that values are also intellectual in concept and construct. Values are big ideas and big ideas underpin every subject discipline; that is how disciplines grew, through exploring big ideas.

Any unit of study – whether a linear set of subject discipline lessons, a theme taking a half term, a lesson, or even just a few minutes in the classroom – needs to ensure learning is taking place and can explore some key elements. The teacher should consider:

- Big ideas – What do I want the children to understand or conceptualise?
- Enquiry Questions – What do I want the children to wonder about?
- Knowledge – What do I want the children to know?
- Entitlements – What will every learner experience?
- Polished Products – What skills will the learners need to create, make, or design quality products?
- Local to Global – What is the relevance to the learner and the wider world?[1]

Values come into all of these questions and all of these questions come into every subject discipline. It is just that the subject discipline usually takes the lead because it is 'defined' and 'structured'. As children work on products, they bring the values of commitment and determination and that joy of producing something appreciated by others. It is the top two items on the list above that really expose values as children study science, art, history, geography, or technology.

If we exemplify this approach through a consideration of a theme, the issue becomes clear.

---

1   This summary is produced with permission from the Olympus Academy Trust, Bristol.

Children might study the theme of 'Identity' in Year 6 or Year 7. This could be done either in an integrated way in the primary school, or in separate but intellectually connected lessons in secondary schools, or better yet as a transition theme through the end of one and the start of the other.

Through learning about identity over time, with the historical development of tribes, nations, and super-powers, they learn about the interconnectedness of race, slavery, enfranchisement, class, and government. They learn about democracy and dictatorship, freedom, and restraint. Through each of these runs the thread of values that make some people dominant and others subservient, puts some into battle against others, and allows some to be sacrificed in pursuit of power or freedom. The study of history will be much the better for an emphasis upon the values that drove people to act as they did; whether to dominate, tolerate, or rebel.

Identity in science would take us into the world of classification of species, genetics, DNA and onto gender, race, and maturity and ageing. How do we see ourselves? How do we identify? Are we first colour and then gender or do we see our size or shape first? Society has only so recently begun to allow women to fulfil a wider range of roles, has been prejudiced towards and slow to recognise the achievements of non-white people, and still struggles to properly integrate those with special needs. Yet these are features of people's identity: who they are. These are values ... but we were studying science.

Our consideration of identity in art would take us into the realms of performance and portrayal ... again often affected by identity. 'Who we are' coupled with what we have witnessed, experienced, enjoyed, and suffered are fundamental big ideas. They link performance with the science of inheritance. While science can validate though experiment and proof, art and culture build a shared story of how the world has developed. Hence, the Bayeux Tapestry literally threads us through an experience of invasion; 'Guernica' portrays the horror of bombardment in stark black and white; Lichtenstein's 'Wham' shows how war can be presented alongside the recruitment posters of World War I.

At the same time, consideration of our identity through everyday human life can be addressed through the likes of Lowry's images of the working classes or Gainsborough's portraits in Britain. Aboriginal art shows us a different identity again; as do the Madhubani paintings of India; or Mynele's work in South Africa. These are all examples of cultural expression from across the world.

With these examples we are learning *about* history *through* art and at the same time we are developing understandings *about* values that help us to understand why civilisation needs to learn from history.

In PE we might discuss the way sport has spread around the world. Why do some nations enjoy cricket and others are left bamboozled by it? How has soccer spread? Why do people identify with their team against others yet come together to support their country's team against other nations?

The same is true across other subjects: in food technology the influences of different cultures play into what we eat; while the need to make music is fundamental to identity.

As we take an identity theme further with maps of migration over time and explore geographical influences, we deepen our understanding. Migration is not a modern phenomenon. People migrate for four main reasons: to escape threat, to seek a more prosperous future, forcible displacement, or the desire to explore (and sometimes to conquer and dominate). Let's look closer at these and identify the curriculum links.

Our first reason that people migrate is that they are trying to escape from danger. In the modern day the people running away from Syria, Afghanistan, or Iraq are under threat, fearful of the war going on around them or afraid of reprisals. They are seeking refuge, either temporary or permanently, in a place far away from the dangers of their current home. Traditionally in British schools, children have been told the story of Moses leading his people across the Red Sea to a 'promised land', just as countries in northern Europe represent the promise of a safer life to refugees nowadays. The story of Moses is recorded in the Old Testament in the book of Exodus and the same story appears in the Quran; a real life, modern exodus appears on television regularly.

There are many historical examples of refugees in the curriculum. These include the story of the *Mayflower* and the Pilgrim Fathers. As early settlers in the 'New World' these people had decided to leave their homeland to avoid religious persecution. Holocaust Day asks us to work with children to try to help them understand the persecution of Jewish people during World War II. Even the child evacuees of World War II, often so enthusiastically taught with role play and in some cases with suitcases and train rides, were refugees. As they set off to the countryside from the cities, they did not know what we now know as history; that they might return in six years. Tibetan refugees have lived outside their own region in China for over half a century. When children study comparative religions, they may be interested to know that the religion of Buddhism is founded on the concept of taking vows of refuge and seeking the answers to problems within oneself.

A second reason for migration is that people seek a more prosperous future. Many of the people who migrate to Europe from African countries in the present day believe that they will have more opportunities for prosperity than they could anticipate if they remain where they are. They believe that Europe offers work, money, and a more secure future. These are often referred to as 'economic migrants', a term which implies that they are somehow less worthy than refugees. However, economic migrants have been common throughout British history: they include the Huguenots who came to England from Holland and France; the English 'settlers' who set off for North America; the many Irish and Scots who migrated to America or Australasia; and many, many more. All of these groups of people were taking their skills and labour to look for work in lands of opportunity. Many schools teach the story of the *Titanic* and draw the distinction between the conditions for those in the wealthy staterooms and those in the steerage. Those in the steerage were heading to America in search of prosperity; they were also economic migrants.

The British Empire was in many ways been built on economic migration: from merchants in India; to settlers in America; plantation owners in the Caribbean; and so on. The end of the Empire saw subjects of the areas that had been ruled by Britain migrating to the British Isles: as Ambalavaner Sivanandan said, 'We are here because you were with us'. Many schools teach about migration in the 1960s, a decade which saw a rise in immigration from Commonwealth areas, such as the Asian sub-continent and the Caribbean. These people were seeking a better life and they had been asked to come to Britain to help rebuild its infrastructure after World War II. Many of them came to work in our hospitals and on our public transport system. Similarly, Britons were encouraged to go to Australia and New Zealand to help their economies, throughout the 1960s, and many took advantage of the £10 Pom ticket for their family to sail all the way to the antipodes.

A third reason for migrations is that some people are forcibly made to move. We teach children that, as the 'wild west' was tamed in North America, the Native Americans – who were at the time anachronistically labelled 'Indians' – were placed on 'reservations', land that the European immigrants had no use for and often away from the native hunting territories and livelihoods of previous generations. The partition of the Indian sub-continent is a curriculum expectation for secondary schools. As India won its independence from the Empire, its British rulers – responding to a rising Muslim separatist movement – partitioned the country in the transfer of power, organising the mass migration of people according to religion, and resulting in large scale bloodshed in transit. In more recent times Britain has a history of offering refuge to displaced communities, for example from Bosnia, Vietnam, and Uganda.

Finally, throughout history some have had a desire to explore, conquer, or dominate their new surroundings. From the perspective of local populations, this can often be seen as invasion. The imposition of culture can leave lasting impact, such as the legacy of Roman Britain on us or the European empires across the world. Invasion usually implies an imposition, force, and subservience which is why there is usually resistance. Britain has historically been both conquered by and repelled invaders, from the Romans, Vikings, and Normans to World War II. Might this be why migrants are sometimes described in the British press with value laden terms such as 'swarms', 'hordes', and 'armies'?

What we need is a gentle and serious on-going conversation with our maturing children to place current events in some context. Of course, British values are important. However, they will better upheld if they are understood and enjoyed rather than imposed, and part of our values ought to be to respect the values of others. Societies mingling means that we see the influence of one on another in fashion, food, measuring systems, and even things like the side of the road we drive.

All of the above are examples of curriculum content linked to one theme: identity. They show how the subject disciplines can be extended while at the same time exploring values and helping children to consider, understand, and influence the world in which they live.

This is not a series of lessons that have an objective stating a value to be absorbed within the next hour. This is an open-ended opportunity to learn aspects of curriculum disciplines in depth: *about*, *how*, and *through* the subject, while also considering values which in turn will enable understanding of the subject disciplines themselves.

This is not about being 'creative' or 'imaginative' but about seeing the interconnectedness of subject disciplines and the opportunities to help children appreciate values: to learn *about, how to* and *through* values.

CHAPTER 21

Does Inspection Value Teaching About Values?

In this chapter Mick Waters looks at the accountability agenda and its impact on a values-based view of schooling – and conversely – how a values-based intent could influence the inspection process and its outcomes for learners.

However much we might agree with the importance and place of values within our schools, and with the suggestions in this book, there is always a nervousness about how far this is appreciated by inspection. We know that the accountability agenda, particularly inspection, drives much of the practice in schools. In England, the inspection arrangements tend to be viewed as more judgemental and creating greater anxiety than in most countries, but everywhere in the world people in schools keep a weather eye on what inspectors are saying and respond accordingly.

Typically, inspection agencies look closely at whether a school is achieving its ambitions, however they are defined. This is the case in England where Ofsted makes a judgement about the impact of the curriculum: judged in terms of the statement of intent that the school sets itself. If our intentions include a focus upon values in all aspects of school, including the teaching of subject disciplines, then whether those values can be seen in the lived experience of all pupils in the school would be a salient question for inspectors.

In the last few years in England, inspectors have given more prominence to curriculum during inspection. There is a recognition that a concentration on exam and test performance has distorted the breadth of learning for children, and so the inspection process now focuses upon the curriculum experience of pupils. As Amanda Spielman, HMCI, has explained, 'We know that focusing too narrowly on test and exam results can often leave little time or energy for hard thinking about the curriculum, and in fact can sometimes end up making a casualty of it.'[2] She has even offered recognition that the inspection process has contributed to this: 'I acknowledge that inspection may well have helped to tip this balance in the past.'[3]

Spielman's own articulation of the purpose of schooling (what we might call her intent) accords with the values we are supporting within this book. She argues:

> To understand the substance of education we have to understand the objectives. Yes, education does have to prepare young people to succeed in life and make their contribution in the labour market. But to reduce education down to this kind of functionalist level is rather wretched. Because education should be about broadening minds, enriching communities and advancing civilisation. Ultimately, it is about leaving the world a better place than we found it.[4]

Inspection currently addresses three 'i's: *intent, implementation,* and *impact.* A school or teacher that believes in the importance of values education – in the way that is expressed in this book – and builds it into their vision statements or commitments, is placing values within their *intent.* If that same school or teacher works to make values become a reality through the experience of subject disciplines that learners have in lessons, backed up by

---

2   Spielman, A. (2018) 'Amanda Spielman Speech to the SCHOOLS North East Summit (11 October 2018)'. Available at: https://www.gov.uk/government/speeches/amanda-spielman-speech-to-the-schools-northeast-summit.

3   Ofsted & Spielman, A. (2017) 'HMCI's Commentary: Recent Primary and Secondary Curriculum Research'. Available at: https://www.gov.uk/government/speeches/hmcis-commentary-october-2017 .

4   Spielman, A. (2022) 'Amanda Spielman's Speech at the Festival of Education'. Available at: https://www.gov.uk/government/speeches/amanda-spielmans-speech-to-the-festival-of-education-2022.

the concern for values throughout the daily rhythms and routines of the school and the events that take place in it, then that is the *implementation*.

The *impact* is what we see all around us in the way learners emerge from their learning experience. Of course, test and exam results are one indication of *impact*, and so are a host of other outcomes. Do pupils enjoy the subject discipline? Do they behave like scientists, historians, mathematicians, and artists? Are learners fascinated, intrigued, and captivated by aspects of PE or design and technology? Are they seeing links between their conversations in religious studies and geography? Are novelists, poets and dramatists being naturally referenced in discussion of historical or technological developments? Is the world of work beckoning with positive choices being made to support career possibilities? Most schools and teachers place enjoyment of the domain and the subject having lasting influence within their aims: are these laudable aims coming through in the way the learners talk about their learning?

The question we need to ask ourselves is whether the outcomes we are seeing match our intentions. We must use professional *insight* to ask ourselves whether the *integrity* of our curriculum is secure as we travel from *intent* to *impact*. As learners move to KS4, are they disappointed to say farewell to some aspects of their learning, or do they see themselves as failing and happy to let go? Do themes in primary school captivate and take children into deep considerations and conundrums, asking big questions and exploring big ideas that demand intellectual engagement and the use of their knowledge and skills? Is KS3 being used as an opportunity to dig deeper into the subject disciplines and further the learning steps taken in primary school? Are children seeing the differentiation between branches of knowledge which we express as subject disciplines: the way a scientist works being different from the way a historian works, or a linguist, artist, or mathematician. Do pupils understand the sub-divisions in the science branch of human understanding into physics, chemistry, and biology? Are they starting to see the twigs of science, the specialisms emerging in the form of astro-physics and micro-biology? As they stand back, do they see these twigs of science interlinking with the twigs of history in marine archaeology, or languages with technology in computational linguistics? When they stand back from the tree of knowledge, do they see the full canopy of the tree – where the twigs are pretty well indistinct and the branches only partially evident –

knowing each small part contributes to the incredible and growing wealth of knowledge that fuels our understanding of our world?

If these sorts of understanding are developing, then the *intent* of curriculum is being achieved. If not, then we need to *improve* and, again, this book will provide the direction.

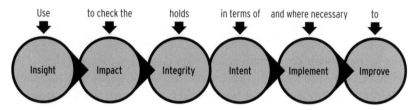

Some worry that inspection focuses upon too narrow criteria and that the wider aspects of school are insufficiently considered.

The framework currently in place does talk about helping children to grow physically and mentally with a clear statement about aspects of personal development.

> *The provider prepares learners for life in modern Britain by:*
> *equipping them to be responsible, respectful, active citizens who*
> *contribute positively to society; developing their understanding of*
> *fundamental British values; developing their understanding and*
> *appreciation of diversity; celebrating what we have in common*
> *and promoting respect for the different protected characteristics*
> *as defined in law.*

While one of the inspection's agency's problems is that of inconsistency, there are few inspectors who fail to give due credit to schools which develop the sorts of values that this book encourages, and a well taught curriculum with values in mind will meet the expectations of the framework.

Elsewhere in the world, inspection is less of a challenge to those in schools. England seems to somehow delight in not valuing its teachers enough to trust them. In New Zealand, for instance, inspection is managed with schools identifying areas of their work they would like inspectors to address and advise upon. In parts of Canada, inspections are carried out by peers from other schools, led by a full-time inspector who acts as moderator. As a general rule it seems that national approaches to inspection both mirror the culture and the extent to which teachers are trusted and respected in various countries. So, Denmark is very decentralised, and Finland places responsibility for school effectiveness within schools themselves. In many African countries, inspection is seen as a vehicle for collecting and assimilating the views and practices of teachers in order to inform their growing systems. Japan incentivises aspects of school improvement rather than looking for failings against set criteria, which inspection can easily become.

The much-valued HMIs who preceded Ofsted in England had the informal motto 'do good as you go'. This meant that inspectors should leave a school better than they found it; always leaving staff with something upon which to build, benefiting from the HMI's experience and insight across so many schools.

Our key message in this book, though, is straightforward. Values matter. They add to, rather than detract from, teaching and learning, and improve outcomes. Inspection might cause us problems and be a driver of behaviour, but we should not let it overshadow our efforts and beliefs.

CHAPTER 22

Sorting out the Wardrobe: A Coherent Approach to Personal Development, SMSC, British Values, and Related Issues

In this chapter Mark Chater examines the roles played by the many non-subject aspects of the curriculum in developing and deepening a values-based approach. In so doing, he explains and untangles the interplay of schools' many competing and compelling duties.

> *SMSC is a broad concept that can be seen across the school's activities but draws together many of the areas covered by the personal development judgement.*
>
> Ofsted School Inspection Handbook, 2021

Introduction

In addition to subjects, values-led schools address a range of statutory or desirable curriculum features that have accumulated in the school system over several years. These include, but are not restricted to, personal development, SMSC (spiritual, moral, social, and cultural development), British values, positive curriculum approaches to preventing extremism (based on the Prevent duty), safeguarding, equalities, faith identity (including both the identities of individual pupils and families, and the legal religious character of the school, if any), collective worship, relationships and sex education (RSE), and health education. Two statutory subjects, citizenship and RE, are often closely related to these strands, but since they are legally recognised as subjects, they are discussed in detail elsewhere in this book. There are also items which do not have current legal enforcement but are still seen as popular and important, such as character education, personal learning and thinking skills, and community cohesion. All these features hold important content and learning that students need. How does a school provide all this within the reality of time constraints, and limits on staff time to prepare? One fundamental principle is to bring all this crucial work together into a coherent plan and practice.

Whatever they might say in Narnia, wardrobes are not magic. Over time they can get over-filled with assorted coats, shoes, belts, hats, and other accessories. The curriculum covering personal development can get a bit like that overcrowded wardrobe: every year new stuff gets squeezed in, old stuff sinks to the bottom, and before you know it you can't find what you need. When there's an inspection – it might be Ofsted or the faith school inspections that are statutory in schools of a designated religious character – you are suddenly madly scrabbling to put on all these garments at once. Where's that relationships and sex education policy we adopted two years ago? Does it connect to the anti-bullying and behaviour strategies? And so on.

Everything in the wardrobe is useful (or at least was once); but it's hard to sort through, or not enough people have the key, or it needs a partial clear-out. This chapter makes suggestions about a coherent, values-led approach to personal development and the other requirements. Many of the definitions and notes of guidance overlap with each other, which means that avoiding duplication needs an eagle's eye view. One key to a coherent plan and practice is leadership. Another is staff and governor understanding and ownership.

The requirements and where they come from

The following links take you to current sources of definitions and guidance for maintained schools in England and Wales. Schools need to be aware that definitions, legal requirements, and guidance can change over time, but these are current at the time of writing (2022).

Personal Development: *School Inspection Handbook* (https://www.gov. uk/government/publications/school-inspection-handbook-eif/school-inspection-handbook#personal-development). Personal development includes preparation for adult life and engagement in society and the expectation that schools will challenge discrimination in all its forms and promote equality of opportunity. This document refers to British values and equalities within its helpful definitions of SMSC.

Another useful source is *How Ofsted inspects 'personal development': The Key for School Leaders* (https://schoolleaders.thekeysupport.com/school-evaluation-and-improvement/inspection/whole-school-inspection-criteria/how-ofsted-inspect-personal-development/).

SMSC: *The School Inspection Handbook* (see above) defines spiritual development to include reflectiveness and knowledge about different beliefs and enjoyment of learning. Moral development means recognising the difference between right and wrong, understanding that actions have consequences, and developing reasoned views. Social development encompasses social skills, participation in society, fundamental British values, and a positive contribution to modern Britain. Cultural development involves understanding and appreciation of the wide range of cultural influences on modern Britain, as well as taking part in a range of artistic, music, and sporting opportunities. Other sources of current expertise and experience can be found at:

- Ofsted definition of SMSC education: https://www.smscqualitymark. org.uk/what-is-smsc/.
- The Linking Network hold SMSC courses for school leaders: http:// www.thelinkingnetwork.org.uk/.
- There is also useful guidance from the RSA: Research Action Centre. https://www.thersa.org/globalassets/pdfs/reports/schools-with-soul-report.pdf.

Fundamental British Values: *Promoting fundamental British values through SMSC* (https://www.gov.uk/government/publications/promoting-fund amental-british-values-through-smsc). The four values which Ofsted inspects are named as democracy, the rule of law, individual liberty, and mutual respect and tolerance of those with different faiths and beliefs.

Prevent: Creating positive curriculum approaches to protecting children from radicalisation has its legal basis in the Prevent duty (https://www.gov. uk/government/publications/protecting-children-from-radicalisation-the-prevent-duty). It can be seen as part of safeguarding and the wider curriculum work to build respect for diversity and challenge prejudice in all its forms that is outlined as part of SMSC and British values. Prevent is one element in a wider strategy to defend the country from the risk of violent extremism. It aims to challenge the thinking and assumptions that can lead a young person towards extremism or terrorism. Its main focal points are currently the risk of white supremacist and far right ideologies along with Islamist and Jihadist ideas. School leaders have a responsibility to ensure that staff know how to spot warning signs and raise concerns.

Safeguarding: Statutory guidance overview: *Keeping children safe in education* (https://www.gov.uk/government/publications/keeping-children-safe-in-education--2). This statutory guidance is updated each year. It covers the four forms of abuse (sexual, physical, emotional, and neglect) and sets out in detail what schools need to do by way of making information available, with procedures for dealing with concerns, disclosures, and allegations. There are multiple connections to anti-bullying, relationships and sex education, and equalities.

Equalities: Guidance overview: *Equality Act 2010: advice for schools* (https://www.gov.uk/government/publications/equality-act-2010-advice-for-schools). The Equalities Act (2010) places a duty on schools, including schools of a designated religious character, to ensure against direct or indirect discrimination in relation to sex, race, disability, religion/belief, sexual orientation, gender reassignment, or pregnancy/maternity.

Faith Identity: *Education Act 2005* (https://www.legislation.gov.uk/ukpga/2005/18/contents). *Section 48 inspections: The Key for School Governors* (https://schoolgovernors.thekeysupport.com/school-improvement-and-strategy/inspection-evaluation/inspection-framework/section-48-inspections-guidance/). Schools of a designated religious character (sometimes referred to as faith schools) have different rules about the provision of collective worship, religious education, and relationships and sex education. These aspects of the curriculum are separately inspected by designated agencies of the faith. For example, Church of England and Methodist schools are inspected by a process known as SIAMS (Statutory Inspection of Anglican and Methodist Schools). These arrangements apply only to schools with a legal designated religious status, not to maintained schools where a particular religious or ethnic group happens to be in a majority.

Collective Worship: The legal requirement is for a daily act of collective worship which should be wholly or mainly of a broadly Christian character (https://www.gov.uk/government/publications/collective-worship-in-schools). This requirement has been in place since 1988 despite several attempts to reform it. Schools can apply for an adaptation to this requirement but cannot stop providing it. Schools of a designated religious character have collective worship as authorised by their Governing Body in accordance with their faith.

Relationships and Sex Education (RSE), and Health Education:
Relationships and Sex Education (RSE), and Health Education (https://www.gov.uk/government/publications/relationships-education-relationships-and-sex-education-rse-and-health-education).
This document scopes out the required content at primary and secondary phases, including links to safeguarding, different forms of families, healthy relationships, and wellbeing. Parents have a legal right to withdraw their child from some elements of this provision.

The following links are also relevant for non-statutory but important aspects of personal development:

Character Education:

- *Character Education Framework Guidance* (https://assets.publishing. service.gov.uk/government/uploads/system/uploads/attachment_ data/file/904333/Character_Education_Framework_Guidance.pdf).
- *A Framework for Character Education in Schools* (https://www. jubileecentre.ac.uk/527/character-education/framework).

Personal, Learning and Thinking Skills:

Personal learning and thinking skills in Foundation Learning (https:// repository.excellencegateway.org.uk/Personal_learning_and_thinking_ skills_in_Foundation_Learning.pdf).

Community Cohesion: *About Community Cohesion – Community Cohesion and Intercultural Relations*, Professor Ted Cantle (https://tedcantle. co.uk/about-community-cohesion/).

While these pieces of law and guidance do have substantial overlaps, there also hidden tensions, for example between the equality requirements and collective worship. There are also exceptions and alternative arrangements for some schools of a designated religious character. In all schools there is a legal right for parents/carers to withdraw their child from RE, collective worship, and elements of relationships and sex education. The overall legal basis for these elements is untidy and the detailed guidance can be lengthy and confusing. At the time of writing, most of these elements are judged in inspections as to their quality and intent, rather than their impact. The more recent DfE and Ofsted documents do show a growing harmonisation between personal development, SMSC, and British values; however, a more unified, coherent, and single-sourced definition is still lacking. That vacuum can cause some levels of strain on schools. It is for school leaders and Governing Bodies to judge wisely as to how they approach these requirements, how they create coherence of intent and quality of provision and what forms of outside help they use.

Coherence and leadership

To meet the challenge of providing all the elements identified above, staff and governors need time to talk, discuss, and reach a strong understanding of what the school intends and provides, who does what, where, and how successful it is. Staff need time to plan and create what will happen. Giving time to this can also create opportunities to reflect on priorities in a particular school, reflecting the school's ethos, legal status, community context, and the needs of the pupils.

Some key questions and principles that can underpin successful leadership for coherent provision are:

- *What are we going to call it?* The elements listed above can be usefully grouped together. Their collective name varies between schools, and so does the title of the leadership role – it may be SMSC lead, personal development lead, or something else. Ensure the vocabulary is known, understood, and used at all levels of the school. For clarity in this section, we will refer to it as personal development.

- *What does it mean to lead personal development?* Be clear about who does this. Identify the knowledge, planning process, and evaluation moments.

- *Where is personal development?* It can sometimes be 'everywhere but nowhere', so it needs strategic attention at leadership level and ownership by all adults in the school. Leaders need to be able to identify where and when it is happening.

- *Does personal development compete with other priorities in the school?* While some feel that personal development can be in danger of being crowded out by the standards agenda, there is no need for schools to choose between the two. Many schools can and do combine passion for high standards of academic achievement with passion for the personal development of every pupil. The two priorities can support each other.

- *What should the personal development leader do?* The analogy of a searchlight might be useful: it is not the leader's job to do everything, but to shine a light, see what needs to be done, coordinate the action, assess the impact, and let the staff see examples of excellence. Look with 'personal development eyes' at your school. For example, carefully examine the pupils' experience of bullying, neglect, or discrimination in all their forms, watch out for resources that could have unintended consequences, see what is working well and can be developed and placed into the curriculum.

- *How do we know if it is going well?* Check policies, including living links between policies – e.g. the profound curriculum connections between Prevent, safeguarding, anti-bullying, behaviour, RSE, and EDI policies. By creating and modelling the ethos and values of the school, ensure that policies are 'lived not laminated'. Evaluate the provision little and often: listen to staff and students and encourage professional reflection.
- *What do the staff need?* Staff training is key to taking staff with you. We all need to be on board. Good and outstanding teachers can still stumble with some elements of personal development, perhaps because they find it sensitive, controversial, or triggering. Encourage staff to ask for help before they need it. Make sure examples of good practice are visible.
- *When Ofsted call?* Know your school's narrative and be ready to share it. Articulate the work of the school sharing the contribution of the whole staff team and all subjects.

Personal development, and its related content across other issues, can seem like 'soup in a sieve' with so many possible actions that a school can take across curriculum, assembly, enrichment, and ethos. Grappling with complexity in order to find a pathway forward that is wise, contextually relevant, age appropriate, and constructive, becomes easier if a coherent approach is taken by leaders who ensure that the school's narrative is owned and shared by all staff.

Understanding and ownership

If schools understand the expectations of new and existing guidance, they can then identify the curriculum, enrichment, and whole school provision already in place that meets expectations, then identify gaps for their students, and plan appropriate action.

The Linking Network, with more than fifteen years of experience in leading CPD for personal development, SMSC, and creative approaches to diversity, identifies the salience of staff training as an essential in successful ownership. Training is based on some underlying principles:

- Schools welcome the support, time, and space that training can offer. Time and space is needed to find a coherent strategy to lead personal development across a school and to translate a range of guidance requirements into a practice that is coherent not piecemeal, and high-value not tokenistic.
- Teachers are generally already highly committed to pupils' personal development and wellbeing. Many of them state this is why they became teachers. Once they have a working understanding of the requirements in their school's context, and particularly some of the more challenging aspects such as how spiritual development is defined, they will gain an equally high confidence in this area.
- Teachers are pleased to learn about the place personal development has in the curriculum and Ofsted framework; it doesn't matter to teachers *what* it is called so long as it is valued.
- Schools in challenging circumstances often find that the need to focus on results can feel relentless.
- Schools often find that although they do a great deal to prioritise personal development, they are not practiced in defining it or articulating their work.
- School leaders at senior and middle level, who are crucial to the school's successful ownership of its approach to personal development, find it helpful to have good examples of other schools narrating their approach, particularly schools in similar circumstances.
- Middle leaders have influence in schools and are close to the development of the curriculum. In both primary and secondary schools, they have a hugely important impact on the tangible spiritual, moral, social, and cultural development of pupils. They particularly value guidance on subject-specific interpretation of SMSC in the context of a broad understanding. Once they have a working understanding of SMSC; a way of translating this understanding into practice in their particular subject expertise; and a sense of the potential limitations for their subject in delivering aspects of SMSC (no subject should be expected to do everything); then they find they can confidently identify SMSC in many aspects of their curriculum and strategically place further opportunities into their offer to their pupils within their subject.

- Training needs to follow a pattern of understanding the school's context in its community; its external expectations; what is already being provided by the school across all aspects of school life (all curriculum areas, all staff, all enrichment, assemblies, school culture, and ethos); and thinking carefully and non-judgmentally about some examples of what might be missing or in need of improvement. Towards the end of a training session, staff readily identify quick wins that are easily in reach, to begin action rapidly. Following this, longer-term strategies can be identified.
- The fundamental need, expressed by all, is for training in understanding what the different aspects of personal development are: what they look like when done well in a school; how a contextual plan-act-evaluate approach can help; how a school can evidence its work; how it links to the school's stated ethos and values; and how best to move this agenda forward through meaningful, appropriate, and effort-effective actions that can be taken within the resources a school has available.

Barriers to excellence

There can be barriers to effective training and provision. Usually the barriers are unexamined mindsets, and the most common of them were identified in the RSA report 'Schools with Soul':

- A fear of controversy, which can lead to an unhelpful sanitization of content.
- Governors, parents, and community are insufficiently connected with the school and the community.
- Leadership and understanding are insufficiently distributed throughout the school staff and Governing Body.
- Not enough time for reflection about purpose.
- A tick-box approach rather than a holistic understanding, or a data-driven approach rather than a good narrative of the school's achievements.

Practical steps for supporting quality of provision

In its sustained work to support schools developing approaches to SMSC, personal development, and diversity, the Linking Network has identified to following useful practical steps:

- Across the whole curriculum there are many spaces for impact: PE provides opportunity to develop social skills, working and socialising with others; maths can contribute to confidence and resilience; history, geography, and citizenship can underpin pupils' understanding of the consequences of human behaviour, the stories and needs of communities, and human rights; RE, English, art, and music develop many aspects of moral and cultural understanding and representation, as well as building empathy and critical thinking; and science helps students consider many ethical issues and critical thinking. Assemblies can share a whole school perspective and make the schools ethos clear. We do not need to ask any subject to shoehorn in issues; rather, all subjects can seize opportunities that are appropriate to the subject's purpose. In a training session, staff can take time to reflect on this and consider what their different curriculum subjects can offer.

- Think strategically about visitors to bring in and projects to engage with. For example, inviting faith/belief representatives to answer questions about their beliefs and actions can help with several aspects of personal development.

- There is a need for tailored resources created in response to current priorities.

- Networks for dissemination can be highly effective. For example, the networks supported by the Linking Network, generate a clear picture of the needs of schools in their communities and respond with up-to-date expertise as well as drawing in input from other schools, youth services, council staff, advisory teachers, and specialist consultants.

- Work around a themed project or topic can be an effective way of combining several of the priorities. For example, a project on human rights, taught at an age-appropriate level, can provide a cornerstone for content and experiences related to SMSC, British values, Prevent, equalities, character education, and community cohesion.

- Pupil voice can give powerful evidence to schools to showcase their work and create levers for change. It can take the form of interviews, presentations, assemblies, or assignments. It can be particularly powerful to interview vulnerable pupils, or those whom the school finds most challenging, or pupils who have arrived midyear.
- Resources can be good indicators of a school's priorities and blind spots. For example, look at representation across all aspects of equalities on walls, website, curriculum themes, books, and writers. This work can be built throughout the life of a school so that every child sees themselves on the walls of the school and sees those who are not present in their school. Look with personal development eyes to see what you can add.
- A wide range of resources are available to schools from The Linking Network. They include SMSC leaders' toolkit, courses for whole school staff, whole-school review, personal development in ITT, guidance for subject areas, pupil questionnaires, curated booklists, assemblies, home learning, linking and classroom resources that promote social cohesion supporting exploration of identity, diversity, community, and equality. Training is available online and face to face. These SMSC resources offered by TLN were developed over time through work with school leaders of schools in many different circumstances. The work emerged from the learning from developing effective Schools Linking programmes between schools in local areas across England.

What schools say

I would just like to thank you for running this course. It was absolutely outstanding, and the information surpassed all of our expectations. It was extremely well delivered, and the information packs and handouts will be very useful in delivering effective insets in school. I was particularly impressed at how the presenters shared real-life experiences and the amount of knowledge and understanding they both shared on SMSC. I came away confident in presenting an inset in school myself. So much fantastic information that I just want to go back to school now and share the whole day with staff. They made such a scary element of the Ofsted framework an exciting adventure. Halina Rooney, Sudbury Primary School, Brent. https://thelinkingnetwork.org.uk/what-we-do/smsc-british-values-courses/.

The Linking Network provides teachers with a tried and tested means of addressing key issues in Spiritual, Moral, Social and Cultural aspects of learning, exploring citizenship, reflecting on British values in an inclusive way and modelling future citizens. It provides an effective means of building inclusive patterns of social cohesion among children and young people and has the capacity to raise achievement. Coventry University. https://thelinkingnetwork.org.uk/wp-content/uploads/2019/09/Schools-Linking-and-Social-Cohesion-An-Evaluation-of-TLNs-National-Programme-July-2018.pdf.

I've attended many SMSC events and have learned a lot in the process. It's been a really valuable experience for myself and the pupils, too. Head teacher commenting on the SMSC Quality Mark managed by Young Citizens. Recognising Spiritual, Moral, Social and Cultural Development (https://www.smscqualitymark.org.uk/).

Some self-evaluation prompts for schools

For a coherent approach to personal development, and the other issues discussed in this chapter, the following prompter questions, based on what Ofsted is looking for, might help senior and middle leaders to take the temperature and promote reflection.

- Do all pupils feel safe at your school? Are there areas of the school which are hostile or don't feel safe?
- Looking at pupil movement in and around corridors and in social spaces, is there a friendly atmosphere? Are pupils getting along?
- Do your pupils have a safe space to talk openly? Do pupils get a chance to discuss contemporary issues affecting them?
- Are pupils able to resolve issues themselves? When staff do get involved, is there a clear process in place to stop things from escalating? Do pupils feel comfortable with raising issues with staff?
- Do you have student mental health ambassadors?
- How well supported are the extracurricular elements, such as after school clubs, practical youth social action, active citizenship, and volunteering?
- Is your curriculum inclusive and diverse? How do you know? Have you audited across all of the equalities and protected characteristics? What are the strengths and where are the areas for development?

- Does your PSHE curriculum cover statutory sensitive issues like sexual health and consent effectively? Have you considered whether your policies relating to behaviour, rewards and punishments, exclusions, and dress and hair codes, are inclusive of all students and avoid impacting on some students more negatively than others?
- Who leads on personal development elements? Do all the staff know who it is? Is their brief clear? Do senior leaders have a clear understanding of responsibilities, areas for development, and how the elements fit together?
- Are the various personal development elements underpinned by policy documents, whether standalone or combined? Do all the staff know where to find them? Do they reflect the school's best practice?
- What training do you provide for your staff on personal development/ SMSC?
- Do staff and pupils have sufficient knowledge of different people's faiths and beliefs including those of no faith? Do they have enough opportunities to reflect on their own beliefs and perspectives on life?
- Is your careers programme offer extensive? Are pupils supported over their long-term career aspirations?
- Is the PSHE curriculum relevant to pupil's everyday lives? Do pupils have their say about what they feel they need to learn?
- Do you make sure that pupils who are not in regular lessons get the same opportunities to learn about life in modern Britain? If so, when?
- What are your processes when difficult global, national, or local events arise that have a distressing effect on students and staff? How do we inform all staff so that we respond in a timely and thoughtful manner?
- Do you have a reward system? Do pupils buy into it? What has been the impact of it so far?
- How does the school deal with any inappropriate views and comments?
- What aspects of your personal development provision are especially worth celebrating and maintaining in the core curriculum, in enrichment, and across the school? Are they visible on the website and in conversations with other schools?

CHAPTER 23

A Word on Special Educational Needs

This chapter looks at how some Special Educational Needs and therapeutic settings are using a values-based approach to meet the needs of their students.

Beyond the mainstream contexts discussed so far Values-based Education has been shown to have benefits in Special Educational Needs, therapeutic, and Pupil Referral settings. The Values-based Education philosophy and its outworking – through modelling, the building and use of an ethical language base, the attention to the 'inner curriculum' (both discussed in the following chapters), and through heartfelt leadership – is just as applicable and just as effective in these contexts. Values-based practitioners in these spheres see values as an integral part of both their practice and their calling.

'Special Education' is defined as calling for educational provision that is 'additional to or different from provision made generally … '. This assumes values related to the 'rights' of individual learners as implied within the education system itself, and the way in which the head teacher, teachers and all other adult staff perceive it. This raises relative value issues in relation to:

- Equity in the allocation of, and access to, time (and content pacing) and other compensatory resources and functions of the school.
- Meeting the specific pedagogic demands of the nature and degree of the individual's needs for effective learning.

- Supporting the self-concept and *strengths* of the individual with special needs.
- The contribution which Values-based Education makes to all children and young peoples' experience of social interaction, e.g. in the context of inclusion issues about grouping of CYPs in schools.

Values and pedagogy

The above considerations are aimed at achieving a values *context* for effective teaching and learning. Ensuring that every child has the best possible experience in school means that their 'special' or additional needs are met, that they are treated with respect, and that their opportunities and experiences are rich, valuable, and compelling.

The language of values, supported through real demonstration, has an intrinsic accessibility. Children with various degrees of language skill develop their understanding of an ethical vocabulary intuitively and emotionally, as well as academically. By focusing on building confidence, self-respect, and resilience, along with appropriate academic support, children with additional needs will grow, develop, and experience success.

Values and behaviour

One of the most cited impacts of the values-based approach in schools is its effect on behaviour. Teachers notice the improvement in behaviour when children are treated with respect in an atmosphere of purposeful calm. People always respond well to warm and kind words. Pupils start to see and feel for themselves a different way of being. They are taught and helped to regulate their emotional impulses and start to glimpse the positive results, both in themselves and in those around them. Success breeds success.

It really is that simple, say the practitioners. Values must go through the school like a stick of rock. You model to the children the behaviour you want to see – and you do it, day in and day out. You must dispel the myth of 'soft values' from the outset, because real working values demand courage, conviction, and utmost patience. It is not easy, and it takes time. Even when you feel you are being challenged again, and again, and again, you must believe in the effect you are having and will have. You have to build your values culture block by block – and then one day, you start to see it right there in front of you.

Every mainstream values-based school can cite poignant and compelling stories of children who 'turn themselves around' as a result of Values-based Education.

The following two vignettes paint a picture of values-based philosophies in practice in whole-school therapeutic settings, which see the effects of this approach day after day and year after year, on whole cohorts of young learners.

Dominic Seamer is headteacher of Wilds Lodge, a therapeutic residential school that has had four consecutive outstanding Ofsted inspections since its opening in 2007, and nine outstanding care inspections. He speaks with the utmost conviction about his beliefs in a values-based approach:

> *It is our responsibility to re-engage the children and show them the worth of learning. The building and maintenance of positive relationships is also of paramount importance. The children in my school have not always had the most positive of relationships with adults and peers in schools.... By making the effort to model relationships with colleagues (which has obvious professional and personal benefits as well), and build these relationships, the children are able to see healthy, reciprocal relationships and the benefits that these bring.*

> *This school offers numerous opportunities for values to be modelled and experienced by both staff and pupils. This is shown through the right needs being identified, and the right support being given, at the right times. This is equally applicable to adults and children across all areas of the school. By everyone feeling safe, secure, and that they matter, everyone is then more able to be effective in whatever their role may be.*

The values of Wilds Lodge can change and evolve on a regular basis but the main underpinning principles are:

- *Respect* – between peers, between colleagues, between children and adults and between our school and other professional bodies.
- *Resilience* – working with the pupils to help them to understand that they are capable, they are worth something, they can overcome

difficulties, and that they are not defined by a diagnosis, condition, or by the circumstances they find themselves in.

- *Honesty* – the importance of honest, authentic relationships where both adults and children feel empowered to speak openly and to accept honest and helpful criticism.
- *Empathy* – practising and modelling understanding and empathy towards each other is essential. Everybody is carrying 'baggage' of some kind with them. We try to make sure that our pupils understand the importance of empathy and are given the opportunities to see it being modelled, experience it themselves, and demonstrate it towards others.

David Bartlett, headteacher of The Pear Tree therapeutic school has conceived an innovative modern-day and purposeful values-based curriculum for his students built around a sequence of events to encourage learning and development. It is demonstrably the outworking of their mantra:

- *Inspire.*
- *Motivate.*
- *Educate.*
- *Train.*
- *Employ.*

He writes:

> *Above everything else we must ensure our students have achievable goals, aspirations with self-belief, and the confidence to move forward with their development and life planning. They must be shown that the world of work is fun, enjoyable, and rewarding. Our culture actively promotes this from the beginning of the student's time with us following admission regardless of age. Our population has often come from a culture of many generations of unemployment and negative outcomes. Therefore, demonstrating an alternative culture needs to start as soon as the child arrives.*

We invite you to visit the websites of these schools to see more of the transformational effects of their work.[5]

---

5   See https://www.wildslodgeschool.co.uk and https://peartreeprojects.co.uk.

CHAPTER 24

Values-based Learning and Teaching in the Early Years

In this chapter Bridget Knight shows how the early years settings naturally embodies the essence of a values-based curriculum. Early focus on a values-based curriculum sets a child on a positive pathway for learning.

This is where it all begins! Through Values-based Education, we are instilling a life-long way of being, living, and learning.

Schools that use a values-based approach in their reception classes attest to its efficacy and desirability. When we consider that the formulations of habits and outlook begin at the earliest age, it makes great sense. Furthermore, we know that the development of language is central to the whole process of learning. The gentle introduction of the language of values equips children from the youngest age with some of the key tools they will need to form relationships with others and the world around them, and to develop the sophisticated skills of self-understanding and self-regulation.

The guiding principles that shape practice in early years settings are by their very nature values-based. The early years framework already gives voice to the values-based ethics that enable successful personal, social, and academic development. Namely:

- *Every child is unique, constantly learning, and can be resilient, capable, confident, and self-assured* – the basis of the early years approach, and the premise of Values-based Education, is the honouring of children as valued, beautiful individuals who, if properly nurtured, can make a difference to the world through who and how they are.

- *Children learn to be strong and independent through positive relationships* – pivotal to a values-based approach to learning are positive relationships, based on unconditional positive regard. Young children flourish as they are nurtured in growth.

- *Children learn and develop well in enabling environments with teaching and support from adults, who respond to their individual interests and needs, and help them to build their learning over time. Children benefit from a strong partnership between practitioners, parents, and/or carers* – a values-based culture that creates climates of delight, in which children can grow and flourish, along with their families, builds the best conditions for success.

- *The importance of learning and development. Children develop and learn at different rates* – a Values-based Education prepares and enables children to be the most successful learners that they can be: academically, personally, socially, and spiritually.

An ethical vocabulary

Lots of values-words are common parlance – friendship, kindness, love, peace, etc. – and they abound in children's stories, storybooks and characters, and rhymes. A values-focused approach to teaching and learning with this age group deepens understanding. We are, it's true to say, continuously amazed by small children's ability to comprehend in an instinctive way, the importance of values and by their readiness to absorb a values-based way of doing things. They notice other children and themselves, demonstrating determination when learning how to write a new letter form, or resilience when they have fallen over and got up again for the umpteenth time in the playground. Moreover, there can be a proud joy in learning new words – empathy, for example, is something little children can readily show and once they know the word for it, they can talk about it too!

Teaching action rhymes (see appendix 3) is a brilliant way of communicating the meaning of the values to younger children. They love joining in! In the resources section in the appendix are lots of rhymes we have written especially for reception children.

Values-based learning through play

Lots of the best learning in the early years comes through stories and play. Playing in the sandpit, with the Small World play, while at an easel and painting – so many opportunities arise for gentle exemplification of values: how we are drawing our friend, showing kindness by sharing, acting out the value of care, or simply enjoying being in the moment. The vocabulary and meanings of values are shared and realised through these times. We start talking about and drawing attention to values in the early years, so that the values themselves become like friends. Promoting the ethical vocabulary happens from the start. Children quickly see and absorb the meaning of values in action and become adept at using them in context.

Let's look at the early years framework and the specific early learning goals (ELG) to see how well values fit in:

Communication and language ELG: Listening, attention and understanding			
Children at the expected level of development will:	What the adults will do through a values-based approach:	Making an enabling environment	Resources
Listen attentively and respond to what they hear - with relevant questions, comments, and actions - when being read to and during whole class discussions and small group interactions. Make comments about what they have heard and ask questions to clarify their understanding. Hold conversation when engaged in back-and-forth exchanges with their teacher and peers.	Model respectful, affirmatory listening, by tuning into the child as a unique individual, implicitly communicating your relationship of unconditional positive regard. Model the language of values and exemplify values through your own actions linked to language. For example, asking the child how they are today and showing you are listening by responding to their answer.	Create a language-rich environment, exposing children to the language of values, e.g. How will we show friendship in our role-play area today?	See values story book list and our values action rhymes (appendix 3), written especially for early years children!

ELG: Speaking

Children at the expected level of development will:	What the adults will do through a values-based approach:	Making an enabling environment	Resources
Participate in small group, class, and one-to-one discussions, offering their own ideas, using recently introduced vocabulary. Offer explanations for why things might happen, making use of recently introduced vocabulary from stories, non-fiction, rhymes, and poems. Express their ideas and feelings about their experiences using full sentences, including use of past, present, and future tenses and making use of conjunctions, with modelling and support from their teacher.	Tune into each child, creating opportunities for children to engage with ideas that are meaningful to them. Give children time to talk and think. Respond positively to children's efforts, repeating back to give affirmation and consolidation.	Create lots of opportunities for children to regularly express their growing understanding of emotions and feelings, for example, Circle Times to share 'today, I am feeling ... '.	See our values story book list and our values action rhymes (appendix 3), written especially for early years children!

Personal, social and emotional development ELG: Self-regulation

Children at the expected level of development will:	What the adults will do through a values-based approach:	Making an enabling environment	Resources
Show an understanding of their own feelings and those of others and begin to regulate their behaviour accordingly. Set and work towards simple goals, being able to wait for what they want and control their immediate impulses when appropriate. Give focused attention to what the teacher says, responding appropriately even when engaged in activity, and show an ability to follow instructions involving several ideas or actions.	Demonstrating understanding and empathy, using the language of values or emotions, e.g. 'I think you might be feeling shy today but how could we show x that you would like to be his friend?'	Find ways of celebrating individual achievement and class achievement through your own values-based reward system, such as a Values Tree or a Values M. Build in regular opportunities for calming and self-regulation such as circle time using music and reflection.	See how to play Special Person - a game guaranteed to increase self-esteem.

ELG: Managing self			
Children at the expected level of development will:	What the adults will do through a values-based approach:	Making an enabling environment	Resources
Be confident to try new activities and show independence, resilience, and perseverance in the face of challenges. Explain the reasons for rules, know right from wrong, and try to behave accordingly. Manage their own basic hygiene and personal needs, including dressing, going to the toilet, and understanding the importance of healthy food choices.	Talk about, notice, and model the values of resilience and perseverance, offering stories and discussion time. Use puppets and role-play to de-personalise and exemplify positive and undesirable behaviours. Give children time to talk, think and respond. Model modifying opinions in the light of reflection ... 'Mmm, I wonder if I was right ... perhaps ... ?' Respond positively to children's efforts, repeating back to give affirmation and consolidation.	Create lots of opportunities for children to regularly express their growing understanding of emotions and feelings, for example, Circle Times to share 'today, I am feeling ... '. Affirmative displays in the classroom of children's own work and of their ideas builds this sense of community.	See our Reflection Time ideas at the end of this chapter.

ELG: Building Relationships

Children at the expected level of development will:	What the adults will do through a values-based approach:	Making an enabling environment	Resources
Work and play cooperatively and take turns with others. Form positive attachments to adults and friendships with peers. Show sensitivity to their own needs and those of others.	Prioritise relationship-building through connection with pupils on an individual as well as collective level. Tune into individual's interests and passions and find ways to show connection through this. Ask sensitive questions, noticing and commenting gently on needs and feelings. Value children's responses meaningfully. Be sensitively curious about children. Let children see you forming relationships that are positive with their parents or carers. Give children time to talk, think and respond. Model the use of valuing language, such as 'I like the way you are putting those crayons away' or 'What good reading today!'	Create a positive community. Talk explicitly and openly about all the ways in which we support each other in our class. Take opportunities to celebrate each child as a unique individual, and encourage others to do likewise – for example, have birthday rituals for the children and the adults in the class. Encourage children to bring occasional objects such as photographs from home to share and discuss. Create lots of opportunities for children to regularly express their growing understanding of emotions and feelings, for example, Circle Times to share 'today, I am feeling ... '.	See how to play Special Person – a game guaranteed to increase self-esteem.

ELG: Physical development ELG: Gross motor skills			
Children at the expected level of development will:	What the adults will do through a values-based approach:	Making an enabling environment	Resources
Negotiate space and obstacles safely, with consideration for themselves and others. Demonstrate strength, balance and coordination when playing. Move energetically, such as running, jumping, dancing, hopping, skipping, and climbing.	Build in the language of values, such as sharing, caring, kindness and co-operation alongside and woven into all physical activities, thereby demonstrating the relevance of values to all aspects of our lives.	Prioritise as much as possible being out and among nature, relishing its wonders and learning to care for it as well as ourselves - walking around growing flowers, fingering and touching (but not pulling off) leaves on the trees, and appreciating moments of calm and stillness after lots of physical activity under the sky.	See our Values in the Forest ideas at the end of this chapter!

ELG: Physical development ELG: Fine motor skills		
Children at the expected level of development will:	What the adults will do through a values-based approach:	Making an enabling environment
Hold a pencil effectively in preparation for fluent writing (using the tripod grip in almost all cases). Use a range of small tools, including scissors, paint brushes, and cutlery. Begin to show accuracy and care when drawing.	Create numerous opportunities for children to make meaningful connections with their own emotions and lives through learning - writing about their families and friends, making cards for them, and so on. This deepens their connections and their understanding of themselves in relation to those around them as well as creates motivational reasons for writing development.	Celebrating our connections with our close families, friends, community, and the larger world through setting store by well-executed displays in the classroom, opportunities to make high quality gifts for others, etc.

ELG: English reading, writing and comprehension

Children at the expected level of development will:	What the adults will do through a values-based approach:	Making an enabling environment	Resources
Comprehension: demonstrate understanding of what has been read to them by retelling stories and narratives using their own words and recently introduced vocabulary.	Choose stories, poems and rhymes, and other stimuli that engage children and underline and exemplify values at an age-appropriate level. Encourage children to use their growing vocabulary that exists around each value word.	Start a values library in the book corner; encourage children to look for values in books and explain how they work in the story. Give children post-its from time to time to use on individual books!	See the values action rhymes (appendix 3), written especially for early years children!
Anticipate, where appropriate, key events in stories.			
Use and understand recently introduced vocabulary during discussions about stories, non-fiction, rhymes, and poems, and during role-play.	For example, friendship: friendliness; happiness; trust; understanding; fun; enjoyment; learning; etc.		
ELG: word reading children at the expected level of development will:			
Say a sound for each letter in the alphabet and at least 10 digraphs.			
Read words consistent with their phonic knowledge by sound-blending.			
Read aloud simple sentences and books that are consistent with their phonic knowledge, including some common exception words.			
ELG: writing children at the expected level of development will:			
Write recognisable letters, most of which are correctly formed.			
Spell words by identifying sounds in them and representing the sounds with a letter or letters.			
Write simple phrases and sentences that can be read by others.			

ELG: Mathematics

Children at the expected level of development will:	What the adults will do through a values-based approach:	Making an enabling environment
ELG: number children at the expected level of development will: Have a deep understanding of numbers up to 10, including the composition of each number. Subitise (recognise quantities without counting) up to 5. Automatically recall (without reference to rhymes, counting or other aids) number bonds up to 5 (including subtraction facts), and some number bonds to 10, including double facts. ELG: numerical patterns children at the expected level of development will: Verbally count beyond 20, recognising the pattern of the counting system. Compare quantities up to 10 in different contexts, recognising when one quantity is greater than, less than or the same as the other quantity. Explore and represent patterns within numbers up to 10, including evens and odds, double facts, and how quantities can be distributed equally.	Help children to be aware of their own learning and review their progress and successes.	Value number and mathematics as part of our everyday life through interactive and interesting displays in the classroom.

ELG: Understanding the World

Children at the expected level of development will:	What the adults will do through a values-based approach:	Making an enabling environment
Past and present: Talk about the lives of the people around them and their roles in society; appreciate some similarities and differences between things in the past and now, drawing on their experiences and what has been read in class. Understand the past through settings, characters, and events encountered in books read in class and storytelling.		

ELG: Understanding the world

Children at the expected level of development will:	What the adults will do through a values-based approach:	Making an enabling environment
People, culture and communities: Pupils describe their immediate environment using knowledge from observation, discussion, stories, non-fiction texts and maps. Similarities and differences between different religious and cultural communities in this country, drawing on pupils experiences and what has been read in class. Similarities and differences between life in this country and life in other countries, drawing on knowledge from stories, non-fiction texts and, when appropriate, maps.	Model respectful approaches to finding out about our local area and wanting to do things to improve it. Involve children in local charities and in knowing about, and therefore caring for, some of the things on our doorstep. Model respectful attitudes towards differences between religious and cultural communities and countries. Refer often and meaningfully to children as being 'global citizens' of the world.	Make time to go out into the local community for visits and exploration. Make friends with representatives from the local community so that children are helped to establish a sense of connection. Encourage inter-age relationships and use opportunities for pictures and writing to promote these relationships. Display and refer to world maps and other countries.

ELG: The natural world

Children at the expected level of development will:	What the adults will do through a values-based approach:	Making an enabling environment	Resources
Explore the natural world around them, making observations and drawing pictures of animals and plants. Explore similarities and differences between the natural world and contrasting environments around them, drawing on their experiences and what has been read in class. Understand some important processes and changes in the natural world around them, including the seasons and changing states of matter.	Model curiosity, awe and wonder at our natural world. Thread the language of values through all activities and experiences, talking about them in relation to our natural world: how do we show respect, care, and kindness for our world? How can our values of hope and friendship apply to our world?	Take opportunities to help children engage at first hand with the natural world through regular Forest School and outdoor learning. Use technology to bring the wonders of the world to the classroom.	See our Values in the Forest ideas at the end of this chapter!

ELG: Expressive arts and design: Creating with materials			
Children at the expected level of development will:	What the adults will do through a values-based approach:	Making an enabling environment	Resources
ELG: Creating with Materials. Safely use and explore a variety of materials, tools, and techniques, experimenting with colour, design, texture, form, and function. Share their creations, explaining the process they have used. Make use of props and materials when role playing characters in narratives and stories.	Take opportunities to exemplify a value through art, for example, why not let children develop their cutting and sticking skills by decorating a huge heart with 'jewels' for the value of love? Encourage children to express their ideas as they create, thinking about what the value means to them, how they can show it themselves, when they have experienced it from others.	Create a celebratory climate for learning and a beautiful classroom decorated with artwork illustrating values, combining words, design, colours, and texture.	

ELG: Being imaginative and expressive			
Children at the expected level of development will:	What the adults will do through a values-based approach:	Making an enabling environment	Resources
Invent, adapt, and recount narratives and stories with peers and their teacher. Sing a range of well-known nursery rhymes and songs. Perform songs, rhymes, poems, and stories with others, and, when appropriate, try to move in time with music.	Think in terms of music, art, and literature to help children see and express values. Take opportunities to regularly enjoy and appreciate works that touch the spirit. Enjoy each other's efforts and talk about how they make us feel.		Values action rhymes (appendix 3).

Reflection time

Early years classes who are given the opportunity to take part in reflection time every day become collectively as well as individually calmer and better able to self-regulate. During this time, a calm, quiet and still atmosphere is created in the classroom, and both adults and children take part.

Kayleigh Evans, early years leader at Eardisley CE Primary School, describes how this works in practice in her school:

All of our reflections are related to our school's value of the month and they are set as meaningful and relatable experiences. We sit in a circle – I sit in the circle too and model calmness and quietness. Sometimes we hold hands and there's a wonderful feeling when everyone is still. Each reflection begins with a discussion, where children are invited to talk about our value and share any ideas they may have; the children's contributions are greatly praised and are noted in observation notes for their learning journey. A candle is then lit to signify it is our time to be especially still in our minds and to think more deeply. The children quickly tune in to the ritual of this and benefit from its regular practice.

During the silence, children are invited to focus on the candle and think about the discussion that we have had. During this time, children really develop their ability to be both still and comfortable with silence, and to use this calm to focus more deeply. They love it – and they become so responsive!

From time to time, children are presented with a linked question or a scenario that they are asked to discuss. Their responses are meaningful and heartfelt. Reflection is something that the children take part in right from when they first start school and has been found to be a calming and meaningful activity. Children often carry out their own reflections and help promote a calm and peaceful atmosphere in the classroom. We love it – it's one of the best things we've ever done.

CHAPTER 25

Values and Sustainability – How Nature can Inform the Curriculum

In this chapter we explore the Harmony Project, a framework to develop and deliver teaching and learning based on principles of harmony from nature.

The first chapter of this book acknowledges the importance of a dynamic curriculum that serves pupils and their needs, both now and in the future, and the role that values play in achieving this.

The Harmony Project recognises among these needs that pupils develop the skills, understanding, and agency to engage with the environmental challenges we collectively face – and they will face in the future – and to find ways to solve or mitigate them. Having a values-based framework is essential if pupils are to navigate these challenges successfully, something which is acknowledged, although not explicitly, in the Department for Education's Sustainability and Climate Change Strategy:

> *The challenge of climate change is formidable. For children and young people to meet it with determination, and not with despair, we must offer them not just truth, but also hope.*[6]

---

6   Department for Education, (2020) 'Sustainability and climate change: a strategy for the education and children's services systems', Available at: https://www.gov.uk/government/publications/sustainability-and-climate-change-strategy/sustainability-and-climate-change-a-strategy-for-the-education-and-childrens-services-systems.

What are 'determination', 'truth' and 'hope' if not values?

Our approach to education provides a framework for teaching and learning, and for a whole-school, values-based belief system, which has principles of harmony from nature at its heart. These principles can be thought of as the features of natural systems that sustain and maintain their health, and they align closely with values, as we will go on to explore in this chapter.

By using these principles to inform the curriculum, we provide pupils with models of what sustainable systems 'look like', because some of the best of these are found in the natural world. Having these points of reference and exploring how these features or principles can be applied to our own lives is essential if we want pupils to learn to live more sustainably. So, what are these principles, and how do they align with values?

The Harmony Project works with seven principles of harmony from nature:

- Cycles enable natural systems to be self-sustaining and self-regulating. In the natural world, nothing is wasted as everything feeds back into the system. We talk about throwing things away, but, as we are starting to appreciate, there is no 'away'.
- Diversity ensures the resilience of any system, both in human society and in nature.
- Interdependence teaches us that all life works in relationships. It is systemic. Everything is connected.
- Health shows us how the dynamic balance inherent in all natural systems maintains the health of that system.
- Adaptation illustrates that nature is in a constant state of change. Living things adapt to their environment over time and this helps them to stay well and to survive.
- Oneness reminds us that natural systems are the sum of their parts and that every living thing, ourselves included, is part of something larger than itself.
- Geometry allows us to see that there is a pattern and order to the natural world on a micro and a macro level. The patterns we see in nature are present in us, too, and this reminds us that we are part of the natural world and are not separate from it.

These seven principles help schools develop and deliver an educational experience for pupils in which they not only learn *about* the natural world, *in* the natural world, but also *from* the natural world, and how to care for it better. They provide a framework for both teaching and learning, and for a school's core values, which shape the context in which that learning takes place. As an example, the principle of *interdependence* can be used as the starting point for discussions across the whole school about values such as friendship and co-operation, trust, and responsibility. The principle of *adaptation* reminds us of the importance of adapting our own behaviours and attitudes to the circumstances in which we find ourselves, to the challenges we face and to the needs of those around us. It can be a lens through which to explore values such resilience and determination, courage, and hope. Meanwhile, the principle of *health* lends itself well to explorations of values including care, empathy, and happiness.

A fuller overview of how natural principles and values can be aligned is shown is shown below..

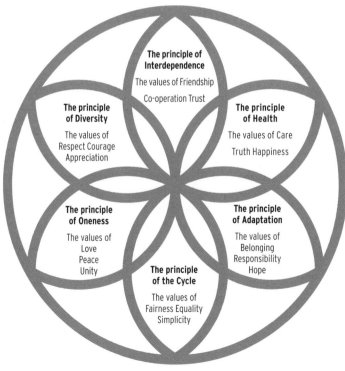

How can nature's principles inform teaching and learning?

Schools that follow a Harmony approach to education link the teaching and learning that takes place in each year group over each half term to a principle of nature, or, in some cases, several principles. Each half-term, pupils are posed an overarching question which signposts teaching and learning in all subjects, and which provides a stimulus for pupils' reflection on their learning. For example, Year 1 pupils are asked 'Which is my favourite wildflower and why?', which signposts learning linked to the principle of the *cycle* and the lifecycle of flowering plants. Similarly, in Year 3, pupils explore the question 'Why should we protect the rainforest?', this is linked to the principle of *diversity* and the importance of valuing and preserving the diversity of life in these environmentally critical habitats. Further up the school in Year 5, pupils find ways to respond to the question 'How can we ensure our oceans stay amazing?', with reference to the principle of *interdependence* and the impact of human behaviour on ocean ecosystems.

Regular opportunities are planned into the learning journey for pupils to explore these overarching questions through the lens of the principle of nature that guides the learning. In Year 2, one half-term's learning focuses on the question 'Why are bees so brilliant?' and this is linked to the principle of *interdependence*. Pupils learn how bees in a colony are dependent upon each other to carry out functions and roles that contribute to the collective wellbeing of the whole; about the symbiosis that exists between bees and flowering plants; and why we are so reliant on bees for our own survival (in science). They collect data to better understand the local bee population and its behaviour (in maths) and learn about the threats to bees caused by human activity (in science). They use their knowledge and understanding to plan how they can make the local environment more bee-friendly (in geography) and produce non-fiction texts to educate others about how we can care for bees (in English).

Pupils are encouraged to reflect on the relationship between needs and responsibilities, and to express how this understanding can be applied to our own lives to ensure the health and wellbeing of our communities, as well as the health and wellbeing of the planet.

In this model of education, principles of nature, and the values inherent in them, permeate all subjects, encouraging pupils to make connections between different areas of their learning and bringing cohesion and coherence to the curriculum.

The focus on enquiry that is central to this approach encourages pupils to take a proactive approach to their learning as they seek to find answers to the question they have been posed, creating a culture in the classroom (and beyond it), that places real value on the child's role as co-creator of learning and agent of change.

What is the impact of this approach?

As explored in the introduction to this book, teachers are often drawn to their profession by a desire to 'touch the future', to have an impact on the futures of the young people they teach.

This impact is both specific to the individuals they teach over the course of their careers, and to the contribution those individuals make to the world around them. By helping pupils to develop the knowledge, understanding, and values framework needed to make more sustainable choices about how they live, teachers have the opportunity to touch the future of all humanity, of all living things, of our entire planet.

The Harmony approach to education supports young people in developing a sense of agency by casting them in the role of active participants and co-creators of their learning. This sense of agency is a powerful lever for change. It is achieved through an enquiry-based approach to teaching and learning linked to values and principles of nature, and by promoting sustainability actions. In this way, issues of sustainability are both taught and lived out.

Harmonia, or harmony, is the Greek word for 'joined together'. Through the Harmony approach to learning, we want pupils to understand how nature works according to principles that enable natural systems to work well together, and how these same principles can guide and inform how we work together, too. We want them to learn to live in harmony.

What do teachers and practitioners say?

Reviewing our curriculum through the lens of harmony pulls together the school's vision and values to prepare our children (and their families) to become 'agents of change' for a more sustainable future.

Roy Sewell, St Mary's First School & Nursery

St Bartholomew's is fully engaged with harmony and delivers our version of a harmony curriculum. Importantly, the principles and concepts are reinforced through all curriculum areas, which we believe is crucial for pupils to make connections to the world around them.

Ian James, headteacher, St Bartholomew's Primary School

Further reading

Dunne, R., (2020) *Harmony: A New Way of Looking at and Learning About our World – A Teachers' Guide,* The Harmony Project.

CHAPTER 26

Who Decides the Curriculum?

In this thought-provoking chapter Mick Waters speaks to us about the differing groups of people whose voice and interests create a 'push and pull' on a school's curriculum and invites us to re-examine the core purposes of education.

Most books on how we should address the curriculum in a school are naturally aimed at teachers but of course there are other interest groups, often called 'stakeholders'. What do others want from the school curriculum? Are values important to them? What do communities expect?

One of the problems with talking about groups of people is that collective nouns suggest an artificial homogeneity. Just as with 'teachers', all 'parents' do not agree, all 'employers' do not share the same views. In any mass of population that collective noun problem is enormous. Any two people can have opposing outlooks or agree on some things and differ on others.

There are contrasting ideas, opposing views, and sometimes factions of opinion. Many people hold views which appear to contradict themselves. Too often conversations are polarised and become arguments, and just as often individuals struggle to understand the issues and build an opinion from the information that they have available to them. And, of course, within any organisation that offers a view or standpoint, there are individuals who have very different opinions. Two parents might share the same general outlook but differ on an aspect of detail. For example, they might think dressing smartly for school is important for all sorts of reasons but disagree about the benefit of a school uniform. Most of us reflect on our own school days as part of the experience which colours our view of the way children of today should be taught: 'It wasn't like this in my day,' is an easy refrain ... some would say 'thankfully', just as others say 'sadly'.

Oddly, there is no agreed set of principles for what we are trying to achieve in our school system, no agreed common purpose.

If we were to gather a group of any thirty adults in a room, there would be many different starting points for establishing priorities. Some would begin with what a good adult life would hold and see school as a stepping-stone on that path. Others would begin with what our children need and build from there. Some would start with employment essentials, other with predictions for the future, yet others would see schooling a providing some 'basics' to supplement what family and community provide. As we move the conversation into how any of that should be achieved some fundamental extremes would emerge based on how learning is seen to happen in schools. There would be those who tend towards allowing children to explore and discover where possible, ensuring rigour, while others would believe that the economic way to teach is through a formal process, made enjoyable. Sometimes the debate would get stuck around simplistic definitions and assumptions.

The most interesting part of the conversation might well happen when people discussed the reasons for their assertions. Why? What are we trying to achieve? In our country there is more consensus about this than we often realise.

In our book, *About Our Schools*, Tim Brighouse and I list some of the purposes of schooling that we believe would be accepted by most in our country.[7] While there is disagreement about some of the wording or emphasis, there is a broad consensus about these principles.

We should want our children to understand through their schooling that:

- *It will be their duty as adults to guard and participate in a representative democracy which values national and local government. To that end schools will progressively involve students in many aspects of school life and the community in which the school and the families are located.*

---

7   Brighouse, T. and Waters, M., (2022) *About Our Schools: Improving on Previous Best.* Carmarthen: Crown House.

- *Their religious faith and beliefs will be respected and they will be encouraged through their schooling to respect all faiths and the humanist position.*
- *That the many differently rewarded jobs and careers, which are vital to the wellbeing and practical operation of our society and others elsewhere in the world, are open to them. These include producing our food, construction and manufacturing, providing energy, medicine and care, logistics, information and entertainment, defending us and making and upholding our laws, cleaning up our mess and doing the tasks that only few can face, caring for our world, and working to support less fortunate people and causes, offering solace ... and helping others to learn, whether in classrooms, libraries, galleries or museums. This kaleidoscope of employed and self-employed opportunities, available in the private, public, and voluntary sectors, is ever changing and expanding under the influence of accelerating political, economic, social, and technological developments.*
- *These careers require differing talents and students' schooling experience will be based on valuing them as individuals and equipping them with the values, attitudes, knowledge, and skills to make a successful and rewarding contribution to society as adults in and out of work.*
- *They will be encouraged and expected to think for themselves and act for others through their life at school and in the community. They will be aware of how decisions are reached and how actions can work to solve or create problems. In doing so they will explore and understand the range of obligations, contributions, rights, and choices open to them in our own and other societies.*
- *They will be offered a range of learning opportunities that will reap more benefit if they commit to learning and seek further learning experience in other positive contexts.*
- *They will encounter through their schooling experiences expert help in acquiring a foundation of skills and knowledge which will allow them to survive and flourish in our own or another society.*
- *They will be thirsty to learn about the way civilisation has sought to solve its problems and made incredible discoveries and achievements while also, at times, making mistakes.*

- *They will have the ability to navigate media, including social media, and become critical and discerning users of developments in this field.*
- *They will be equipped to make good arguments for a just cause, understanding the views of others, and thereby to influence their social and political environment.*
- *They will understand and appreciate that our world is comprised of people from different cultures, races, and orientations, and be aware of the ways that power can be exercised with care or can be abused, and that people can be respected and valued, or exploited and persecuted. Their actions in the present and the future will reflect an understanding of our civilisation's past accomplishments as well as acknowledging that some of those achievements have come at the cost of prejudiced and flawed thinking.*
- *They will recognise their responsibility to protect the planet and contribute by living sustainably with the aim of preserving biodiversity and limiting global warming.*

All of these principles require pupils to be versed and immersed in subject disciplines and, importantly, able to apply them in the contexts and circumstances that they meet as citizens, as parents, and in employment ... or as travellers, hosts, colleagues, friends, politicians, volunteers, or good neighbours in whatever role they find themselves.

Implicit within those roles is a set of values and acceptance that a society has to support itself and its membership or it fails. Is that not a key purpose of schooling? One of the lessons from studying history is that, while they had heydays, societies as varied as the Ancient Greeks, Romans, Aztecs, and Egyptians, all eventually crumbled.

We teach children about these and other historical periods to encourage understanding of civilisation through example. Each of these cultures knew about order in society: they organised governance, trade, education and health, all variable depending on influence and wealth. They explored art and culture and believed in influences beyond human understanding. In each of these typical civilisations studied in primary school, a proportion of the population was subjugated to the power of the rulers. Each civilisation eventually collapsed – though all left their legacy on the modern day.

Empires such as these have often been understood in terms of cycles. In their early life they expand their boundaries, increase their territories, and have major wars. As they over-extend, or even just consolidate, the expansion slows or reverses, and they look inward and stagnate, idolising their heroic past. The British Empire – another example of civilisation studied in our schools, followed that pattern – as did, arguably, the Romans. Britain's Empire expanded rapidly from the sixteenth century through trade and colonialism, at its height ruling almost a quarter of the world. It survived the loss of its American colonies in the eighteenth century, but in the twentieth it was weakened by the two World Wars, independence movements across its colonies, and the creation of the British Commonwealth (which many would say is a misnomer). Like other historical empires it shaped the world in which we live in profound ways, though the meaning of its legacy continues to be contested and sometimes contentious as Britain come to terms with its imperial past.

Do we simply teach children about these civilisations as separate studies: a series of events, dates, people on a timeline in a specific region? Or do we help our young people to develop an appreciation of what a good and successful society is and does so that they might wish to support their own as a decent citizen or in a role in governance?

When we study art and design, do we want our young to simply name artists, know to which 'school' they belong and describe their techniques and some key moments in their life? Or do we want our children to learn to produce good art for themselves in a range of media? Do we want them to go further and recognise the power of artists to comment on society as they see it and influence their world? Do we want children to realise that artists, like most of us, gravitate towards others who seem to be on their wavelength and build movements, whether that be arts and crafts or cubism or impressionism? Do we want children to recognise the value society puts on art whether that is in the astronomic cost of 'masterpieces' changing hands or the way, for example, Holbein was able to exploit his talent and renown with the wealthy merchants of the Hanseatic League, in Tudor times when trade routes pointed in a different direction from London?

When children meet mathematics, do we want them to marvel that the ancient Greeks saw mathematicians as part of society's improvement, with, for example, geometry used to construct underground tunnels to transport water as well as beautiful temples? Indeed, while scribes did number crunching, the quest for understanding patterns took mathematicians in ancient Greece and beyond into trigonometry, algebra, and arithmetic, and that is still the case today.

Do we want our children to wallow in the power of language in Shakespeare's writing, or just to tactically pick the bones out of a soliloquy to get an A star resulting in, 'I'm never going to do that again'?

Is science, do we merely seek the understanding of a series of increasingly complex concepts in biology, chemistry, or physics, or the wider recognition that scientists' work has made society safer and more adventurous. Practising personal hygiene has made a dramatic impact on life expectancy since Victorian times, and inoculation has contributed to population growth as scientists collaborate to solve problems or to break barriers to understanding. Do we want our young to realise science is a live, collaborative subject discipline with so much still to discover?

In the modern world technology pulls on the younger generation with all the attraction of the biggest magnet. While most do not need teaching about how the latest applications and connectivity work, or what they can offer, do we want them also to know the pitfalls, the risks, and dangers of these technologies and how to avoid them?

The above examples from subject disciplines have been offered as questions, but few of these choices really need to be binary. Surely in most cases, the answer is 'both' (except perhaps the Shakespeare example). Surely, we want our children to both know about subject disciplines, and then to apply what they know, and to do so through an immersion in the discipline that enables them to become people who can actively draw and paint, sing, code, write, calculate, build, make, play, experiment, research, and map. All these verbs make our subjects living arenas of learning. In engaging with the subject disciplines children need, use, and extend values.

Of course, individuals who see the purpose and impact of a subject discipline can also become engrossed and lost in writing, inventing, performing, painting, or investigating. Our children will find solace in producing a piece of art, experience the satisfaction of a problem solved, push themselves to a peak of performance and feel the appreciation of an audience, win with grace, lose with dignity, and enjoy the pleasure of eating a meal cooked or wearing a dress made by themselves. They will learn about values by being valued, and these feelings of value will last into adulthood along with a fascination in the subject disciplines.

The influences on schools

The overarching influences of various 'stakeholders' are there in any school's approach to curriculum, but schools are also affected by the prevailing climate. Schools are often looking over their shoulder to what others expect – whether politicians, employers, or parents – and often these groups are used as a justification.

Of course, at the sharp end, there is also inspection which in theory is society's watching brief on schooling and addresses and represents the concerns of each of these stakeholders. Let's look at each in turn.

Politicians

Politicians set a curriculum and measure its effectiveness through a qualification system that currently emphasises knowledge. At the same time, they are quick to place upon schools a responsibility for any issue of concern that becomes topical or in the public view. Obesity, climate change, racism, women's safety, plastic, animal welfare, and all manner of other topical issues are met with the refrain, 'of course, it begins with education.' Or, 'we need to start in our schools.'

Politicians pronounce on character, then British values, or relationships and sex education, for example, and then urge schools to follow their guidance … as though schools have any spare time after they have finished preparing children for the tests and exams that carry significant community and professional consequences.

When children take to the streets and go on strike on Fridays to protest about climate change and rally with a Scandinavian climate change protester, they are told by politicians that they should be in school and not missing lessons, as though lessons are the only place to learn. It is noticeable how few such mass climate change protests for teenagers seem to happen at weekends or in school holidays … though it would of course not be a 'climate strike' if held on time off. However, beyond the need to make politically useful comments at appropriate times, politicians are the same as most of us: parents and members of communities.

Employers and employability ... and more political influence

For many years, employers generally have argued for a more rounded curriculum. The Confederation for British Industry (CBI) has produced report after report calling for a workforce more suited to modern employment practices. The call for changes in the way qualifications and curriculum are constructed is an ongoing feature of English education.

Often this is characterised as employers wanting young people to leave school versed and practised in what are called 'soft skills'. These skills are not easy to learn; they are not 'soft' at all. Skills such as determination, responsibility, adaptability, and collaboration have to be practised in context, discussed and, from the teachers' point of view, planned and developed. Employers complain that the 'production line' ethic of schooling – which sees examination results as the outcome – is selling them short in terms of the skills our young people will need in the future. Having said that, employers, like the rest of us, are quick to notice when a youngster seems lacking in functional skills such as managing money or time, or when an apostrophe appears in the wrong place.

In 2004, the Tomlinson Report proposed the establishment of a range of diplomas that would bring together academic and vocational aspects of learning. These were to be developed though partnership between education and business and offer a challenging and high-status qualification for young people. Pilot diplomas in four domains were developed and taught in schools and colleges across England: and somewhere there are about 20,000 adults who have these rather unique qualifications in construction, hair and beauty, engineering, and health.

Although progress was made in getting them underway, it was short lived. The principle of the diplomas split opinion, not only because the vision or purpose was questioned, but more because their existence and growth threatened the established A levels. Digby Jones, at the time the president of the CBI, was at odds with the diploma from the outset even though his organisation had given evidence to the Tomlinson enquiry calling for exactly such a development. Politically it was a bad time too. Leading up to the 2005 election, Tony Blair was keen to avoid controversial debate around his 'Education, Education, Education' agenda and committed to A level remaining as the 'gold standard'. From thereon, the diploma was 'dead in the water' and, when Michael Gove ended it for all of the twenty proposed programmes in 2010, there was barely a political whimper.

Ten years on, Gavin Williamson, then education secretary, announced the development of 'T levels' as a blend of vocational and academic learning leading to qualifications that fit young people to the changing world of employment. It will be many years before the programmes are properly developed and, in the meantime, the world of employment is moving on. Artificial intelligence is massively influencing workplaces. While a generation ago robots beginning to build cars was seen as revolutionary, it is now the norm, and robotics and AI are in many aspects of industry and business.

Employer behaviour is changing. Employers are sifting candidates for work less on the basis of GCSEs and qualifications. They know that qualifications are a proxy and so they are becoming devalued. In shrinking jobs market, where most applicants have a similar set of GCSEs and A levels, the employer wants to know about the candidate. They are checking for teamwork, leadership, creativity, responsibility, and initiative. If a pupil can only recall a special project on imagination in Year 4, or a role play that happened in Year 9 on teamwork, it is probably not going to leave a good impression in an interview.

Large companies are now reaching agreement with media and software companies to offer degrees online and micro-credential development is helping them to grow their own talent. People are gaining qualifications as they are paid rather than face what they see as debt. This will eventually disrupt the traditional university system, encouraging and forcing greater partnership with employers. The increasing employment and corporatisation focus of education is already happening, companies are edging towards it, regardless of government and changes in qualification and schooling.

Where does this fit with values in subject disciplines and schools?
We are often told that we need to teach what employers need and value. If that is the case, then we need to get our children to see that change and the future are not something to be scared of but are something they can

shape. We should encourage entrepreneurship in our young people and show them that they can play a part in this changing world.

More and more parents will wonder whether university is right for their children; and that traditional rite of passage will be further questioned in the face of 'earn as you learn' opportunities.

And so we come to parents

Of course, parents are the most significant influence on their children's education. They could have been the first port of call in this chapter but, in reality they feature towards the end of the consideration of what the curriculum should offer. It has been so since the Elementary Education Act of 1870 when significant numbers of parents resented schooling for taking away a source of their income. Schooling was made compulsory with the implication that the state knows best. Partnership with parents is a relatively recent concept, having grown in the late sixties and been promoted by the Plowden Report (1967).

The pressure of home learning was one that many parents had to cope with during the pandemic, again variably. Some found it a burden and overwhelming, others enjoyed it. For those who really engaged with it, many parents found home learning taught them more about what their children learn at school than they realised. When asked what they have done at school, many children have always replied, 'not much', no parent could see what 'not much' means. Periodic media interest in fronted adverbials, or vertices, or Samuel Pepys and the Great Fire and such like, also fuelled comments and questions about why our children should learn these things.

For some parents, such content seemed abstract and irrelevant to the lives of their children, now and in the future. For other parents, such content was the same as when they were at school and they wondered why things hadn't moved on. For others still, content was different from when they were at school, and they wondered why these new topics were now important. We accept change in our shopping, clothing, transport, and home life; schooling is different. Both schooling and being a parent are complicated.

While parents typically find the content of the curriculum intriguing, bewildering, confusing, or essential, they know it must be 'covered'. That's why we have schools: because children must learn things.

Most parents have one over-riding concern and that is that their children are happy at school and in childhood. The same issue comes out of survey after survey of parents about what they want from a school. They want their children to be happy.

That, of course, begs the question of what we mean by happiness. Is it day by day contentment? Is every moment idyllic? Is it laughter and frolicking and friendship? Does it mean they are never to be sad or worried or anxious?

Most of us know that if our children are to grow up to be secure in adulthood, then they need experiences that gradually prepare them for the world beyond the perfect: the stumbles, falls, mishaps, unfairness, cruelties, and problems. Part of our role in school is to enable children to come to terms with complexity in life. They need to learn how humans work, how they are different on different days, how some people have different outlooks, and some become friends while others remain acquaintances. We all live and work in communities and learning to 'give and take' is essential, seeing other points of view is vital, as is knowing why we agree with some and not with others.

All of us, though, would surely want children to have a joyous and purposeful childhood.

CHAPTER 27

A Curriculum That Educates Rather Than Teaches: Should we Address Contentious Issues Within our Subject Disciplines?

Here, Mick Waters takes us into what many call the 'hidden curriculum' – the less charted waters of real-life matters – where consideration of values is pertinent, meaningful, and while sometimes contentious, always important.

The Black Lives Matter movement has led to calls for the de-colonising of the curriculum and this has led the school system to question its influence and how it should respond.

The discomfort felt by many in the school system arises because it has never been good at dealing with 'contentious issues'. While the spotlight is currently on 'Black History', it could equally be the Holocaust, or the legacy of the Japanese involvement in World War II, or the impact of nuclear testing in the 1960s. This discomfort is not confined to history but exists around issues such as gender, sexuality, ethics in science, or the portrayal of contentious issues in art.

Our national curriculum was developed in part to 'rein in' the growing tendency in some schools to debate with youngsters some issues that were perceived to be troubling if society at large started to 'think'.

When state schools were established in 1870, the curriculum of the day reflected contemporary and popular aspects of society, along with some things that had been the diet of public schools. The classics were deemed not particularly appropriate for the masses. There was concern that we were going to lag behind other countries in developing science in schools. History was taught as the British Empire in all its grandeur. We currently tell young people a great deal about World War II, in part to recognise those who fought in it; in 1870 a similar span of time had passed since Trafalgar and Britain was just out of the Crimean War. While the country moved towards mass education to fuel the industrial growth, it still needed volunteers to fill the mass graves of war, so schooling could not risk anything other than to preach allegiance to the crown and teach of its victories. Indeed, even the nation's defeats were often described in terms of heroic successes.

Geography taught about British explorers. Livingstone had recently crossed Africa and it was exactly a hundred years since Cook popped into Botany Bay and claimed Australia. It was only 40 years since Wilberforce had persuaded parliament to abolish slavery and, while the inhumanity of the institution was acknowledged, there was no teaching about the enormous wealth it had generated.[8] Perhaps teaching about exploitation might have made those in Victorian times realise just how much they themselves were being exploited by the mill owners and mine developers. Dickens had died in 1870 and he formed the 'modern' section of the literature curriculum – a bit like teaching Margaret Atwood or David Walliams today. The Arts and Crafts movement was influential and current ... and 'art and craft', including symmetrical patterned potato printing, was taught as a subject in English schools right up to the 1980s.

From the outset, it was held that children should be taught that Britain was a model nation, successful and right. This same unregulated curriculum continued largely untroubled until the 1970s. A national curriculum arrived for many reasons. One was the growing mobility of families, the wider realisation that schooling was variable, and also that children who moved school would repeat learning. With awareness of variability came

---

8   See for example the work of the Centre for the Study of the Legacies of British Slave Ownership: https://www.ucl.ac.uk/lbs/.

growing disquiet about quality in schooling which became a convenient rationale for the central control of schools.

In the 1960s, University exam boards, which ran GCE O levels and A levels began to bring in 'strange' subjects. One such was the 'British Commonwealth History' O level, which encouraged consideration of the East India Company and the triangular trade, and in which pupils were invited to discuss issues of power, wealth, heritage, and equality. One of the reasons for the establishment of the private exam boards (and their replacement with awarding bodies) by Baker was the perceived need to stop the universities from encouraging the kind of critical thinking which would upset the balance of society. Indeed, one of the drivers for the national curriculum was to rein in the discourse that was growing about the extent to which pupils might be allowed to meet and discuss controversial matters. The raising of the school leaving age in 1947 and then 1971 had meant that 16 years olds were now at school so, in effect pupils who were previously seen as men and women were debating right and wrong in aspects of government and, by implication, the actions of their rulers. Hence, Thatcher decreed that teachers could only be registered if their degrees were in subjects of the national curriculum. Psychology, sociology, and philosophy were all outlawed at the time because they were seen as potentially dangerous.

The national curriculum in 1988 tightened everything. There was sop to 'cross curriculum issues' – which included such things as civics, health, technology, and careers – but this was quietly dropped after about a year because teachers were genuinely promoting cross curriculum thinking and ministers wanted certainty and control, in history in particular. Instead, there was a nod to PHSE and personal development … and civics which was neutered as much as possible. This meant these aspects got about an hour a fortnight, which ensured they had as little impact as possible.

There is always resistance to change. When Christian Barnard did the first heart transplant there was a moral and ethical outburst. Not only was it an affront to religion in many people's eyes, it involved a woman in the donor role. How could a woman's heart be placed in a man's body? When Louise Brown was born, the outcry against test tube babies was significant. For these things to be discussed in school would risk raising a thinking generation. The pressure to increase the content and volume of exams was a useful strategy to stop teachers bringing learning into the real world ... and the real world into learning.

And so vast swathes of real life have simply passed schools by until suitable time has elapsed: the Cold War; the Troubles in Northern Ireland; the battles with unions; the poll tax; the migration crisis; the MeToo movement, have all received barely a mention except perhaps, after due time, in history. More recently even the relatively uncontentious finding and relocation of Richard III's body got virtually no mention, even in history ... because teachers needed to 'get on'. The grooming of girls in towns across Britain went largely unmentioned in schools. This is not surprising; teachers have become so pushed to ensure success in the exams for passing groups of pupils, that their capacity to build interest, excitement, or intrigue in their subject discipline is limited. They teach 'an exam course'. The change of the clocks twice a year is hardly mentioned, children study phases of the moon in a one-hour lesson without being asked to look at it. The wonder of ancient science or mathematics is lost in the clerical routine of schooling for exams.

Since schools began, they have been in part seen as a haven for children away from the realities of life. One of the explicit reasons for compulsory state schooling was to protect children from the exploitation of child labour. Schools have always been places where kindly people protect children from the travails that adults in society are facing: wars, bombing, and, very recently, looking after vulnerable children in epidemic. There has always been an effort to preserve children's innocence; shelter them from the harsh world outside and to leave to their families the embarrassing or the difficult to explain. Hence sex education was a quicksand that teachers were better avoiding until the media and entertainment industries let the previously hidden birds and bees escape. Steering clear of religious issues was seen as fine when church and Sunday school were prominent, yet with our new complexity of belief systems, schools usually fail to fulfil legal obligations in terms of worship, condoned by inspectors who themselves turn a blind eye to contentious issues.

Contentious issues, though, have always vexed and governments avoid them in the knowledge that the teaching profession is unlikely to object to not being required to enter a minefield. So contentious issues tend to be addressed tentatively: Black History gets a month (in some schools); LGBTQ+ gets a fortnight and consciences are assuaged or issues dodged. Works such as *To Kill a Mockingbird* elbow in alongside the GCSE texts but pupils add to the pressure on teachers to focus on passing the exam through addressing extracts rather than explore thoroughly the social issues it exposes.

Our teaching of World War II encourages understanding of the blitzkrieg and British fortitude with little mention of allied bombing of Dresden. The opening ceremony of the Olympic Games in London portrayed a history of the nation which we could celebrate, naturally avoiding the aspects over which we might be embarrassed. We celebrate British success in sport and schools are implored to seek marginal gains, yet the level of bullying and abuse that has become apparent in cycling, gymnastics, and swimming creates an awkward discomfort.

Of course, environmental concerns and the battle for the planet were allowed by Michael Gove as minister for the environment, though he determined that such issues of sustainability had minimal place in his 2013 draft of the national curriculum. The environment has become less contentious as it has reached prominence as a global issue and it has become increasingly impossible for schools to ignore. COP26 provided an opportunity for government to 'promote' a strategy now that the issue was no longer contentious. The sad thing here has been that teachers' new-found zeal for real issues seems to stop at muttering about plastic. At the same time, the daily sticking in of printed sheets into exercise books leading to the destruction of trees simply to act as place holders for photocopying goes unremarked … even in so called eco schools.

A few years ago, the government had another chance to assert itself again and introduced fundamental British values. Worried about fundamentalism, they introduced not just British values, but 'fundamental' ones. Given the gaming of the system to do well with Ofsted, this was often seen as a relatively easy win for many schools. A display near the entrance door with images of the Queen, prime minister, union flags, a telephone box, and a bag of chips … a quick assembly … job done!

Curriculum design often perceives learning as a linear process both in 'coverage' of content and in the building of knowledge, skills, and understandings. However, true geographers, scientists, mathematicians, and historians all make connections between spheres of learning. They see the potential tangents in science, the patterns in mathematics, the roots in languages, the influences in art, and the cause and effect in geography; and they see these facets in each other's disciplines. True historians do not see a linear progression of events but a 'corkscrew effect' of history repeating aspects of itself in the lives people experience.

This was at the heart of the Crick Report in 1998 that heralded 'citizenship' as a curriculum topic. It asserted that 'we should not attempt to shelter our nation's children from even the harsher controversies of adult life, but should prepare them to deal with such controversies knowledgeably, sensibly, tolerantly and morally.' Citizenship along with PHSE took a battering from Gove's reforms.

We need teachers who are at ease with discussing contentious issues but many are not. Partly because of the fear of parent reaction – as with the gender demonstrations and blockades in Birmingham in 2019 – but also because, due to the curriculum of their own schooling, many do not understand the impact of their subject discipline on society beyond its exam status.

Communicating the joy of the subject discipline – the intriguing stories of those who have practised as its specialists, the effect of the discipline on civilisation for good or ill, its application to the real world and the relationship it has with others – are the true roles of the teacher and this is where leadership has to step beyond the compliance to a results regime and instead engineer true education.

So let's come full circle on contentious issues. In Kensington Gardens sits the statue of Edward Jenner, who is credited with having developed the process of vaccination to fight smallpox and which has been used globally against multiple illnesses. The statue was originally erected in Trafalgar Square in 1858 but was moved to its quieter and less prominent location four years later in response to protest. The first protests came from people who disagreed with vaccination, including many in the medical profession, and also from many who objected to a civilian being honoured with a statue alongside military heroes.

Statues have again become contentious with the sacking of the monument to merchant, philanthropist, and slave trader Edward Colston in Bristol in

2020, bringing to a climax the tensions around the historical associations of public figures. How do we help our children to learn, as they mature, that society is grappling with contradictions and complexities, and addressing them rationally is part of being educated? It comes back to conversations about values. Essentially, everything we do in school is about personal development and teaching history, geography, languages, science, art, maths, and other disciplines is all about working with youngsters to open their eyes through the subject discipline … to educate them.

CHAPTER 28

The Future of Education: Creating and celebrating an ethics-centred international Curriculum

In this chapter Neil Hawkes aims to inspire you to join him in seeing the future of global education, as one that empowers ethical intelligence through Values-based Education.

I am always delighted to talk with groups of educators and others about my passion for Values-based Education. At the start of my talks, I always say that my aim is, 'To inspire you to be more conscious of the role of values in all aspects of your life'. My hope is that you will see the tremendous good for humanity, if collectively we envision education in the way that values-based schools do throughout the world. Such schools are taking the lid off the potential of their students, enabling them to have a meaning and purpose for their lives, powered by the energy of positive human values.

Over the last twenty years I have been privileged to visit schools that aspire to be values-based in Europe, Africa, The Caribbean, North and Central America, Asia, and Australasia. These visits have shown me that basically all people are similar, with the same needs, fears, and hopes. I have seen that teachers do their best often in quite challenging circumstances. Education systems are highly complex; often politically driven by dogma and doctrine that find it difficult to adopt new ways of thinking, based on the current needs of students and their communities. Despite the resistance of the status quo, I am proposing a reimagining of education based on sustainable values that give students enhanced basic education and the knowledge and experience that will help them to be ethically intelligent.

I would like to ignite your imagination, giving you a glimpse of aspects of the future that are already present in some amazing schools. Choosing just a few has been daunting, as there are now so many examples of good practices that I could share with you. However, let me describe a few; forgive me if your school is not among them. I have deliberately not chosen any UK schools as there are numerous outstanding Values-based Schools, which I have described in a previous chapter in this book.

My starting point is May 2018, when my wife Jane and I were welcomed to AFNorth International School, at Branssum in the Netherlands, by its director Kathy Wood MBE. AFNorth International School is a Dutch Foundation, established around its dynamic international community. Students, families, and staff enjoy the 'best of both worlds,' in that they gain a wonderfully rich and culturally diverse experience. They live in an international environment, yet under the safety and security of their own national system. The school provides an education commensurate with the national requirements of its four founding nations – Canada, Germany, the United Kingdom, and the United States. The expectation, as agreed by all four nations, is to develop a mutual understanding of a shared school culture – hence its passion for Values-based Education.

Kathy is an inspiring educator, whom I first met when she was a headteacher at Brookside School in Bicester, Oxfordshire. I was privileged to be her school's adviser. She then went to be the head of Hornbill, British Forces School in Brunei. It is in this school that she underpinned the school's educational philosophy with Values-based Education. When I visited the school I awarded it the Values Quality Mark, issued by the IVET Foundation. Kathy built on this experience by taking her great educational knowledge, insights and passion for values to AFNorth. Kathy invited us to help her deepen the staff's understanding of the power of values by conducting training sessions.

We had an amazing time in this unique international school, which has children from kindergarten to high Sshool graduation. Recently, the students made two inspiring videos to be used at an international pupils' conference about the importance of positive values and the effects they can have on the world. The videos feature several students who do not have English as their mother tongue and some students with special needs (SEND).

When I first watched the videos, I was so moved by the quality of thinking and the passion behind what was being so articulately presented. For me, they represent the outcome and impact of a values-based school. Values are seen as the positive essence of students, who are inspired to put this into action in their lives. Imagine the transformative effects on our world, if students from all schools were able to articulate how their values can make the world a better place. This is what Krzysztof Bryla says in one of the videos:

> *I think values such as trust, empathy and responsibility make the world a better place, by helping us to positively change the way we perceive things around us. They help us to see the good in people. They lead to mutual respect and trust, opening pathways to international collaboration for everyone. A person with values will always help others and will not stop until the goal is accomplished. Shortly put, values make the world a better place by creating global citizens, who are empathetic, caring, responsible and eager to explore new ideas when they meet people.*

How do we first empower students to think about values in this decisive and inclusive way? I believe we must begin in the early years. Our aim is to give children an ethics-centred, holistic education. This inspires them to be the best version of themselves that they can be. Such an innovative school I observed in Iceland, at Leikskolinn Alfaheidi Kindergarten for children between the ages of 2-7. I visited with my wife Jane on two occasions – 2014 and 2017. The school has implemented Living Values Education (LVE), which is a global program. I was one of its founders and have been the Chair of LVE in the British Isles since 1994. I love its heart-based programs, such as the values activities for children 3-7, which help schools to focus on creating a positive atmosphere for children and adults. I was first invited to the school to educate the staff in the LVE approach to developing a values-based school. The school gives the children a wonderful caring values-based atmosphere, filled with mutual respect. All staff model the school's values, and the children have access to a child-focused curriculum that helps each child to develop naturally and love learning. The calm and purposeful atmosphere is tangible. The headteacher said that the whole school feels the values philosophy – it's in the walls.

This atmosphere is also present on the other side of the world. In March 2020, just before the UK's first Covid-19 lockdown, I revisited Snells Beach Primary School in New Zealand. I had first visited it eleven years earlier when it was a new school. I was deeply moved to see that their values journey had blossomed. The principal, Kathryn Ramel, who on my first visit had been the deputy, was proud to show me how the values work had been developed and influenced the whole of the school's curriculum. The uniqueness of each child is recognised and nurtured. Agency is a high priority, which encourages pupils to take responsibility for themselves and their learning. The principal said that many immigrants from the UK find it difficult to understand why a school such as hers does not have fences around it to keep people out. Are their children going to be safe? In this school the community is welcomed as an integral part of its resources for learning and is not looked on as a potential threat.

One early years teacher was so proud to show me the values training book that I had used with the staff on my first visit. A newly appointed teacher told us that she was enjoying the values approach to learning. The experiences that are given to the pupils attending the school are in many ways like those in values-based schools in Sweden, Belgium, El Salvador, Jamaica, Thailand, Nigeria, Singapore, and many other parts of the world. Importantly, the curriculum is designed to match pupils' needs both as learners and as human beings. I thought it poignant that Jasmine, a teacher at Mahurangi High School, the local secondary school, shared with me that her colleagues see a very positive difference in pupils transferring from Snells Beach School. Their attitudes to learning and their respectful behaviours are so positive, compared with pupils who are not helped to understand the transformational power of positive human values.

I hope you enjoyed reading about these remarkable schools. In recent months, I have been thinking deeply about how education can be improved globally. I feel that education is lop-sided. There is a huge emphasis on the acquisition of basic subjects with scant regard for nurturing the human qualities that will ensure a sustainable future.

The schools I have highlighted in this chapter educate young people to see the world and behave through a positive values lens. I have been actively supported in developing my thinking into a coherent proposition by Dr. Marco Tavanti, professor, School of Management at University of San Francisco. Marco has a deep understanding of education as seen from the global perspectives of the UN, UNESCO, and the OECD. In October 2021, we wrote a chapter about empowering education for sustainable global and ethical values. This is part of the V20 (values experts) protocol to the G20 leaders, arguing that they should look at sustainability from a human values perspective.

In thinking about the future of global education, I would like to share with you some of my ideas, which need to be acted on to transform education. I hope this will help you to feel empowered to take appropriate actions in the setting and context in which you are based. How do we create a global system of education that meets the needs of individuals, while ensuring a common future for human coexistence, environmental interconnectedness, and sustainable prosperity for all?

Humanity is faced with a monumental existential global challenge, elements of which include: Covid-19; climate change; loss of biodiversity; social and racial injustice; and economic inequalities.

The resolution of these global challenges is linked to enabling students to fully appreciate their scope and nature; how each of us can contribute to their solution. To achieve this awareness, education must be forward looking. It must inspire students to be the best version of themselves that they can be, so that they can be the change that is needed in the world. Such an education must give students quality holistic education that embraces sustainability at its core, espousing ethical values such as integrity, solidarity, empathy, justice, cooperation, and sharing.

One aspect of the current education system that prevents a more relevant curriculum, is the pressure many schools experience from an educational culture that is standards based and outcome focused. In such systems, basic education is narrowly defined; schools teach discrete subjects, which have isolated knowledge and skills that are measured in exams. Alarmingly, much of the current curriculum fails to give value to enabling students to understand themselves; to know how to care for their internal world of thoughts, feelings and emotions, and the external natural world. The dominant economic model for education narrowly focuses on student exam grades, which determine their usefulness to society and an individual's sense of self-worth.

In the UK, the evidence for a growing lack of student self-worth can be measured in the rising numbers of young people suffering from mental health issues. The current way that the school curriculum is generally conceived and implemented makes only a marginal impact on the development of respect, empathy, and compassion for others. This is despite teachers being generally caring and dedicated. Teachers share with me that they cannot build a strong sense of resilience in students because of the extremely limited amount of curriculum time given to learning about what it means to be a human being in today's complex world. For instance, areas of the curriculum that help to develop a secure sense of self, such as the creative arts, have been increasingly marginalised. Standardisation of schools with a focus on 'back to basics' has increased in government-controlled schools, which prefer to show that their schools do well on comparative data as measured by such as the Program for International Student Assessment (PISA).

A great inhibitor for change in education, is the vested interest in the status quo and the huge economic investment in it. For instance, as Ava Shabnum Hasan, who runs a UK organisation called *Mentally Well Schools*, pointed out to me, 'The materialistic, consumerist society has a monetary interest in all forms of addiction that generates so much trauma in people.' The videos posted on social platforms such as Instagram give witness to this pandemic level addiction. No wonder there is so much mental ill-health and that many students feel disengaged from their education.

Is there a way out of this impasse? What can I propose that would make a transformational difference to the way education is currently perceived and organised? How can we advance the purpose of education to assure a common future for human coexistence, environmental interconnectedness, and sustainable prosperity for all?

Primarily, I think there is an urgent need for education to adopt an ethics-integral approach, such as Values-based Education. This would mean that the culture of each school or educational setting would be values-based, meaning that everything the school is and does is underpinned by a community agreed set of universal, positive human values such as respect, integrity, kindness, and sharing. Culture, simply put, is about what we do here! It reflects the values, atmosphere, mindsets, narrative, character, routines, and structures of the school.

As we travel towards a global education, my vision is that all students would have the right to access quality holistic basic education – not merely literacy and numeracy – which would help them to make sense of the world; gaining knowledge in the form of skills, understanding, and concepts contained across the various forms of knowledge currently expressed as subjects in the curriculum. These forms of knowledge need, especially in the beginning stages of education, to be sufficiently integrated to create in the learner an understanding of our world. A world in which they see themselves not just as an onlooker but an active part. Such education is inclusive, equitable and lifelong, as stated in the United Nations Sustainable Development Goal (SDG) 4. Students will sense that they are global citizens promoting peace and non-violence, understanding gender equality, sustainable lifestyles, human rights and responsibilities, appreciating cultural diversity, and of culture's contribution to sustainability and action.

Besides access to these basics students require an education that equally nurtures their innate capacity to espouse and act on ethical sustainable values. This was clearly expressed by Krzysztof Bryla the student at AFNorth quoted above. A values-based school is designed to give students access to a vocabulary which develops their ethical intelligence; their ability to self-regulate their behaviour ethically. The outcome is that young people develop the personal power of ethical intelligence and the qualities and dispositions to deal with life's complexities, including difficult and contentious issues. They can create, evaluate, analyse, critique, apply, understand, and remember.

Simply put, I propose that schools balance equally the provision of basic education, on which other chapters in this book have focused, within ethics-centred education. This transformation will inspire students to behave ethically: having the sustainable knowledge to play an active role ensuring that we and our planet can flourish.

This aim was at the heart of my headship in Oxfordshire. As most teachers do, I wonder about the impact I have had on the lives of students. The following is from a letter sent to me by former pupil Stephanie Giles. I hope it acts as an inspiration for you, to have the courage to adopt the form of Values-based Education that I have described in this chapter.

> *Dr Hawkes, I wanted to thank you for implementing your truly inspirational values system. Thank you for making my childhood at West Kidlington Primary School so memorable and enjoyable. Thank you too for teaching me values, which I have held so closely since leaving 20 years ago throughout my adult life. I will be eternally grateful that I was lucky enough to be a pupil of West Kidlington when you were headteacher, and to have experienced the Values-based Education you implemented. Words simply cannot express my gratitude. Please just know that even after all this time, your work has had a truly transformational and lasting impact. It has made a real difference to my pathway in life – thank you.*

Now over to you ...

What is the Point of Values in Learning?

Values-based Education has traditionally occupied the territory of behaviour, personal development, and well-being and SMSC. If values guide our thinking and our behaviour in social contexts, then values can surely guide our thinking and attitudes to learning too. In our profession, we all understand that learning is an emotional event. Our attitudes to it as well as to ourselves make the critical difference.

Values-motivated practitioners have been looking for some time for ways of making the values impact on learning much more meaningful and explicit. Teachers have described how values are effective because they create a 'hook' on which to hang all aspects of what we do. Values can become our 'learning hooks' as well as our 'living hooks'.

Moreover, and most importantly, teachers who make regular and explicit reference to values in both planning and leading lessons find that they have proved to be immensely apposite in improving learning behaviours. Children grasp readily and enthusiastically apply them. There is a deep connection between these classroom values and the regular, monthly whole-school values that guide our behaviours, and the outcome is seamless.

Through this book, we have demonstrated that all the subject disciplines offer myriad deep-seated opportunities to develop values-based thinking and learning, offering a path to wisdom for our children.

Try them out for yourselves and see the impact!

Conducting a Values Audit in your School

When considering developing a values-led approach in your school, it can be helpful to use these three questions:

- What are we trying to achieve?
- How will we organise the approach so that it is reflected in the curriculum and in pupils' learning?
- How will we know if our changes have been successful?

Use the following tables as a starting point in developing a values-led approach by observing conditions 'on the ground', examining school documentation, and talking with staff and pupils. Then consider the wider points raised in our follow up questions.

As you move through the school	
Key Questions	**Evidence**
Your vision: What do you want to be known for as a school? What kind of learners do you want to nurture?	Is your vision visible in action in the classrooms, corridors, and campus? What messages do the displays and environment give? Would your vision be borne out in what you hear people say and see people do?
Do you have a current, 'big picture' vision? How do values underpin your school's curriculum planning and how does policy translate into practice?	Does your curriculum intent show how values flow through all aspects of the school's life? Does every subject have an opportunity to celebrate and further these values?
How are the principles and aims reflected in your day-to-day approaches?	Consider your customary school routines and working patterns day-to-day – do they reflect your principles and aims? What kind of conversations do adults have with each other and with pupils?

How well does your curriculum promote personal development?	Does teaching and learning encourage pupils to work in a principled way, collaboratively, and creatively?
Is the curriculum geared to the enjoyment of learning, and to meeting the needs and aspirations of learners by capitalising on their strengths?	Can you see highly motivated learners working competently and confidently, showing resilience and persevering in tasks which are more difficult?
Are adults ambitious for learners and do they have high expectations of learning?	When observing staff in action are high expectations of all learners maintained?
What do the school displays tell you about the quality and range of the curriculum?	Consider the range of subjects shown and the quality of pupil work. Are displays used to motivate and celebrate?
What is the quality and effect of leadership?	Do children have an opportunity to lead in this school? How much leadership is distributed among staff?

As you consider school documentation or talk with staff

Key Questions	Evidence
How well does the values-led curriculum contribute to good outcomes for all outcomes for pupils? How does the school currently measure the impact of curriculum design on learner outcomes?	How can we use data analysis to learn more about the impact of curriculum design? How do you monitor success through qualitative learner outcomes?
Is this action set out in a strategic way within the overall School Development Plan? How is it monitored and evaluated?	Do outcomes fuel your SEF and SDP?
Do you regularly review how well you are meeting your own aims to ensure that they are responsive to the needs of its pupils?	How rigorous is your approach to evaluating the effectiveness of provision? Are stakeholders familiar with the agreed aims of our curriculum? What kind of success criteria have you identified to check that you are achieving your aims?
To what extent and how effectively has the values-based curriculum, including the enrichment curriculum, been extended and improved through collaborative partnerships with families and the community?	With whom do you work in partnership and what contribution do these partnerships make to our pupils' learning experiences?
Are there meaningful opportunities for values-led learning across the curriculum?	Which features of your curriculum seem most/least relevant and meaningful to our pupils? How can you organise learning to maximise on this/ increase their relevance? To what extent does your curriculum reflect global 21st century issues?
What opportunities are there for values-based learning outside and beyond the classroom?	How do you ensure that these experiences are high quality?
What does the school layout and timetable tell you about the quality and range of the curriculum? Does anything need to change?	Does your physical context and timetable strengthen your offer or constrain it? Where might change enhance outcomes?
What do pupil attendance and punctuality figures tell you about the effectiveness of this approach? What do pupils themselves tell you? How often do you ask them? What are parents' views and thoughts?	Do you experience fluctuations in attendance and punctuality that could be attributed to how learning is organised? What are your children telling you?!
How effective are your arrangements for internal and external transition for pupils?	Is the values experience equally good in all parts of the school? To what extent do you work with pre-schools and secondary schools to ensure continuity and coherence?

Follow up questions

- How do you celebrate the strengths and successes of values?
- Who needs to know what we do well? How do we let people know?
- How are curriculum developments evaluated and how is this information used? How could you refine your approach?
- How often do you audit the curriculum to see how far it reflects your philosophy and ambition?
- Do you pay sufficient attention to auditing and evaluating your curriculum in detail, or do we tend to drift into habitual practice?
- How does the school ensure coherence of curriculum design across the school and equality of opportunity for all its pupils?
- Can we be confident that all pupils have access to a rich and values-led curriculum offer?
- What CPD provision is now needed to enable your school to move forward with curriculum development?
- Where might staff identify training needs triggered by this evaluative process?

A Values Glossary

Care

Care is the process of protecting someone or something and providing what that person or thing needs; caring enough about someone or thing to give it serious attention.

Corresponding values: love, respect, kindness, tolerance, democracy, and consideration.

Key concept or question	Aspects of learning
What can care mean for me?	Caring for myself.
	Health and hygiene.
	Personal safety.
	Self-worth.
	Knowing our own rights.
	Personal goals, hobbies, likes and dislikes and aspirations.
	Working hard - self-belief and pride.
What can care mean for others around me?	Caring for our families, friends, and pets.
	Pets who have cared for people!
	Anti-bullying.
What can care mean for my community.	Caring for others.
	Caring for the school and school resources.
	Our responsibilities towards others.
	Ways of showing our care in action.
What can care mean for the world?	Laws that help us care for each other.
	Groups and charities that work together for the good of the world.
	Caring for the planet - sustainability issues.
The paradox.	Caring too much, about the 'wrong' things and the imbalance this brings in ourselves and/or our world.

Compassion

Compassion is a strong feeling of sympathy and a gentle and sometimes courageous desire to help others in their trials.

Corresponding values: love, respect, kindness, tolerance, courage, democracy, and consideration.

Key concept or question	Aspects of Learning
What can compassion mean for me?	Understanding that we need to treat our bodies, minds, and spirits with care to keep healthy.
	Developing a balanced understanding of ourselves, our strengths, and our weaknesses.
	Enjoying and using our talents.
	Using reflection and mindfulness to improve our wellbeing.
	Using positive affirmations to affirm our capabilities.
What can compassion mean for others around me?	British values - individual liberty and tolerance - understanding and respecting others and their differences.
	The importance of ensuring others feel included.
	Looking out for and helping others at a time of need.
	Anti-bullying messages
What can compassion mean for my community?	British value - democracy - being aware of inequalities.
	Looking at compassionate role models around us - what difference do they make?
	Discovering the needs of our own communities, whether in terms of the environment, wildlife, or groups of people and looking to make a difference through our actions.
What can compassion mean for the world?	British value - rule of law - laws that help us care for each other.
	Groups and charities who work together for the good of the world.
	Caring for the planet - sustainability issues and ways in which we can each make a difference.
The paradox.	Ensuring that our self-compassion does not become self-absorption; how great is our capacity for compassion - understanding there will be limits to our ability to help the world and how we have to do what we reasonably can.

Courage

Courage is about being able to face and then take some control over our fears and being willing to deal with something that is dangerous, difficult, or unpleasant. It is as much about inner, moral courage as about brave acts. It comes from strength of will.

Corresponding values: co-operation, compassion, care, love, understanding, resilience, respect, individual liberty, rule of law, and democracy.

Key concept or question	Aspects of learning
Courage for myself.	Understanding that fear is a natural form of self-protection.
	Understanding the British value of the rule of law.
	Understanding that as humans we have rights that are enshrined in the United Nations.
	Being able to say no and to withstand peer pressure.
	Using positive affirmations to affirm our capabilities.
Courage for and from others.	Recognising that courage grows in community with others - working together to achieve a difficult goal.
	British values - individual liberty and tolerance - understanding and respecting others and their differences.
	The importance of ensuring others feel included.
	Looking out for and helping others at a time of need.
	Anti-bullying messages.
Courage for my community.	British value - democracy - being aware of inequalities.
	Looking at different examples of professional roles carried out by those in our communities - what different kinds of courage are involved - moral, physical, and social?
	Discovering the needs of our own communities, whether in terms of the environment, wildlife, or groups of people, and looking to make a difference through our actions.
Courage for the world.	Examples of courageous leaders and actions throughout history that have brought about positive change in the world.
	Groups and charities who work together for the good of the world in the current day and the courage needed to carry out their actions.
	Caring for the planet - sustainability issues and ways in which we can each make a difference.
The paradox.	The limitations of courage. While we have to do what we reasonably can, fear is a useful in-built protective emotion. There are purposeful limits to our need to act courageously.

Determination

Determination is about having the tenacity to see something through, to be able to listen to your inner voice when you need to be able to take that extra big step. It is fired by self-belief and a desire to make a positive difference in the world.

Corresponding values: resilience, tolerance, courage, and patience.

Key concept or question	Aspects of learning
Determination for myself.	Identifying the many times in our lives when we need to keep going in order to succeed. Having the courage of our convictions.
	Recognising that this ability springs from and at the same time builds a reservoir of inner strength and conviction.
	Dealing with disappointments.
	Using positive affirmations to affirm our capabilities.
Determination in the context of those around us.	Recognising determination in others and supporting them in their endeavours.
	Enacting a determination to think and act in a way that is kind to others – anti-bullying messages.
Determination for my community.	British value – democracy – being aware of inequalities.
	Finding out what needs to be done to improve the lives of those around us and taking appropriate action with others.
Determination for the world.	Developing understanding and opinions about world issues, including sustainability and preservation of our natural world, speaking out against injustice and being advocates for positive change.
	Taking inspiration from the natural world and from stories throughout history to inspire us.
The paradox.	Identifying when we are going in the wrong direction; developing the ability to listen to others and keep an open mind – it isn't always good to be set on something!

Empathy

Empathy goes beyond just sympathy. It is when we use our ability to connect with one another to really imagine ourselves in someone else's shoes. These are the compassionate and tender thoughts that ensure we understand and help one another.

Corresponding values: love, compassion, understanding, friendship, and care.

Key concept or question	Aspects of learning
Empathy for myself.	Understanding the range of our own emotions is the basis for understanding other people. Using positive affirmations to assert our capabilities.
Empathy for others.	Friendships can enable us to be aware of others and the feelings and emotions they are experiencing. Starting to look outwards beyond ourselves can help us grow. Being aware of the feelings and needs of animal and bird life. How do we notice those who need our help? How can we put aside our own frustrations when we don't know how someone else is feeling? How do we support those experiencing difficulties? Anti-bullying messages.
Empathy for my community.	Understanding that caring for someone or something else is part of becoming the best we can be. By focusing our care on another person/animal, we become better people. Caring turns us from self-absorption into a healthier 'me'. Looking outwards to notice the needs in our wider community and taking local action is a great start to developing an empathetic outlook on the world.
Empathy for the world.	Developing understanding and opinions about world issues, including sustainability and preservation of our natural world. Speaking out against injustice and being advocates for positive change. Taking inspiration from the natural world and from stories throughout history to inspire us.
The paradox.	Being aware that we need to keep a balance and appropriate sense of detachment if we are to best help others. Be aware of being empathetic without applying discrimination.

Freedom

Freedom is independence of thought as well as action, rooted in an appropriate sense of responsibility towards both ourselves and others.

Corresponding values: individual liberty, responsibility, courage, forgiveness, resilience, and determination.

Key concept or question	Aspects of learning
What does freedom mean to me?	Understanding that freedom/individual liberty involves choices - and making the 'right choices' brings responsibility.
	Understanding that we have the right not to be coerced or enslaved.
	Being able to stand out from the pack and, if necessary, justify our thinking.
	Understand that learning and language is freedom: freedom of speech.
	Self-belief and self-esteem.
	Understanding that freedom will also demand courage at times.
What does freedom mean for those around me?	We need to identify the quality of our own freedom and recognise what freedoms we then need to allow others - our friends and our families. When do our freedoms impact badly on others and how can we hold this in balance?
	Anti-bullying messages.
What does freedom mean for a community?	Working for justice for various groups and causes brings people together to form pressure groups that aim to change things for the better. Understanding this needs courage, resilience, and determination at its roots if it is to be successful.
	The need for forgiveness and responsibility for any community to be able to function freely.
	Need for courage to attain freedom.
What does freedom mean for the world?	Recognising that all people can show the value of justice and this impacts on freedom and equalities.
	Understanding freedom means human basic needs are met.
	The importance of freedom of speech and the freedom to choose one's own religion.
	The United Nations Rights of the Child.
	What about freedom for our wildlife and captive/farmed animal populations - what are the implications?
	Freedoms and responsibilities in relation to caring for the planet.
	Inspirational role models and their role throughout history.
	Consideration of the World Wars, remembrance, and current conflicts.
	Nelson Mandela and campaign against apartheid.
	Anti-slavery.
	Anti-bullying - all have the right to feel safe and valued.
The paradox.	The understanding that one person's freedom can impact on others detrimentally. Does freedom have a 'stop point?' When is freedom undesirable/frightening/unhelpful?

Forgiveness

Forgiveness can mean letting go of resentment and hurt as well as allowing peace and love to take their place in your mind, outlook, and actions. When we forgive and when we are forgiven – by others or by ourselves – there is a liberation to do better next time, to start afresh.

Corresponding values: love, respect, peace, understanding, tolerance, and democracy.

Key concept or question	Aspects of learning
What can forgiveness mean to me?	Remember doing something wrong – how you felt – did you put it right? What did it feel like to be forgiven? Have you ever forgiven anyone? What happened? How did it feel to forgive? How did it feel after you had forgiven someone?
	The importance of personal safety and the right to be free from hurt (anti-bullying/safeguarding/antislavery).
	The importance of forgiving ourselves and the place of positive affirmations and reflection to help us in this.
What can forgiveness mean for those around me?	The wisdom in forgiveness in the context of family and friend relationships.
	How we can 'make good' after hurting someone intentionally or unintentionally.
What can forgiveness mean for a community?	Working for justice for various groups and causes brings people together to form pressure groups that aim to change things for the better as a precursor to forgiveness.
	The rule of law and its role in enabling people to have forgiveness.
	The importance of atonement and 'giving back' to heal wounds.
What can forgiveness mean for the world?	The wisdom in forgiveness.
	Examples through history of how people have enacted forgiveness and have been able to proceed with their lives even after suffering.
	World matters that remain unresolved: change, sustainability, slavery, etc.
The paradox.	The understanding that personal safety and the safety of others needs to have priority over forgiveness.
	When is forgiveness not appropriate? Are there things that shouldn't be forgiven and what are the implications for this?
	The rule of law and its role in enabling people to have forgiveness.

Gratitude

This value is about realising our thankfulness, both for the small and the big things in our lives – and being open to the wonder of the world.

Corresponding values: care, democracy, friendships, and respect.

Key concept or question	Aspects of learning
What can gratitude mean to me?	Why this value is important to us on a day-to-day basis.
	Recognising and being proud of our own skills and talents – having a good sense of our self-worth and the contribution our particular personality and character can make to those around us.
	Reflection on the aspects of our lives we are thankful for – friendship, love, wisdom, play, sunshine, etc.
	Do we see the good things in life as a blessing and a gift rather than a right?
	How do we become thankful for more than just material possessions?
What can gratitude mean in relation to those around me?	Why gratitude is important.
	How we feel when someone is grateful.
	The importance of saying thank you to those we are grateful to.
	In what ways are expressions of appreciation and thankfulness built into the life of our school?
What can gratitude mean for a community?	Realising that peace and mutual support in any community are prized values – these enable us to function well and they bring out the best in people.
What can gratitude mean for the world?	Developing our understanding of nature and the way our eco systems work so that we can better protect the planet.
The paradox.	Gratitude relies upon wise judgement – we need to understand the true value of what we are being grateful for and be aware that this value, like any other, can be weaponised to keep others subservient.

Friendship

Friendship is a special, loving, caring relationship with other people, ourselves, or the planet we live on.

Corresponding values: love, respect, peace, understanding, joy, happiness, quality, care, and courage.

Key concept or question	Aspects of Learning
What can friendship mean to me?	Having a good relationship with ourselves is the starting point of any other relationship. Understanding that we are valued, valuable, and worthy gives us the self-respect and self-worth we need to then form equal relationships with others.
	The place of positive affirmations and reflection to help us in this.
What can friendship mean for those around me?	What makes a good friend? How can I show I am a good friend?
What can friendship mean for a community?	Becoming someone who is willing to take part in local good causes to raise money, raise awareness, and change things for the better.
What can friendship mean for the world?	How can I be a good friend to the planet?
	How can I be a good friend to people across the world.
The paradox.	When can a friendship be bad? Unhealthy relationships where there is a power imbalance - where there is coercion, bullying, or where it simply doesn't feel right - these are matters of personal safety and have safeguarding implications.

Hope

This value is about looking for and seeing the best of situations, people, and circumstances. It is built upon the understanding that people can work together to show and develop positive outlooks, impulses, and actions.

Corresponding values: patience, resilience, determination, wisdom, and the rule of law.

Key concept or question	Aspects of learning
What can hope mean to me?	Personal and academic goals.
	Developing our own self-worth to achieve these aims.
	Reflection, mindfulness, and positive affirmations as a way of developing wellbeing.
	Patience, determination, and resilience – hopefulness often involves waiting!
What can hope mean for those around me?	Friendships and relationships: 'building one another up' and offering supportive, or even critical advice is a fundamental part of personal and learning relationships.
	Seeking mutual support to achieve a positive outcome.
	Anti-bullying messages.
	Recognising the attributes of other people opens our own eyes to possibilities.
What can hope mean for a community?	Becoming someone who is willing to take part in local good causes to raise money, raise awareness, and change things for the better.
	Consideration of good role models.
What can hope mean for the world?	How can I help to bring hope to the planet?
	Understanding and awareness of sustainability, ecological, and protective issues, and moral dilemmas.
	Examples of historical and current actions by individuals and groups who are making a positive difference in terms of peacebuilding, supporting groups of people or animals, and protecting the world's wildlife and ecological systems.
The paradox.	The potence of 'false hope' and the way in which this value, like all others, can be weaponised to be used for purposes that are unhelpful to us personally. We must use our own wisdom to weigh up arguments while holding on to a fundamental desire to do all we can to bring and live in hope.

Love

Love means holding someone or something in very high regard. Love must not be 'just words'. It means something only when it is expressed in action and practical care.

Corresponding values: kindness, friendship, generosity, care, and gentleness.

Key concept or question	Aspects of learning
What can love mean to me?	Who loves me, and how do I know that I am loved? Who do I love and what does that look or feel like?
	Developing an appropriate sense of self-worth so that we understand our own value and the fact that we are uniquely valuable.
	Personal wellbeing.
	Having high aspirations for ourselves as an aspect of self-love.
	The use of reflection, mindfulness, and positive affirmations as a way of developing good emotional and mental wellbeing.
	Being able to receive as well as give love – being able to say thank you and being able to be gracious when others are kind.
What can love mean for those around me?	Putting other people's needs before your own. What makes a good friend? How can I show I am a good friend?
	Acting with generosity. Developing our responses to one another. Being alert to how others are feeling and reacting.
	The importance of kind words and deeds.
What can love mean for a community?	Looking out for those in need of help and support.
	Anti-bullying messages.
What can love mean for the world?	Expressing love for the world through taking an aspect of it to be especially caring of.
	How can I be a good friend to people across the world.
	The spiritual concept of *agape* – love without personal gain.
The paradox.	Can we ever love too much? Or in the wrong way?
	Misplaced notions of love can have safeguarding implications so we need to be able to analyse the motivations behind love and be able to trust the instincts that lead to it.
	The idea of 'tough love' – being able to be honest with others and tell them if we don't think they are on the right track.

Patience

Patience is about waiting with dignity and grace, knowing that we do not have to have everything straight away; trusting that sometimes things take their own time in which they will unfold and this needs to be honoured. It can mean not giving up, coping with temper, recognising strengths and weakness, and not being too hard on ourselves because we all make mistakes.

When we are patient, we allow ourselves to be alive to the universe around us, to notice things more deeply and this allows us to use that new knowledge and wisdom in our lives.

Corresponding values: kindness, friendship, generosity, care, gentleness, trust, resilience, determination, tolerance, and respect.

Key concept or question	Aspects of learning
What can patience mean to me?	How good are you at waiting for something? What makes you impatient? How long can you sit still? How can you stop losing your temper?
	Understanding ourselves, recognising our qualities and achievements, and setting our goals for the future in the knowledge that skills, talents, and achievements develop over time and with persistence.
	A respectful approach to our own lives, reminding us that life operates to timescales that are not always just about us.
	Personal wellbeing.
	High aspirations for ourselves as an aspect of self-love.
	Reflection, mindfulness, and positive affirmations as a way of developing emotional and mental wellbeing.
What can patience mean in relation to those around me?	Valuing and honouring our fellow human beings; our friends and our family.
	Others can sometimes frustrate us but recognising everyone is different makes us more tolerant. We need to take 'the long view', giving people time. Patience helps us to 'walk a mile in their moccasins', leading to the development of empathy.
What can patience mean for a community?	Learning to live together and to tolerate one another in any community requires patience. When we practise this value, we start to find that we are better able and equipped to look out for those in need of help and support. Being patient is being prepared to wait for something good to happen. When we learn to wait for something we usually appreciate it. It involves long term commitment to a task. We can remind ourselves, 'Rome wasn't built in a day', doing something worthwhile takes time and taking the long view gives us perspective.
	Antibullying messages.
What can patience mean for the world?	Taking lessons from nature. Farmers wait until the summer rains to make their valuable crops grow. Be patient ... and don't give up. As we learn to wait for things to grow, we understand that change takes time – and the more complex the problem, the greater the time it takes.
The paradox.	Misplaced patience: sometimes our impatience is a helpful and pragmatic trigger, reminding us that bland acceptance of a situation can actually be unhelpful or even harmful.

Peace

Peace is more than just the opposite of conflict and war. Peace is more than just the absence of something: it is a force for good, and helps us to notice things more deeply, in turn allowing us to apply new knowledge and wisdom in our lives. It is possible to attain, and to operate through, a deeply centred inner peace that manifests in our thoughts, words, and actions.

Corresponding values: courage, love, resilience, rule of law, tolerance, care, and friendship.

Key concept or question	Aspects of learning
What can peace mean to me?	Inner peace can be achieved in different ways: good conscience and knowing you have done your best; through physical activity; or through mindfulness and reflection. Gaining a degree of control over inner peace can affect your whole life and that of all of those around you. Understanding what brings us peace - and knowing what we can do or where we can go to achieve an equilibrium when ours is disturbed - is an important part of self-knowledge.
What can peace mean in relation to those around me?	Some people can achieve and demonstrate a remarkable degree of inner and outer peace. These are not just Nobel Prize winners but may also be people you know. Talk to them: where does their peaceful motivation come from? We can also think here about the crucial matter of feeling or being at odds with someone - how can we go about making peace? Conflict resolution is something any of us can potentially arbitrate if we learn the basic skills. How can we become the peacemakers in our world?
What can peace mean for a community?	Where does peace reside in our community? It comes from each one of us and what we emanate, and it can be helped by peaceful spaces. Natural spaces, where there is opportunity for growth, are always good at enabling peaceful vibrations. What can we do to make our school a more peaceful place? Anti-bullying messages.
What can peace mean for the world?	How do organisations, countries, and world leaders bring about peace? What price are we willing to pay for peace. History provides many-layered examples of the things people have considered worth sacrificing peace for.
The paradox.	While peace is always a desirable end goal, we also have to be able to understand the appropriate place of peace. For example, not speaking out against injustice may achieve a transitory peace but sacrifice a longer term or more sustainable peace. These judgements are carefully weighed alongside other values, such as justice and equality and are among the hardest and most complex conundrums of the human condition.

Respect

Respect is a highly regarded value because it denotes a tacit agreement to treat one another well: with good manners, care, thoughtfulness, and sensitivity. It means there is an equality of relationships so all will be regarded and looked after.

Corresponding values: care and kindness.

Key concept or question	Aspects of learning
What can respect mean for me?	Being able to truly respect others starts with self-respect and feeling it's okay or it's good to be me. This means valuing our individuality with its strengths and weaknesses.
What can respect mean in relation to those around me?	Knowing and being able to use basic oral and written good manners in a range of settings: please and thank you, good table manners, knowing how to greet and respond to people in different social and formal situations. Treating people from different age groups and cultures respectfully (not only as a convention but also because we want to). Being able to respond to others because of our common humanity. Not having a fixed mindset about people. Allowing ourselves to be curious about and surprised by others. Anti-bullying is a strong theme here. Who commands our respect and how do they do it? If there are elements of coercion or aggression this has safeguarding implications.
What can respect mean for a community?	What do we respect in our local community? How do we show this respect in our wider community? Who are the role models for this value in our community and how do we do we demonstrate our respect with tangible action?
What can respect mean for the world?	Personal justice. Social justice. Global justice. Respect for our natural world and for the sustainability of the planet.
The paradox.	As with any value, blind or unthinking respect for something or someone may be unwise and even dangerous - so our respect needs to be well-considered and to have its basis in reasoned decision making.

Responsibility

This is a very active value and comes from a resolve to make efforts to be the best person we can be, taking a full and active part in our community, and using our judgement wisely. Responsibility can be seen as the other half to our rights in the world and both aspects need to work in balance.

Corresponding values: care, kindness, and justice.

Key concept/question	Aspects of learning
What can responsibility mean for me?	What am I self-responsible for? What do I need other people to help me to do? Safeguarding aspects relating to this value are crucial - power imbalances in relationships, and our responsibility to keep ourselves and one another safe in different contexts.
What can responsibility mean in relation to those around me?	How do we show responsibility and receive it from our friends and family? Good manners play a big part here, as do selfless and caring outlook and acts. Anti-bullying themes. What responsibility do we have to our animals and pets who rely on us? What about those who are older or younger than us? How can we show our responsibility in school?
What can responsibility mean for a community?	What do we do to help in our local community? Who are the role models for this value in our community and how can we help to do our bit? What do we achieve that shows our commitment?
What can responsibility mean for the world?	Our responsibility to the planet. There are many organisations and movements that are already focused on this theme, and it is one in which many children and young people are already engaged.
The paradox.	As ever, having a good sense of where our responsibility in practical terms stops as well as starts is healthy. Feelings of guilt and an inappropriate sense of duty can be aroused through misplaced sense of responsibility so a balanced approach is so important with this value, as with all values.

Trust

This value is essential to human life and lies at the heart of all relationships. Corresponding values: care, democracy, friendship, respect, and rule of law.

Key concept or question	Aspects of learning
What can trust mean to me?	Why this value is important to us on a day-to-day basis.
	Recognising and being proud of our own skills and talents – having a sense of our self-worth and the contribution our personality and character can make to those around us. This leads to self-respect, which is about trusting ourselves. We need to have a self-identity that recognises we are a trustworthy and loveable person.
	Reflection on aspects of ourselves.
	Trusting our own judgements and building the skills to be able to do this.
What can trust mean in relation to those around me?	How do we trust and who should we trust? What are the indicators that will guide us? How we feel when someone is trustworthy? This encompasses friendship, how to be a good friend, and expecting trustworthiness from your friends, as well as the safeguarding issues around safe relationships with others.
	The importance of saying thank you to those we are grateful to.
	In what ways are expressions of trust built into the life of our school? What can we do when trust has been broken?
What can trust mean for a community?	Looking at how our communities work on trust – focus on the work of groups of people and our national laws that help create and maintain trust so that we can function well as a society.
What can trust mean for the world?	Developing our understanding of the way our eco systems work so that we can learn from the way the natural world has to work in harmony to survive. Using this learning to better protect the planet and understanding that trusting in one another is key because we have to work together and use our combined skills and intent to make a positive difference.
The paradox.	Trust has to be underpinned by wise judgement otherwise it is misplaced and can be exploited. Understanding this means we are equipped to weigh things in the balance and to be aware of how trustworthy our own actions are.

Understanding

Understanding is the bridge to other values; it helps to break down barriers and aligns closely with empathy. It is an insightful value, enabling us to move beyond ourselves and to connect on a deeper level with others.

Corresponding values: love, respect, kindness, tolerance, responsibility, democracy, consideration, and empathy.

Key concept or question	Aspects of learning
What can understanding mean for me?	Understanding ourselves is a lifelong business but we can make continuous steps by understanding it is normal to experience a range of emotions in response to different causes. Being able to increasingly recognise and control those emotions appropriately happens when we gently start to understand ourselves.
What can understanding mean for others around me?	Sometimes we have to help other people to better understand ourselves. This starts with being gentle with them and using words that will help them to see us well. We can be good role models in this by demonstrating our willingness to understand others, by being politely curious about those around us, and by noticing their feelings. Anti-bullying questions and issues can be examined through this value – when we start to unpick why bullying happens it is often because of a lack of empathy.
What can understanding mean for my community?	How do we declare ourselves as an understanding community? This revolves around continuous role-modelling and is everyone's responsibility.
What can understanding mean for the world?	Laws that help us care for each other. Groups and charities that work together for the good of the world. Caring for the planet – Sustainability issues.
The paradox.	We need to appreciate that we cannot reasonably expect to be fully understood all the time. There are many times when our own needs, desires, and wishes have to be subsumed for the greater good. We have to be self-responsible and seek resolutions that best meet the needs of everyone.

Values-based Resources for Early Years

Action rhymes

A wonderful way to enable children to play with values is through teaching action rhymes. The traditional rhyme, Incy Wincy Spider perfectly exemplifies determination! Here are others, written especially for and used with early years classes. Older children love teaching them to their younger friends too.

Happiness

When we smile,
It makes life worthwhile.
When we share our smiles,
They go on for miles.

Make a smile action with the mouth and a finger to draw a big smile in the air; turn to one another to share smiles.

Kindness

Little acts of kindness,
Little words of love,
Help make the earth happy,
And as peaceful as a dove.

These things make the world go round,
It's up to you and me:
We can make a peaceful world,
That's as lovely as can be.

Cup one hand, as if holding the world – with the other hand use the index finger to draw round and round it as you say the words.

Determination

One, two,
Whatever you do –
Start it well,
And carry it through.
Three, four,
Try for more –
Be proud of
Your highest score.

Make hands in to fists to make building blocks and use to build towers as you say the words.

Friendship

I value my friend,
And this is why:
He is he,
And I am I.

I value my friends –
As you can see,
Friendship is the
Way to be.

Cup one hand over the other and hold up, then rock both hands from side to side while saying the words.

Joy

Make every day,
A joyful day.
Turn your frown into a grin –
That way – let the sunshine in!

Use the thumb and index finger on both hands (tucking other fingers away) to make frowns and then turn them the other way up to make smiles! Finish the verse by making 'sunshine' by spreading all the fingers out.

Gratitude

Thank you for the present,
That you gave to me.
When I show my gratitude,
I'll make a gift for thee.

Thank you for the thoughtfulness,
That you showed to me.
When I show my gratitude,
I'll show I thought of thee.

Hold out hands to 'receive' an imaginary present from an imaginary person in front of you. Repeat the action in reverse so that you are giving back a gift as you say the words.

Kindness

Sow the seeds of kindness,
Be kind in all you do.
Make a world of gentleness,
That's right for me and you.

Hold an imaginary bowl under one arm and with the other hand, plant seeds using tip of finger and thumb as you say the words.

Grace

Gentle words.
Useful deeds.
Wish for the good and,
For the best.

Make butterfly wings with your hands by using fingers and thumb to make a bow shape. You can make your butterfly gently fly.

Compassion

Compassion is,
To do and say,
The kindest things,
In the gentlest way.

Have an imaginary cat in your lap and gently stroke it as you say the words.

Understanding

Stepping-stones, stepping-stones,
One, and two, and three.
Lay them carefully on the ground,
And they'll bring you to me.

Place imaginary stepping-stones out in front of you – one, and two, and three – point to another person and then to yourself as you say the words.

Empathy

Walk a mile in my shoes,
Hear how my story goes;
Feel how it is to be me,
From my head down to my toes.

I'll walk a mile in your shoes,
Hear how your story goes:
Feel how it is to be you,
From your head down to your toes.

Hold one palm out flat. Use two fingers on the other hand to walk as you say the words. Swop hands for the second verse.

Humility

I am part of all things,
That are both great and small.
Let me bring my skills and talents,
To be a gift for all.

Put arms out in front of you, palms upwards and with fists closed; gradually unfurl hands to show your gifts of skills and talents.

Peace

Shhh ...
Let me live in peace.
Let my hands be kind hands,
Doing good to all,
Let my heart be gentle,
In big deeds and in small.

Put index finger to mouth to make a gentle shhh sound. Hold out hands, palm upwards, and then place hands over the heart along with the words.

Responsibility

Pour the sunshine in,
To the darkest place.
Fill the world,
With my good grace.

Hold an imaginary bucket with both hands and tip it up to pour out the sunshine as you say the words.

Love

This is my heart I share with you,
When you share yours,
You love me too.
This is my love I give to you,
When you share yours,
You love me too.

Use the index fingers and thumbs on both hands to make a heart shape that can be given and received by moving hands away from and into the chest.

Forgiveness

I forgive you –
We can start anew.

You forgive me –
And my heart feels free.

Use hands with palms together in a forgiveness symbol.
Heart symbol made with fingers and hands fly away.

Promote children's ethical vocabulary, language comprehension, and love of reading with these values-based stories!

The very act of sharing stories and books together promotes the values of:

- **Friendship** – sharing a book deepens bonds between people and enables relationships to grow.
- **Joy** – sharing a book creates joy together.
- **Responsibility** – books can open our eye hearts and minds to our responsibility to one another and our world.
- **Respect, Empathy and Tolerance** – through books we start to understand and appreciate our differences.
- **Courage** – reading books about courage builds up our own bravery.
- **Peace, Unity and Justice** – books can open our eye hearts and minds to important issues.

... to name but a few! The following picture books are ideal for class reads and discussion with the early years:

Value Theme	Book
Friendship	*Woolly* by Sam Childs
	Little Penguin by Patrick Benson
	Mr Bill and Clarence by Kay Gallway
	Do You Want to be my Friend by Eric Carle
	Ping by Chae Strathey and Marion Lindsay
	Well Done, Little Bear by Martin Waddell
	Little Beauty by Anthony Browne
	The Sleepy Owl by Marcus Pfister
	Gorilla by Anthony Browne
	The Tunnel by Anthony Browne
Peace	*Five Minutes Peace* by Jill Murphy
	Peace at Last by Jill Murphy
	A Little Moment of Peace by Jenny Meldrum
	Tusk Tusk by David Mckee
	Two Monsters by'David Mckee
	Long Neck and Thunderfoot by Helen Piers

Freedom	*This Moose Belongs to Me* by Oliver Jeffers
	Elmer by David McKee
Love	*Guess How Much I Love You* by Sam McBratny
	The Heart and the Bottle by Oliver Jeffers
	Love is my Favourite Thing by Emma Chichester Clark
	Bog Baby by Jeanne Willis
	Hey I Love You by Ian Whybrow
Unity	*All Kinds of People* by Damon
	The Smartest Giant in Town by Julia Donaldson
	A Balloon for Grandad by Nigel Gray and Jane Ray
	Who is the World For? by Tom Pow
	The Jolly Postman by Alan and Janet Ahlberg
	Where the Forest Meets the Sea by Jeannie Baker
	Room on the Broom by Julia Donaldson and Axel Scheffler
Courage	*Frightened Fred* by Peta Coplans
	Bear Feels Scared by Karma Wilson
	Silly Billy by Anthony Browne
	The King That Missed by David Melling
	Duck, Death and the Tulip by Wolf Erlburgh
	Hiccup, the Viking Who Was Seasick by Cressida Cowell
	Billywise by Judith Nicholls
	Alfie and the Dark by Sally Miles
	Bear Feels Scared by Karma Wilson
Humility	*Willy the Wimp* by Anthony Browne
	Look What I've Got by Anthony Browne
	Zog and the Flying Doctors by Julia Donaldson
	The Wind and the Sun (traditional)
Hope	The Nativity Story (traditional)
	The Lion and the Mouse by Jerry Pinkney
Kindness / Compassion/ Generosity	*Little Beauty* by Anthony Browne
	The Giving Tree by Shel Silverstein
	Penguin by Dolly Dunbar
	Let Me Tell You About Compassion by Sue Webb
	The Selfish Crocodile by Faustin Charles and Michael Terry
	The Tiger Who Came to Tea by Judith Kerr

Respect	*Rainbow Fish* by Marcus Pfister
	Cinderella (traditional)
	The Three Bears (traditional)
	I Don't Care! by Brian Moses and Mike Gordon
	Journey to the River Sea by Eva Ibbotson
Determination	*The Huge Bag of Worries* by Virginia Ironside
	Avocado Baby by John Burningham
	The Magic Paintbrush by Julia Donaldson
Co-operation	*Handa's Surprising Day* by Eileen Brown
Gratitude/ Thankfulness	*A Place to Call Home* by Alexis Deacon
	Noah's Ark by Lindy Norton
	The Fish Who Could Wish by Korky Paul
	A Kitten Called Moonlight by Martin Waddell
	Grandmother and I by Hellen Buckley and Jan Omerod
Responsibility/ Care	*Where the Forest Meets the Sea* by Jeannie Baker
	Dear Greenpeace by Simon James
	Here We Are: Notes for Living on Planet Earth by Oliver Jeffers
Forgiveness	*Mr Magnolia* by Quentin Blake
	Cinderella (traditional)
	The Gentle Giant by Michael Morpurgo
Joy /Happiness	*Cheer Up Your Teddy Bear* by Cressida Cowell
	Funnybones by Alan and Janet Ahlberg
	Mr Percy's Magic Greenhouse by Anthea Kemp
	How to Catch a Star by Oliver Jeffers
	The Incredible book Eating Boy by Oliver Jeffers
	The Cat in the Hat by Dr Seuss
Self-Belief	*Giraffes Can't Dance* by Giles Andrae
	Amazing Grace by Mary Hoffman
	The Gruffalo by Julia Donaldson
	The Paperbag Princess by Robert Munsch
	Elmer by David McKee

Values in the natural world

Learning outdoors, in the forest or a garden, is a natural context for Values-based Education to take place, promoting as it does all the virtues of exploration, awe and wonder, while enhancing individual wellbeing. Here are some joyful values-activities that can be done together:

Values	What you can do
Exploring values of trust and friendship ...	Playing hide and seek in pairs - using animal voices to help your partners find you! This game quickly establishes rapport.
What examples of values can you find today?	Through individual exploration find examples of values in the natural world: it might be the first sign of flowers after winter (determination? joy?); or, if you are lucky, a bird's nest in a tree or hedge (love? care? gentleness?).
Care, compassion, kindness, and courage.	Is our natural place alright? Does it need us to do anything to take more care of it? Pick up litter? Plant more plants? Tidy up fallen twigs, etc.?
Beauty, joy, and wonder.	Take a picture frame, viewfinder, or card of any shape with a hole cut out of the middle - use it to find a value in nature. For example, a flower open in the sun might suggest peace; two plants naturally supporting each other might suggest service, etc. The children will become really perceptive in their observations.
Care, teamwork, unity, compassion, respect, and friendship.	Build a den with your friends ... or work together to build a house for a tiny pixie/hedgehog, etc.
Reflection and contemplation.	In a log circle, close your eyes and listen to the sounds of nature; or lie on your back and watch the clouds ... what do these activities do for your mind and body?

APPENDIX 4

Subject Associations

Subject	Association name	Title	Web address
Art and design	The National Society for Education in Art and Design	NSEAD	www.nsead.org
Citizenship	Association for Citizenship Teaching	ACT	www.teachingcitizenship.org.uk
Citizenship	Young Citizens		www.youngcitizens.org
Citizenship	Community		community-tu.org
Citizenship	The Compassionate Education Foundation	CoED	www.coedfoundation.org.uk
Computing	Computing at School	CAS	www.computingatschool.org.uk
Design and technology	The National Association for Education Technology	NAACE	www.naace.org.uk
Design and technology	The Technology, Pedagogy & Education Association	TPEA	tpea.ac.uk
Design and technology	The Design and Technology Association	D&T	www.data.org.uk
English	United Kingdom Literacy Association	UKLA	ukla.org
English	National association for the teaching of English	NATE	www.nate.org.uk
Geography	Geographical Association	GA	www.geography.org.uk
Geography	Royal Geographical Society (with Institute of British Geographers)	RGS	www.rgs.org
History	Historical Association	HA	www.history.org.uk
Mathematics	The Joint Mathematical Council of the United Kingdom	JMC	www.jmc.org.uk
Mathematics	The Association of Mathematics Education Teachers	AMET	www.ametonline.org.uk
Mathematics	Association of Teachers of Mathematics	ATM	www.atm.org.uk

Mathematics	Mathematical Association	MA	www.m-a.org.uk
Mathematics	National Numeracy		www.nationalnumeracy.org.uk
Mathematics	Science Technology Engineering and Maths Learning	STEM	www.stem.org.uk
Modern foreign languages	The Association for Language Learning	ALL	www.all-languages.org.uk
Music & Drama & Dance	National Drama	ND	www.nationaldrama.org.uk
Music & Drama & Dance	One Dance UK		www.onedanceuk.org
Physical education	Association for physical education	afPE	www.afpe.org.uk/physical-education
Personal social health education	Personal, Social, Health and Economic Association	PSHE	pshe-association.org.uk
Religious education	National Association of Teachers of RE	NATRE	www.natre.org.uk
Religious education	Religious Education Council of England and Wales		www.religiouseducationcouncil.org.uk
Science	The association for science education	ASE	www.ase.org.uk
Science	The Royal Society		royalsociety.org
Science	Primary science teaching trust	PSTT	pstt.org.uk
Science	British science association	BSA	www.britishscienceassociation.org
Special Educational needs	National Association for Special Educational Needs	NASEN	www.nasen.org.uk
Special Educational needs	National Autistic Society		www.autism.org.uk
More Support	National subject association for English as an additional language	NALDIC	naldic.org.uk
More Support	The National Association of School-Based Teacher Trainers	NASBTT	www.nasbtt.org.uk
More Support	The Curriculum Foundation	CF	www.curriculumfoundation.org
More Support	The British association for early childhood education	EE	early-education.org.uk
More Support	National Association for Primary Education	NAPE	www.nape.org.uk
More Support	Chartered College of Teaching		chartered.college

More Support	Values based Education	VbE	valuesbasededucation.com
More Support	Association for the Study of Primary Education	ASPE	www.aspe-uk.eu
More Support	The Forest School Association	FSA	forestschoolassociation.org
More Support	Mantle of the Expert	MoE	www.mantleoftheexpert.com
More Support	National Association of Environmental Education	NAEE	naee.org.uk